SOVIET STEEL

STUDIES IN SOVIET HISTORY AND SOCIETY

edited by Joseph S. Berliner, Seweryn Bialer,
and Sheila Fitzpatrick

SOVIET STEEL

The Challenge of Industrial
Modernization in the USSR

BORIS Z. RUMER

CORNELL UNIVERSITY PRESS

Ithaca and London

To my mother, Elizaveta Gordon

How could it have happened that in our wasteful [*zatratnoy*] economic system everything has become so distorted, has been turned upside down!

Aleksandr Nikitin
Literaturnaya gazeta
April 29, 1987

Contents

Acknowledgments

Much of the material in this volume is derived from a study that was funded by the U.S. government. I am wholly and solely responsible for the data, analysis, and conclusions presented here—all of which are based on open Soviet sources.

I am indebted to Joseph S. Berliner and Holland Hunter for their interest in my project and for their invaluable advice. I also thank my colleagues and the staff of the Russian Research Center, Harvard University, for having provided me with an intellectually stimulating environment.

BORIS Z. RUMER

Cambridge, Massachusetts

SOVIET STEEL

Introduction

Industrial modernization is the key concept of the economic program of the new Soviet leadership. The term "reindustrialization," popular in the West, applies also to the task formulated at the Twenty-seventh Congress of the Communist Party of the Soviet Union in 1986.

The foundation of Soviet reindustrialization is upgrading of the machine-building sector of the economy. Investment in machine building is expected to increase by more than 80 percent over the level of the last five-year plan. Speaking in early 1987, however, General Secretary Gorbachev admitted that the machine-building sector was encountering "great difficulties." His economic adviser, Abel Aganbegyan, described the accomplishments of the first year of the plan period in machine building as "not encouraging."

One of the most important problems facing the machine-building program is the shortage of steel, from which 95 percent of the industry's output is produced. This is not a new development, either for the Soviet economy as a whole or for its machine-building sector, as shortages of steel have persisted from the very first days of the Soviet regime. The current situation can best be illustrated by a letter to a newspaper written by the director of a large oil- and gas-drilling equipment plant in Kuybyshev. In June 1987 the plant's performance fell to the lowest level in twenty years, and the director asked:

Why is the plant in such a bad shape? . . . The cause is in insufficient deliveries of steel. . . . We are complaining "Help us, the plant is standing idle!" The reply is "look for reserves." [But no matter how hard we try, we cannot find any reserves.] Inspectors from the State Supply Committee confirmed that the plant was short 4,764 tons of steel. After that the ministry sent 2,794 tons. . . . But for 1988 the deficit is again approximately 4,000 tons of steel.[1]

This desperate plea for help appeared in 1988, from a plant that is the only one of its kind in the USSR and that manufactures the most important sorts of oil- and gas-drilling equipment. In 1987 steel deliveries to customers across the Soviet Union fell millions of tons short of the plan target.[2] The crisis of the steel industry is escalating despite governmental decrees aimed at improving the situation.

Since World War II the share of world production of steel by the USSR and its satellites has more than doubled and, by the mid-1980s, was 40 percent of global production. In relative terms, the USSR produces more steel than any other country in the world, yet it continues to lag substantially behind the industrially advanced countries in both the quality and the assortment of its steel production.

The slogan "Give us more metal!" has long been a stereotypical element in Soviet economic planning and management. An extensive rather than intensive approach to development has been characteristic of the Soviet steel industry. That is, quantitative growth of production takes precedence over qualitative improvement, but that approach has meant ever greater expenditures of raw material, energy, capital, and labor resources per unit of increase in output. The lag in steel industry output in a qualitative sense has become an obstacle in the path to technological progress in machine building and construction.

Thus the mounting deficit in steel, together with the failure of its user characteristics to satisfy objective economic requirements, constitutes one of the cardinal problems for economic development in the USSR. To be sure, since the mid-1970s efforts have been made to overcome the inertia of extensive development of ferrous metallurgy, which has been dominant ever since Soviet industrialization began in the late 1920s and which is so wasteful in resources. These corrective measures have thus far not yielded the anticipated results. At the same time, however, the significance of qualitative improvement and more diversified assortment in rolled steel—the

TABLE 1.1
Production of basic forms of ferrous metals in the USSR[3]

Product type	Production (in millions of tons)					Annual average rate of growth (%)			
	1950	1960	1970	1980	1985	1950–60	1960–70	1970–80	1980–85
Pig iron	19.2	46.8	85.9	107.3	110.0	9.4	6.3	2.3	0.5
Crude steel	27.3	65.3	116.0	148.0	155.0	9.1	5.9	2.5	0.9
Rolled steel	20.9	43.7	80.7	103.0	108.0	7.7	6.3	2.5	0.9
Steel pipes	2.0	5.8	12.4	18.2	19.4	11.2	7.9	3.9	1.3
Iron ore (commercial)	39.6	106.0	197.0	245.0	248.0	10.4	6.4	2.2	0.3

primary construction material for machine-tool production—has risen in association with the technological revolution that the Soviet leadership has planned for the machine-tool construction sector of the economy.

The Soviet steel industry, as a branch of heavy industry, is highly concentrated, complex (its vertical integration includes the procurement of raw materials and their processing), and centrally managed. As to the dimensions of its development, Table 1.1 provides a good index to its expansion and rate of growth. In an organizational sense, as a branch of industry in the classification of Soviet statistics and governed by the Ministry of Ferrous Metallurgy of the USSR, the Soviet steel industry represents a conglomerate of extractive and processing industrial subdivisions, unified in terms of the final production. This conglomerate includes:

1. The extraction and enrichment of raw materials for ferrous metallurgy (iron, manganese, and chromium ores)
2. Extraction of raw materials other than ore that are required for ferrous metal production (fluxing limestones, heat-resistant clays, dolomites, quartzites, magnesites, etc.)
3. Production of ferrous metals (pig iron, production of blast furnace ferrous alloys, steel, rolled steel, products for further finishing, and powdered ferrous metals)
4. Production of pipes and tubing (steel and cast iron)
5. Production of electrical steel
6. Coke by-product industry (production of coke, coke-oven/gases, and coke by-products)
7. Production of refractory materials (refractory, chrome-manganese steel, and other types of refractory brick; various kinds of refractory products and powders)

8. Secondary processing of ferrous metals (enterprises for the shoveling of scrap and by-products of ferrous metals)

9. Production of metal products for producer purposes (steel wire, cold-rolled steel tape, steel cable, nails and fastening products, welding electrodes, metallic screens, screws, bolts, etc.)

The basic and commanding position in this complex belongs to the production of ferrous metals.

Soviet ferrous metal production, in economic terms, is distinctive in several important respects. First, it demonstrates a high degree of concentration of production, which is limited to a relatively small number of huge enterprises. In quantitative terms, approximately one-third of all enterprises produce about 90 percent of all pig iron and 70 percent of all steel in the USSR.

Second, Soviet ferrous metal production involves a high degree of vertical integration. Thus enterprises with a fully self-contained production cycle produce all pig iron and 85 percent of all steel and rolled steel in the USSR.

Third, Soviet ferrous metal production is characterized by a high consumption rate of material resources in steel production. Thus, 1 ton of rolled steel consumes 7 tons of raw materials and fuel. The steel industry uses one-quarter of all coal (and 10 percent of all natural gas) consumed annually in the USSR.

Fourth, Soviet steel production is distinguished by a high volume of electricity consumption. In terms of the level of electricity consumption, ferrous metallurgy occupies the leading place among all industrial sectors. To put the point in quantitative terms, let us merely note that the established capacity of all electrical motors and electrical apparatuses in Soviet metallurgy constitutes over 15 percent of all such electrical installations in Soviet industry.

It should also be noted that one of the most important distinguishing characteristics of Soviet ferrous metal production (which sets it apart from analogous sectors in other countries) is its self-sufficiency in raw materials. This peculiarity creates special conditions that sharply distinguish the operation of Soviet steel production from that in other countries and, at the same time, generates certain problems unique to Soviet ferrous metal production.

It is important, too, to underscore the significance of the steel industry in the USSR. Thus the capital stock of ferrous metallurgy represents about 9 percent of the capital stock of Soviet industry and approximately the same share of its labor force. So significant a

TABLE 1.2
Mean annual growth rates for rolled steel production in five-year plans (in percent)[4]

1951–55	1956–60	1961–65	1966–70	1971–75	1976–80	1981–85
11.2	7.4	7.1	5.5	4.0	0.8	0.9

utilization of capital, labor, and mineral resources naturally emphasizes the role of ferrous metal production in the Soviet Union. That is true not only for the production of metal but also for this sector's significance for the rational utilization of economic resources, especially at the present time, when a reduction in the resource increment (according to the five-year plan) is to be offset by corresponding economies in production.

The demand for steel continually rises. As a result, ferrous metal production operates under conditions of unceasing, indeed mounting shortfalls in production, with constant and even increasing pressure from the side of the consumer. At the same time, since the late 1970s we have witnessed an unprecedentedly low tempo of growth rates in production—something virtually unknown in Soviet economic history. That retardation in growth is plainly revealed in data on the production dynamics for the final stage of production—rolled steel—in the postwar period (see Table 1.2).

How is one to explain the steadily rising demand for steel? What are the fundamental structural demands inherent in the Soviet economy? Does the demand derive from objective economic demand or from the peculiarities of the Soviet economic system? What are the causes of the declining growth in production: the maximal utilization of productive capacities, an exhaustion of reserves, or the peculiar characteristics of the Soviet economic system? In this book I seek to answer these questions and to assess the possibility of rectifying the existing situation with respect to steel in the foreseeable future.

Before we embark on our explorations of the complexities and intricacies of Soviet ferrous metallurgy, it should be made clear that this book is not a definitive study of the subject. Rather, my aim is to present several tightly argued and closely focused analyses of those problems most pertinent to an alleviation of shortfalls in Soviet steel production. This is, it should be noted, one of the primary objectives in Soviet economic development. At the same time, this is not a narrow "case study" that treats the Soviet steel industry in a vacuum. A narrow approach cannot be effective: it is important to illuminate phenomena that are stereotypical not only for ferrous metals but also for industrial production in general. Hence I invoke materials of a general economic nature at appropriate places in order to analyze ferrous metallurgy within the framework of broader industrial development. This more comprehensive approach should not only ensure a deeper understanding of conditions prevailing in a particular industrial sector but also shed light on the broader dynamics—and paralyzing forces of inertia—in the Soviet economy at large.

CHAPTER 1

Dynamics and Peculiarities of Steel Consumption in the USSR

Among the reasons for the economic slowdown in the USSR, cited both in speeches by the Soviet leadership and in publications on economic topics, the problem of growing shortages of steel has come to occupy one of the leading positions. Given the peculiar nature of the Soviet economic system, it is appropriate to ask the following questions: is the hunger for metal so great? Is there as great a shortage of high-quality steel and steel products as Soviet industrial executives and managers say and Western observers think? Is the decline of the growth of steel output really such a tragedy for Soviet machine building and construction? Is the Soviet industry ready for effective consumption of such products if they become available as it is provided for in the plan? These questions can be answered only by analyzing trends in the requirements for steel in the real conditions under which Soviet industry functions. Specifically, we must consider two important factors.

First, the slowdown in the growth of steel production in absolute terms is taking place under conditions of a sharp decline in investment activity, and it is precisely the investment sphere of the economy where the demands on metallurgy form.

Second, certain successes in the qualitative improvement of steel and in expanding the range of steel products have been achieved.

It is logical to start with identification of the real demand for steel.

We will do this fragmentarily, examining only the basic factors that determine steel requirements, taking into account particular features of the current stage of development of the Soviet economy. Such a formulation of the question determines the following scheme of analysis:

Methodological approaches to the study of trends in the requirements for steel

Approximation of the growth of requirements for steel on the basis of growth of capital investments in the economy

Analysis of trends in the relative metal intensiveness of output of basic metal-consuming branches of the economy—the machine-building and construction industries

Particular features of the planning of the production and use of steel by the State Planning Committee of the USSR (Gosplan) and the State Committee on Material-Technical Supply (Gossnab) and the actual existing mechanism for the circulation and distribution of metal

Methodological Approaches to the Study of Trends in the Requirement for Steel

In a market economy, studying requirements would mean studying demand. Strictly speaking, the same also would be true under the conditions of a normal, textbook-planned economy. But under the conditions of the present-day reality of the distorted Soviet economy, *technical requirements* and *demand* are by no means equivalent concepts. Under conditions of shortage for almost all types of industrial products and the unplanned, uncontrolled market bartering not taken into account by the state—a bartering that encompasses all spheres of the economy and develops independently of the planning system, where steel functions as a medium of exchange—demand for metal products as such does not reflect the actual requirements for it in the economy. Under these specific conditions, demand is dictated not only and, often, not so much by productive needs or technological specifics as by (a) the need to create reserves as insurance against instances of disruption in supply, and (b) the creation of a market stock of metal for exchange and sale. For the market stock, steel of any type, size, and quality will do, independent of what the enterprise actually needs based on its production conditions.

The following frank pronouncement by V. Yefimov, deputy director of an institute of supply, attests to the fact that planners do not believe the requirements that are determined by consumers:

> It is a proven fact that the requirements that consumers themselves determine are not always substantiated. The consumer does not experience the burden of excess orders for material goods. As long as the old principle "a reserve doesn't pull on your pocket" operates, he always has the temptation to overshoot the mark in his claims on what in the economic literature are called "material valuables." It is no accident that between 1969 and 1981 the rate of inventory turnover in days slowed by 23.7 days, which means excess inventory accumulation of 72.5 billion rubles.[1]

A game situation is created: the consumer enterprise and ministry give Gosplan overstated claims for goods, knowing in advance that they will receive less than they ask for, while Gosplan in turn, also knowing that claims are overstated, cuts off the "fat." Neither the consumer nor Gosplan are governed in this game by either data on true requirements or technological calculations.

Even the creation of norms for the planning of requirements for metal plays almost no role since requirements are not calculated on the basis of real technological, economic, transportation, and organizational conditions under which enterprises function, and they are not oriented toward the operation of the supply system.

They are in essence a compromise in the deal between ministries and Gosplan. Both the ministries and Gosplan treat them skeptically, and to put it briefly, as an instrument of planning they do not fulfill their function. The operative criterion for determining the amount of metal allocated to a consumer is the level of consumption attained in the previous planning period (year, five-year period). It stands to reason that given such a base, it makes no sense even to speak of planning steel requirements that approximate consumers' real requirements. But in this case we also cannot speak of planning of production that corresponds to true requirements in a quantitative and qualitative sense.

The influence of the consumer on the producer in an economy of shortages—which the Soviet economy is—is on the whole insignificant. The centralized system of planning does not carry out its task as regulator between production and consumption. Obstacles to this are political and general economic factors that, in the context of this work, it is not expedient to examine and, of course, the archaic methods of planning.

Thus, in fact, unlimited demand is created for all types of metal products, a demand that does not coincide with the current level of requirements. And not knowing requirements, how can one judge whether steel production is high or low, sufficient or insufficient, or how much indeed is needed?

Given the objectives of our study, it seems acceptable to resort to indirect methods of studying trends in the requirements for steel, approximating it on the basis of one or several indicators of economic trends. It remains only to find the most reliable indicators, which correspond to the greatest degree to steel consumption. Such indicators should satisfy the following conditions.

First, they should be as free as possible of the burden of distortion of the two-level Soviet economy and should reflect requirements for steel objectively as conditioned by factors of an economic character and the level of development of technology.

Second, they should not be indicators that characterize results already achieved since these results are to a certain degree a function of the extent to which metal needs have been met.

Third, these should be indicators that in essence reflect the intensiveness of metal use in the economy to the greatest degree.

The indicator that to the relatively greatest degree meets the first two conditions is the planned volume of capital investment in the economy, while the indicator corresponding to the third condition is the output of machine building and construction—the most metal-intensive branches of the economy.

We have settled on these indicators for the following reasons. Given our objectives, the advantage of plan indicators over *ex post* criteria is that targets for branches of industry (including, of course, the steel industry) which are formed at the planning level are relatively free of the limitations and distortions of the real economy. They correspond to a much greater degree to the expected rates of growth and structural changes in the economy, to potential technological possibilities. The shortcoming of plan indicators is that they take insufficient account of resource limitations. But even considering this, we believe that plan indicators permit a more reliable assessment of requirements.

Why do we prefer capital investment? Would it not be more correct to use national income? National income is inappropriate for approximating metal requirements due to the lack of correspondence of the structure of national income by branch of origin to the branch structure of metal consumption in the economy. The largest amount of metal is consumed by branches of heavy industry and construction. An insignificant amount goes to the remaining branches, but their contribution to national income is significant. National income can change substantially under the influence of nonmetal-intensive branches of the economy, but this would not be related to changes in requirements for steel.

Capital investment seems the most appropriate indicator for approximating steel requirements because about 90 percent of the metal consumed in the USSR goes for expanding and increasing fixed capital,[2] and consequently the trend in requirements for steel depends to a decisive degree on the trend in capital investment.

Among branches of the economy, the greatest consumption of steel is in machine building and construction—40 percent and 20 percent, respectively. Hence the rates of growth of production of these branches also serve as reliable yardsticks in the study of trends in the requirements for steel.

Steel requirements are determined not only by economic growth. They also depend on relative expenditures required per unit of growth—indicators that are not reflected in growth alone. Therefore, a no less important aspect of the analysis of requirements is the analysis of trends in relative metal intensiveness.

We may speak of the metal intensiveness of the gross social product, national income, or gross output of branches of the economy (industry, agriculture, construction). But inherent in all these indicators are significant distortions related to well-known shortcomings of price formation in the USSR. Furthermore, the more aggregated a given economic indicator, the greater its error of a structural and price nature. Eliminating the influence of structural change in the economy and putting the necessary time series in comparable form from the standpoint of prices is a task that in our opinion can not be done, especially not within the framework of this study.

For these reasons, there seems to us no sense in studying the trend in metal intensiveness using value indicators. The level and trend of relative expenditures of steel per unit of output forms directly under the influence of primarily technological and not economic factors. In point of fact, we must study the trend in the coefficient, which has as numerator the quantity of steel expended in tons or square meters and as denominator some sort of characteristic of power, capacity, speed, or other type of useful result related to the production of a particular product.

Only the relation of metal expended to the result obtained gives the most expressive indicator of the steel intensiveness of production of a given product. And if the most representative types of production are chosen, the conclusions that are reached can be extended to the economy as a whole. It is precisely this approach that we use in this work.

Approximating the Trend in Steel Requirements Based on Capital Investment and Machine-Building Output

First, we note that plans for capital investment in the economy are generally fulfilled and in the past two five-year periods have even been overfulfilled: for 1971–75, growth of 36–40 percent compared with the previous five-year period was planned, and actual growth was 41.6 percent; for 1976–80 compared with 1971–75, the corresponding figures were 24–26 percent and 28.6 percent; for 1981–85, these figures were 12–15 percent and 17.4 percent.[3] We are not concerned here with the very important question of the growing disparity between the financing of capital investment and the provision of investment goods. The correspondence of planned indicators to actual is emphasized in this context for one reason: to support the validity of using these indicators in our analysis.

The 1970s were characterized by a planned reduction of the rate of growth of capital investment; the end of that decade and the eleventh five-year period were marked by an actual decline. Average annual rates of growth were 7 percent in 1971–75, 3.4 percent in 1976–80, and 3.5 percent in 1981–85.[4] Such an investment slump, unprecedented for the Soviet economy, cannot but have the effect of lowering the requirement for steel.

But a final judgment can be made only by taking into account structural changes in investment during this period. We are interested, of course, in structural changes that have an impact on the steel intensiveness of investment. Shifts in the branch structure of capital investment in the economy as a whole were manifested in a slight trend toward growth in the share of industry in the 1970s and a more appreciable emergence of this trend intended for the first half of the 1980s.[5] Since industry is the most metal-intensive branch of the economy, the trend noted obviously leads to a certain increase in the metal intensiveness of total investment. But also within industry itself the investment quota increased, if not for the most metal-intensive branches (machine building), then for branches that are in any case quite metal intensive—the oil and gas industries—in connection with the development of pipelines, one of the largest users of high-quality, low-alloy steel.

Changes in the regional structure of capital investment, manifested in an increase in the share of investment in eastern and especially northeastern regions and the shifting of centers of investment activity to the north to regions with extreme natural and climatic conditions, are leading to growth in the requirements for special low-alloy steels.

A substantial influence of steel consumption on the investment sphere is exerted by the correlation between expenditures on the acquisition of equipment and on construction work. The higher the share of expenditures on equipment in the total amount of capital investment, the higher, obviously, is the requirement for steel per unit of overall capital expenditures. Data on this aspect of the structure of investment, however, are contradictory. Moreover, the above-mentioned distortions related to pricing introduce themselves here. In our opinion, based on previously completed studies,[6] the share of equipment in industrial investment is not growing. Considering all pros and cons, it seems reasonable to neutralize this factor in the analysis.

Thus on the one hand changes taking place in the structure of investment lead to an increase in requirements for steel, while on the other hand the rate of growth of investment itself has been sharply reduced. Changes in the structure of investment are not so great that their influence offsets the impact of the slump in investment. It is just too great. In the opinion of an authoritative Soviet economist, Konstantin Val'tukh of the Siberian Division of the USSR Academy of Sciences, growth of investment in the economy in real terms has essentially stopped.[7] Therefore it is our impression that the trend in investment is evidence of a relative decline in the requirement for steel, even when structural changes are taken into account.

A direct consequence of the investment slump is a slump in the construction industry. The average annual rate of growth of construction work fell from 6 percent in 1971–75 to 2 percent in 1981–85.[8] In reality, considering the growing inflation that is not openly admitted in the USSR but that in our opinion is tending to accelerate in the economy as a whole and in construction in particular, it is fully justifiable to speak of an absolute decline in construction output in recent years. Consequently, the growth of requirements for structural parts used in construction and, thus, the requirements for steel in the construction industry must also decline.

Another branch of the economy that cannot but be affected by the decline in investment is machine building. Given the relatively low rates of replacement of obsolete and worn out equipment characteristic of the Soviet economy, the majority of machine building output is channeled into capital investment in the expansion of the stock of machinery. Therefore the rates of growth of machine-building output should be planned in relation to the planned rates of growth of capital investment in the economy. Of course, we are not interpreting this as a strict quantitative dependence but have in mind only a tendency. And concrete data confirm this tendency.

The planned rates of growth of machine-building output declined during the 1970s and continue to decline in the first half of the 1980s: the average annual rates of growth projected in five-year plans were 11.2 percent in 1971–75, 9.9 percent in 1976–80, and 7 percent in 1981–85. The actual rates in increase were 11.6 percent in 1971–75, 8.2 percent in 1976–80 and 6.2 percent in 1981–85.[9] The reduction in rates of growth of machine-building output were due to a sharp decline in the rate of growth of investment in machine building and metalworking: the average annual rate of increase fell from 9.6 percent in 1971–75 to 4 percent in 1981–85.[10]

For several types of machine-building products that are most important for the economy, no increases in production were planned. Thus planned volumes of production in 1975 were 2.1 million automobiles and 575,000 tractors; for 1980 the corresponding figures were 2.1 million and 580,000.*[11] Therefore the planned (and, all the more so, actual) slowdown in machine-building output could not possibly have stimulated increased growth in requirements for steel.

In spite of the drop in rates of growth of investment in the economy, which became obvious by the beginning of the 1970s, the idea

---

*In subsequent years data concerning production of automobiles disappeared from Soviet statistical sources, which suggests a drop in production.

of growing requirements for steel was firmly retained in all planning projection calculations. This idea is immanent in the mentality of Soviet planners. It stems from the ideology of Soviet planning, one of the basics of which is the notion of the necessity of uninterrupted increase in the rates of growth of heavy industry. Here is a characteristic pronouncement by an official of Gosplan in the Ukraine, which produces about 40 percent of the steel in the USSR: "High rates of development of machine building, an increase in the volume of construction, and growth of metal consumption in other branches of the economy will lead to a continuation of the strained situation in supplying the economy with ferrous metals in the forecast period" (the reference is to the period 1976–90).[12]

Following the logic of this assertion, one must suppose that a decline in the rates of growth of the development of machine building and construction must lead to a lessening of "the strained situation in supplying . . . ferrous metals."[13] And if this does not take place, then what remains is to propose that perhaps the relative expenditures of metal in the production of a unit of construction and machine building will rise. Only this could objectively justify growth in the requirement for steel.

The Metal Intensiveness of Construction

The basic expenditure of steel in construction, which consumes about 20 percent of all steel produced in the USSR, is in the production of structural shapes.[14] It is precisely in this area that a reduction in relative steel expenditures has taken place, due, first, to intensive replacement of steel structural shapes with reinforced concrete and, second, to a significant increase in the share of prestressed concrete.

The replacement of steel structural parts by reinforced concrete during the 1960s and 1970s was the basic direction of modernization of the construction industry in the USSR, a process that hypertrophied, contradicting technological and economic expedience. The production of prefabricated reinforced concrete continues to expand at rates exceeding not only the production of steel structural parts but also the growth of construction as a whole. During 1960–85 the volume of construction output increased approximately threefold, while the production of prefabricated, reinforced concrete grew more than fourfold. During 1975–80 the annual growth

rates were 1.4 percent and 2 percent, respectively.[15] At the end of
the 1970s the correlation of growth of the production of steel and
reinforced concrete structural parts was 1.0 to 1.3.[16]

Paralleling the growth of the volume of prefabricated, reinforced
concrete and its displacement of steel structural parts has been a
reduction in the expenditure of steel per cubic meter of reinforced
concrete production. While the production of reinforced concrete
increased more than fourfold during 1960–81, the expenditure of
metal in its production grew only threefold.[17] This trend is explained primarily by the growth in the share of prestressed structural parts in the total volume of reinforced concrete production (at
the beginning of the 1980s one-third of all reinforced concrete structural parts were prestressed). Per cubic meter, 8–10 kilograms less
steel is used in prestressed than in ordinary reinforced concrete.[18]

In recent years, a turning point has become evident with respect to
the use of steel structural parts in construction. The ineffectiveness
of using reinforced concrete in many projects and the expedience of
using steel, especially in the construction of industrial enterprises
in regions with extreme climatic conditions (the north of Siberia), is
understood by many specialists in the USSR. Gosplan and ministries are beginning to depart from the global introduction of reinforced concrete and are turning to expanded use of steel structural
parts. In the second half of the 1970s thirteen large plants for the
production of light metal structural parts were built.[19] But the entire
ideology of construction design and the majority of standards are
directed toward the primary use of reinforced concrete, and it will
take many years to overcome this inertia. The objective barrier is the
insufficient allocation of steel, especially low-alloy, heat-treatment-
strengthened steel. Apparently the trend toward reducing the metal
intensiveness of construction will extend into the foreseeable future.

Metal Intensiveness in the Machine-Building Industry

In 1975 Nikolai Smelyakov, deputy minister for foreign trade,
declared in a book that made a great impression on the Soviet public
that "the metal intensiveness [the steel-output ratio per unit of final
product—B.R.] in the domestic machine-building industry is 25
percent higher than in other industrially developed countries."[20]
Let us look at a number of examples.

The metal-output ratio of the K-700 tractor produced by the Kirov plant in Leningrad amounts to 45.5 kilograms per unit of horsepower, and for the A-14 tractor from the Wagner Corp. (U.S.) it is 25 kilograms horsepower; the MTZ-50 tractor produced by the Minsk plant has a metal-output ratio of 52 kilograms horsepower, while the D-17D tractor's (Allis-Chalmer, U.S.) is 49 kilograms horsepower. The 100-t converter manufactured by the Zhdanov Heavy Machine Building Plant weighs 626 tons,* whereas a converter of the same capacity produced by Faster (Austria) weighs 426 tons. The 25-114 tube-welding mill produced by the Elektrostal'mash Plant weighs 2,750 tons; the West German firm of Friedrich Kocks produces the same type of mill weighing 1,600 tons.[21]

A large number of similar examples may be cited in practically every area of the machine-building industry. How can we account for the higher metal-output ratios in Soviet industry? In discussing this question, there are a number of basic points to consider.

How is the specific metal-output ratio generated in the machine-design process or, in other words, do stress analyses of machine parts assume an optimal correspondence between the consumption of metal and the reliability of the parts in operation?

Do the structure of the output of metal and the range of metal products meet the demand for prudent consumption of metal in the manufacturing of machine parts?

Does metalworking technology, likewise the industrial level and structure of the stock of metalworking equipment, allow for efficient utilization of metal in machine building?

Machine Design

To a large degree, the metal-output ratio of the final product of the machine-building industry is determined in the machine-design process. The very methods of stress analysis are essential here. Soviet engineers use outdated methods of analysis. In many situations, the cross-sections of the beds of metal-cutting machines, the frames of presses and forging machines, and the housings of rolling mills are not computed, and instead what are referred to as "design considerations" are taken into account. Multiples of the safety margin (sometimes five and even tenfold) may be assumed in deciding on the cross-sections of many types of machinery. These extraordi-

*All references in the text are to metric tons.

nary safety margins are the result of insufficient knowledge of the properties of materials and distrust of analyses of stresses arising in structures when in use.

It has long been the practice in Soviet industry to apply a correction factor to the calculated cross-section. This correction factor reaches 1.1 for low-alloy steel and 1.15 for carbon steel. (The purpose has been to ensure the strength of structures by taking into account the nonuniform properties of the steel used.) Just one application of this factor increases the weight of machinery and structures by 11–18 percent, or 8–12 million tons of steel per year.[22] How justified is such an expensive distrust of the quality of steel? Is the quality of steel that low in fact? Could it simply be a matter of habit, the wish to overinsure, and ultimately a lack of material incentives for economizing on the use of metal in the design of machinery?

Large-scale observations conducted in the mid-1970s demonstrated that there is a reason to distrust the strength of only 2–3 percent (at most) of the rolled products manufactured from carbon steel. The other 97–98 percent possess entirely stable strength properties and there would seem to be no good reasons for such overinsurance.[23] But machine designers must be absolutely certain of the strength properties of the steels they use, and the plants that supply the steel do not provide any sort of quality guarantees.

In fact, techniques of industrial and product quality control at Soviet steel plants are primitive, and without modern techniques of quality control the plants are unable to produce rolled products of assured quality. The lack of such quality assurance in turn gives rise to distrust on the part of designers responsible for establishing the safety margins in machinery and structures. Steel quality is increasing, but the safety margins, as before, remain high.

With all these drawbacks, a number of positive steps have nevertheless been taken, intended for decreasing the specific metal-output ratios of machinery and structures. In the early 1980s standards and rules for the analysis of machine designs and structural elements were reviewed with an eye toward ensuring full use of the strength properties of metals under actual operating conditions. We do not have any information as to the implementation of these steps. But in light of the recently adopted resolution calling for increased material incentives to encourage machine designers to economize on their use of metal, along with the greater set of options available to designers as a result of an expansion in the range of rolled products, which now includes a higher proportion of flat-rolled products (we will discuss this point below), there is no reason to doubt that the specific consumption of metal at the stage of machine design is dropping.

Relation between Rolled Product and Cast Product

From the standpoint of the specific metal-output ratio, the extraordinarily high proportion of iron and steel casting is an important feature in the structure of metal utilized in Soviet machine building. In 1975 iron and steel casting constituted 45 percent of the metal used to produce machinery in the USSR, or roughly 200–250 percent that of other industrially developed countries. The proportion of rolled product amounted to 55 percent.[24]

A survey of machine-building plants conducted by the Central Statistical Administration in the early 1980s showed that seventy-one out of every one hundred plants produced iron casting, twenty-seven produced steel casting, and eighty-four forged pieces.[25]

Soviet specialists are well aware that such a high proportion of casting hinders efforts to reduce the weight of machinery and is one of the basic reasons for the high rates of consumption of metal in machine building. But such a statement by itself is oversimplified and requires refinement.

So one-sided and unqualified an approach to casting manufacture is unjustified. In fact, there are advanced techniques for the production of cast products which yield high-quality casting exhibiting a high degree of surface smoothness, with small machining allowances. A greatly outdated mode of production of casting, however, prevails in the Soviet Union; 80–90 percent of the overall output of casting is manufactured in sand molds.[26]

Induction furnaces are almost never used for smelting iron casting. Instead, cupolas are mainly used, with designs dating to the 1930s to 1950s. This is why castings are so heavy and possess low strength properties. By smelting cast iron in induction furnaces—a technique widely used in many industrially developed countries— it is possible to greatly reduce the weight and to roughly double the strength of castings by comparison with castings manufactured in cupolas.

Induction furnaces have only just begun to appear at some Soviet machine-building plants. Very few plants are now equipped with these types of furnaces.

There is considerable room for reducing the metal-output ratio of the machine construction industry through improvements in casting technology. In the Soviet casting industry, the introduction of induction furnaces would be a veritable technological revolution and would lead not only to a number of economic and technical advances but also to a marked drop in the weight of machinery.

For some time the development of this technology has been held back by the absence of plants specially designed for the production of induction furnaces. The first and (as yet) only such plant (at Novozybkov, in Bryansk oblast) expressly intended for the production of such furnaces was constructed in the late 1970s; it has an annual production capacity of 320 furnaces.

What was actually achieved, however, was somewhat less, and not only because of the inadequate supply of induction furnaces; there was also the need to modernize antiquated casting shops. But this means a considerable investment; furthermore, it would be necessary to temporarily reduce the output of cast products, an extremely painful step for any machine-building plant.

Efforts aimed at determining the optimal ratio between rolled and cast products in the overall volume of structural materials used in the Soviet machine-building industry must deal with a number of conflicting issues. The problem has not been solved, and may never be solved as long as the range of rolled product remains entirely inadequate, and as long as an outdated technology for the production of casting, resulting in low-quality castings, remains in use.

The State Planning Commission and machine-building ministries have tried to make a convincing case for doing away with cast product and replacing it with rolled product, more precisely, welded parts made from flat-rolled metal. This would achieve a savings in metal through a reduction in scrap in machining and also through lighter welded parts. But Soviet steel plants are not able to supply the machine-building industry with rolled product of the proper dimensions and shape and, consequently, a considerable proportion of the metal is turned into chips in the course of machining, or scrap in gas-cutting operations.

Because of the limited range of products, no great reduction in the weight of machine parts can be achieved. As a result, the volume of metal waste in the manufacture of machine parts from rolled product is not simply not lower than when casting is used, but in fact is much higher.

From a theoretical standpoint, it might be asserted that rolled product ought to supplant casting where there are no constraints on the range of products. But it is highly unlikely that these constraints will disappear in the foreseeable future. In absolute terms, therefore, the production of steel and iron casting will unavoidably increase. The Soviet machine-building industry has no other way of producing structural metal and billets.

With all these difficulties and conflicts accompanying changes occurring in the structure of the stock of structural metal in the machine-building industry, the proportion of iron and steel casting nevertheless dropped in the 1975–80 period from 30.0 percent to 28.3 percent (iron casting) and from 9.7 percent to 9.3 percent (steel casting), while the proportion of welded structures increased from 48.3 percent to 50 percent.[27]

As is clear from these data, the changes have been occurring at extremely slow rates. Nevertheless, they are occurring. We should not forget the enormous scale at which the industry we are discussing operates. The range of rolled product has also expanded and new sets of relationships are being created; welded constructions are slowly replacing castings.

Though the technology of casting manufacture has not been improved, the weight of welded constructions made from the corresponding types of flat-rolled metal product is still much lower than in the case of constructions made from castings. For example, the weight of welded beds used for grinders and lathes and also for presses is 30–40 percent lighter than the weight of casting iron, and is 30–40 percent more rigid.[28]

Finally, we must recognize that with all the drawbacks in the range of rolled products, the use of welded constructions has tended to expand, a factor that is reducing the specific metal-output ratios in the machine-building industry.

Range and Quality of Rolled Product

The limited range of rolled product manufactured in general and an insufficient output of rolled product with enhanced strength properties in particular has led to the widespread practice of replacing unavailable shapes and dimensions of rolled product of desired quality with larger sizes of sheet of reduced quality.

The results have been an increase in the weight of structures and machinery without any basis in the stress analyses or the technological demands, and extraordinary volumes of waste in the ma-chining process. Here is the reason for the low utilization factors for steel in the chemical machine-building industry (0.7), the auto-mobile industry (0.68), and machine tool manufacture (0.6);[29] these factors have not shown any signs of decreasing.

A far lower proportion of the total volume of rolled products manufactured by the Soviet steel industry consists of flat-rolled metal, by comparison with the situation in other industrially devel-oped countries (40–42 percent versus 60–65 percent).[30]

There are even greater differences in the production of cold-rolled sheet steel. Cold-rolled sheet steel constitutes roughly 20 percent of the total output of flat-rolled metal, which is approximately 30 percent less than is the case in the United States.[31] Note that it is precisely through the use of flat-rolled metal, particularly cold-rolled product, that the greatest decrease in the specific metal-out-put ratio of products may be achieved.

The use of thermally hardened and low-alloy steel sheet and roll-formed shapes is also a major factor in reducing the structural metal-output ratio of machinery. In the latter half of the 1970s low-alloy steel sheet amounted to 13 percent of the total volume of flat-rolled product, thermally hardened rolled metal 5.6 percent, and roll-formed shapes 1.2 percent.[32]

This is insufficient to meet the needs of the Soviet machine-building industry. The production of roll-formed shapes lags con-siderably; by means of roll-formed shapes, it is possible to achieve maximal strength and rigidity of structures and machine parts with minimal consumption of steel.

According to computations from the State Planning Commission, a drop in the rate of consumption of metal in the machine-building industry of 18–20 percent, the goal set for the industry for the 1981–85 period, would require a 200–250 percent increase in the output of low-alloy steel sheet, thermally hardened rolled metal, cold-rolled sheet metal, and roll-formed shaped.[33] We do not believe such a goal is attainable.

An increase in the proportion of rolled product in the form of flat-rolled metal is among the most important indices in long-range plans for the development of the Soviet steel industry. Actual achievements, however, often fall far short of the plans. In the late 1960s a scientific group within the State Committee for Science and Technology concluded that the proportion of rolled product in the form of sheet must be increased to at least 45 percent by 1975 and to 50–55 percent by 1980. In fact, in these years the figures for flat-rolled metal amounted to 40 percent and 42 percent, respectively. In 1985 it was 41 percent.[34]

Nevertheless, despite the appreciable lagging behind international indices, and even domestic plans, positive shifts in the structure and quality of rolled product are undoubtedly occurring in the Soviet Union. Over the past decade the use of flat-rolled metal made from low-alloy steels and roll-formed shapes has increased markedly. The production of cold-rolled strip metal increased in 1981 with the commissioning of new production capacities at the Karaganda, Verkh-Isetsk, Magnitogorsk, and Cherepovets plants.

Though the rates of growth of the production of flat-rolled metal are low despite the commissioning of the new sheet mills, and though the strength properties of low-alloy steels are not high enough (the yield point of most of these steels is at most 50 kilograms per square meter, whereas most of the steel produced in the United States has a yield point in the range 60–90 kilograms per square meter), the Soviet machine-construction industry is receiving increasingly higher-quality flat-rolled metal from the steel industry and, moreover, an increasingly wider range of flat-rolled metal. But there remains the opposite problem: is Soviet metalworking technology ready to make efficient use of improved rolled product?

Technological Adaptability of the Machine-Building Industry to the Use of High-Quality Flat-Rolled Metal

The facts indicate that the introduction of types of rolled steel that are efficient in terms of consumption of metal has lagged behind not only because of insufficient production of these types of steel. The machine building industry itself, and especially metalworking shops, are not ready to make use of high-quality types of output. This is clear from the significant quantities of high-quality types of rolled product manufactured for which there is no demand, and which consequently must be returned to the steel plants for remachining.

For example, the Magnitogorsk plant, after a considerable investment, began producing cold-rolled steel strip from high-tolerance rolled metal with a high degree of surface finishing. In its decision to allocate the investment to the factory, the State Planning Commission assumed an extraordinarily high demand for such high-quality rolled metal, so extraordinary indeed that each ton would be greedily snapped up by machine-building plants. But in fact it turned out that the demand for this type of steel is low, since many plants are not ready to make efficient use of it, and the price is high. As a result, the Magnitogorsk factory has had to suffer great losses.[35]

The result is that under pressure from the State Planning Commission, and wishing to demonstrate their desire to economize on metal consumption through the use of high-quality types of rolled product, the machine-building ministries transmit requests for the production of this type of rolled product to the steel plants. But the machine-building plants themselves are unable to use the metal.

How might we explain the inability of the machine-building industry and metalworking shops to make efficient use of high-quality rolled metal, and how does this inability manifest itself? For many years, Soviet machine designers have suffered from a certain "mindset" arising from constant shortages of flat-rolled metal. They are well aware of the advantages and efficiency of sheet metal. But to actually switch over to the use of flat-rolled metal requires a change in the principles of design and technological "thought," and where there is a shortage of sheet metal (which obviously cannot be excluded), major difficulties and financial losses can be expected. Doubts that flat-rolled product of desired dimensions and quality can actually be obtained are not the only reason why the introduction of flat-rolled product at the stage of machine design and construction lags behind.

No less important a factor—and possibly even more important—is the desire of machine builders to produce heavier output, since plan fulfillment (consequently, awards) depends on the output of machinery as measured by weight.

The stock of metalworking equipment is inadequate for modernizing the metalworking industry. The proportion of the stock of metalworking equipment in the form of forging and pressing machinery amounts to only 16 percent approximately. Metal-cutting lathes predominate. The proportion of machinery used for pressure stamping in the manufacture of forging and pressing machinery is at most 20–22 percent.[36]

At the same time, judging from the experience of other industrially developed countries, the proportion of metalworking equipment in the form of forging and pressing machinery should be at least twice as high. It is worth recalling the low technical level of gas-welding operations at Soviet machine-building enterprises. Soviet industry produces an extremely limited quantity of numerically controlled gas-welding machines and produces almost no minicomputer-controlled metal-cutting machinery that would ensure maximally efficient cutting of sheet metal.

Because of the inadequate technological adaptability of the machine-building industry to the pressing, stamping, and welding of flat-rolled metal, there is still a great demand for steel and iron casting, and the demand for sheet steel lags behind. The Soviet machine-building industry is switching over only very slowly to the use of high-quality types of rolled product and, thereby, is not encouraging steel plants with any degree of vigor to produce these types of rolled product.

In considering the possibility of reducing the metal-output ratio of finished products, and thereby reducing the demand for metal, we should bear in mind qualitative elements in the manufacture of rolled steel. According to projections of the State Planning Commission, the use of rolled product from ordinary carbon steel reduces metal consumption by 20 percent; the use of thermally hardened, cold-rolled sheet steel in place of hot-rolled sheet or of roll-formed shapes in place of hot-rolled shapes reduces metal consumption by 25 percent.[37]

Shortages of precisely these types of rolled product, according to industrial executives, has forced machine-building plants to produce heavier machinery, leading to greater waste of steel in the machining process. This, in brief, is the main reason for the high specific metal content of Soviet machinery and equipment and, in general, why technological progress in machine construction lags behind.

But this oversimplifies the problem, and in fact our discussion has been one-sided. If, somehow, the Soviet steel industry could all at once manufacture rolled product in line with the decrees of the State Committee for Science and Technology, the governmental body responsible for forecasting technological progress in the Soviet Union, would there not arise a crisis of overproduction of rolled product, which has commonly been assumed to be in short supply?

The question is not entirely rhetorical, if we bear in mind the degree of technological adaptability of the machine-building industry to efficient use of this type of rolled product. I. Pashko, chief expert in the steel industry of the State Planning Commission, made the following surprisingly blunt and highly authoritative statement: "The high level of use of steel and iron casting, together with insufficient use of flat-rolled metal (there is now a relative 'oversupply' of flat-rolled metal and a 'shortage' of section metal), indicates that the machine-building industry is not ready to adopt the new technological processes for the manufacture of lighter machinery made of flat-rolled metal."[38]

In this sentence we have the key to understanding the central issue here. It seems that even the limited quantity of high-quality flat-rolled metal that is produced often is not used for its originally intended purpose, and further, this output exceeds the actual (though not the planned) demand, and so there is an "oversupply."

How can the constant declarations about shortages of high-quality rolled product be explained in light of the creation of oversupplies of the rolled product? The reasons for this paradoxical situation may be found in the system of industrial planning and plans for metal consumption, topics we shall discuss below.

Allocations Mechanisms in the Soviet Steel Industry

We have come to the conclusion that neither the dynamics of capital investment nor the dynamics of the metal-output ratio of industrial production and the construction industry is responsible for, or can account for, the growth in the shortage of steel. Even despite some drop in output (2–3 percent), it is clear from our analysis that there exist real tendencies toward an easing in the shortage. But these real tendencies remain buried beneath the weight of pathological features that fill the entire Soviet economy. Nevertheless, information does come through on occasion which in no way supports the general perception of growing shortages. Let us look at an example.

In 1981–82 the Moscow Procurement Office surveyed three hundred industrial enterprises in the city for the purpose of studying their supplies of raw materials, including metal. These enterprises all had an overabundance of metal reserves; further, these reserves were growing, in fact, faster than the growth of production; thus in the 1971–80 period the reserves increased by 84 percent, while industrial output increased by 78 percent.[39] It was thus concluded that the supplies of metal available to the enterprises had improved.

How, then, did the authors of the survey explain the "complaints of those who had been surveyed as to shortages of metal"? In their opinion, "extraordinary supplies at some enterprises seem to have created *artificial* shortages at others" (emphasis added). They even generalized: "such immobilization of resources will lead to artificial shortages of resources throughout the nation."[40] But no enterprise had been found in the survey where shortages in fact existed. We can only suppose that such enterprises were not in the sample.

Here is the pattern, as seen from a survey at a single plant (the metalist factory in Moscow).[41] In 1981 the plant's output plan for the coming year was barely increased, whereas 50 percent more steel was demanded for the plant by comparison with the previous year. The plant managers knew from the beginning that their demand would not be granted. They were guided, however, by the principle that "the more you ask, the more you get." And they were right. As a result, metal supplies at the factory turned out to be somewhat greater than necessary.

The extra metal was added to several years' accumulation already greatly in excess of the assigned reserve quota. There is no place to store all these quantities of rolled metal, which are always in short supply. Different types and grades of steel are piled up haphazardly at the plant site and rust away in the open air.

At the factory, not only is the metal stored carelessly, but the very consumption of metal in the production process is highly inefficient. Thus, the metal-utilization factor amounts to 0.62 (that is, 38 percent of the metal becomes waste). A portion of the rolled metal at the factory (otherwise in short supply) is counted neither in accounting nor reporting documents and, thus, does not seem to exist. As the survey showed, such a pattern may be observed at many other enterprises.

Why should the factories have a need for such large quantities of metal? The accumulated reserves constitute a layer of fat. Just as a camel in the desert can survive for long periods of time without any food because of its fatty deposits, so many enterprises are able to function undisturbed because of this "fat."

Such a state of affairs is natural not only to individual enterprises but also to entire regions. Thus in 1982 the production plan for rolled metal as a whole for the USSR was not met, and as a result

enterprises in Leningrad, the principal center of the machine-construction industry in the Soviet Union, received correspondingly
lesser quantities of rolled metal than had been planned for them.
There was, however, no catastrophe. The Leningrad organizations
responsible for procurement "searched in-house and put to use" the
missing quantity of metal.[42]

But can such greed be explained only by the desire to create
reserves against possible shortages? No, this is not the only reason.
Factories trade in metal and exchange it for different types of goods
and services. As the Soviet press has recognized, "steel has become
a special kind of currency; once the consumer has snipped off what
he doesn't need, he can barter it for whatever he pleases."[43]

The accumulation of "vast reserves greatly in excess of the assigned quota"[44] and the existence of a black market in metal are no
secret to the governmental procurement organization. But officials
put up with it and adapt to the existing state of affairs, as can be seen
from their efforts to regulate buying and selling and exchange operations involving metal.

Trade in metal, which bypasses the governmental planning and
procurement offices, occurring directly between enterprises, is part
of the "shadow economy," as *Sotsialisticheskaya industriya*, the
organ of the Central Committee of the CPSU, terms it.[45] When one
speaks of the shadow economy (or, as it is called in the West, the
"second economy"), it is usually understood that this economy
operates in parallel with the basic ("first") economy. Such a division seems artificial. An economic system now exists and is rapidly
developing.

The upper levels (national income and its distribution into consumption and accumulation, capital investment, distribution of
manpower, wages, defense expenditures, regional economic appor-
tionment) of this economic system are centrally planned, regulated,
and implemented. At the lower levels of this economic system,
however, particularly at the very bottom of the system, there exists
an unrestrained and unregulated market. Here corrections for market deviations, errors, and awkward situations that arise at the upper levels seem to occur. The sluggish centralized planning system,
which is increasingly slipping as the scale of the economy expands,
is increasingly being replaced by the market.

The vast inventories form a base of supplies for this market, a
market controlled neither by the State Planning Committee, the

State Procurement Authority, nor the Central Statistical Administration. But according to official data at the start of the 1980s, reserves of the means of production in the Soviet economy, a large portion of which are in the form of equipment and spare parts and various materials in short supply, amount to over 128 billion rubles,[46] or roughly as much as was spent on new industrial equipment for all the years of the tenth five-year plan.

But government statistics cover only part of these reserves. An inventory of equipment performed in 1972 found at various enterprises tens of thousands of machines and pieces of equipment that had not been accounted for in the statistical reports. A very large portion of these reserves constitutes the exchange or marketing reserve of the enterprises.

Soviet managers are forced to put up with the development of an extensive and intensive sphere of the economy which remains independent, unplanned, unregulated, and unaccounted for by governmental statistics.

The actual quantities of steel that are redistributed through the channels of the shadow economy are impossible to calculate even approximately, though one thing is clear: the flows regulated by the State Planning Committee and State Procurement Authority are only the visible portion of the iceberg.

The liberties permitted by the upper levels of management of the centralized Soviet economy with regard to the marketing activity (in its warped Soviet form) which extends throughout the entire sphere of metal consumption are entirely understandable. The state system of planning the production and consumption of metal and deliveries to enterprises is unable to handle the goals set for it. Let us briefly consider how this system operates.

Note, first, that metal production and consumption planning are maximally centralized and organized according to a standard pattern, that is, in the same way as for production and consumption in the chemical industry, cement industry, and the output of other types of nondefense industries. At the highest level there is the State Planning Committee, which is responsible for deciding the general figures of the balance of production and consumption. Somewhat lower is the State Procurement Authority, which is responsible for regulating and coordinating the activity of regional Central Procurement Administrations and Central Procurement Administrations specialized for each branch of the economy. Below, and roughly at the same level in the hierarchy, are the Ministry of Ferrous Metallurgy and Soyuzglavmetall (Central Administration for Procurement and Distribution of Ferrous Metals), which is under the authority of the State Procurement Authority.

The ministry is responsible for meeting the metal production plan. Soyuzglavmetall plays a central role in determining the demand for steel and steel products. It is the principal body responsible for establishing how much and precisely what grade and category of steel must be allocated to a particular enterprise; as such, it serves as a coordinating center bringing customers together with producers.

Thus studying the centralized metal procurement planning system means studying the activity of Soyuzglavmetall. This system, created mainly in the 1940s, is today an anachronism if we consider the scale and multiplicity of technological relations and structures typical of the modern Soviet economy. It is the source of the basic drawbacks and mismatches of the existing methodology of metal procurement.

First mismatch. The production plan for rolled metal, in a breakdown by category, is developed by the Ministry of Ferrous Metallurgy in May or June of the year preceding the plan year, while orders for rolled metal in a breakdown by type are not submitted to Soyuzglavmetall by customers until September. Thus the Ministry of Ferrous Metallurgy develops the production plan for each plant without having available the plant's itemized demand. This it receives only after the plan has already been essentially developed and transmitted to the steel plant.

Soyuzglavmetall is unable to transmit the itemized steel demand to the ministry in time, since the collection and processing of the orders is a lengthy process, and modern data collection methods based on the use of computers have yet to be implemented. In developing the plan, the ministry is oriented toward the existing breakdown of the structure of rolled metal consumption by category and the rough estimates provided by Soyuzglavmetall on the basis of staff experience and intuition. Hence subsequent corrections of the plans are unavoidable.

Second mismatch. Planning and evaluation of plan fulfillment are based on value and weight indices. The breakdown of the plans by category of rolled metal plays a subordinate and secondary role. The steel plants do not suffer seriously if they meet their production plan in tonnage and in rubles, though their range of rolled metal may not expand. But the customer requires precisely an expanded range of rolled metal, and this is the principal task now confronting the Soviet steel industry. Let us explain this situation in more detail.

The range of rolled metal products is planned by the plants in aggregated indices, and not in detail. For example, it was planned that in 1983 the Novolipetsk plant would produce 500,000 tons of "rolled strip 1.2–3.9 millimeters in thickness."[47] There is considerable difference between rolled metal 1.2 millimeters thick versus 3.9 millimeters thick in terms of the labor intensiveness of the manufacturing process and in terms of utilization properties.

The plant itself is given the authority to determine how much rolled metal of a particular thickness it is to produce at this juncture. If the tonnage plan is not met, the plant workers forfeit bonuses that can be as much as 20 percent of their wages. From the technological and economic standpoints, it is far easier for the plant to meet the plan by producing thicker sheet, which it does.

Customers, on the other hand, have much greater need for thinner sheet. When customers must choose between taking thicker sheet (which they have not ordered) or getting nothing, naturally they agree to accept the thicker sheet so as to either exchange (possibly sell) it or machine it to the necessary thickness, letting half the metal go to waste. It is noteworthy that price does not play a major role either for manufacturer or customer.

Because of this sort of practice, three-fourths of all steel plants were unable to meet their 1982 contractual obligations with customers for deliveries of the desired range of categories of rolled metal. The demand for categories of rolled metal in short supply was met only 40–60 percent of the time.[48]

How does this happen? In fact, the orders Soyuzglavmetall receives from customers are not for such aggregated dimensions of rolled metal, but for far more differentiated dimensions. Does this mean it is unable to require the manufacturing plants to produce rolled metal of the category needed by the customer? Is this not one of the principal functions of Soyuzglavmetall?

Third mismatch. Yes, this is precisely one of its principal functions. But Soyuzglavmetall, which is supposed to keep track of the level of customer-order fulfillment, itself often suggests and decides that one category of rolled metal may be replaced by another (in this case, thin sheet by thick sheet). There are any number of reasons to account for the powerlessness of Soyuzglavmetall.

First, neither the State Planning Committee nor Soyuzglavmetall—the two central bodies responsible for planning and regulating the production and consumption of metal—has available information on the actual capacities of the plants for the production of different categories of rolled metal. Their only information is the overall mean hourly productivity of the rolling mills with respect to an aggregated category. Therefore they are unable to make full use of the actual capacities of the rolling mills. Thus Soyuzglavmetall lacks the ability to regulate the production of metal in accordance with the itemized demand.

Second, even if Soyuzglavmetall had available the necessary information, it would be physically unable to bring demand in line with the production of rolled metal by type and grade at the scale of the entire Soviet economy. Many tens of thousands of customers are served by Soyuzglavmetall, whereas there are over a million shape and size categories required by customers. Allocation of orders to the factories occurs over a period of two months. The use of computers still lies in the future. The most that it can do is to allocate some proportion of the orders to the most important customers by roughly five hundred actual categories of rolled metal and submit orders for other categories of rolled metal to the manufacturers in forty-nine aggregated categories; thus, in the above example, "rolled strip 1.2 to 3.9 millimeters in thickness."

Computers are still not used to handle customer orders, which mainly follow the principle "from the level already attained." The use of the production capacities of the rolling mills is determined on the basis of individual experience and the intuition of the staff of Soyuzglavmetall. Naturally, requests from customers for permission to exchange types of rolled metal they do not need for types they do need get lost in an ocean of paperwork, and since Soyuzglavmetall is unable to regulate each particular instance, it willingly agrees to the substitution. Thus its activity promotes the marketing activity of the enterprises.

In recent years, the State Planning Committee and State Procurement Authority have tried to modernize the outdated system of metal production and consumption planning. These efforts have proceeded in two directions.

Production. It was decided that the production of thinner, high-quality, consequently more labor-intensive categories of rolled metal should be as profitable to produce as thicker, lower-quality, consequently less labor-intensive categories. Therefore, in 1981–82 production planning in terms of "conventional tonnage"—that is, in terms of weight units derived from labor-output ratios for the unified quality standards—were adopted expressly for this purpose and introduced as an experiment at certain factories.

Consumption. The allocation of rolled metal should be computerized in light of its quality properties and in more highly itemized category units than conventional tonnage.

These innovations are supposed to revolutionize the entire system of production and consumption planning and make the system far more efficient.

If production plan fulfillment is measured in terms of conventional tonnage, the wages and bonus rates of the workers at the steel plants would have to be expressed not only in terms of the degree of fulfillment of the tonnage plan but also in terms of the assigned range of categories.

By computerizing the process of planning demand and allocation of orders to steel plants, it is possible to expand and increase the detail to which the production of rolled metal may be specified and, thereby, to coordinate demand with production. The potential for excess buildups of rolled metal would thereby be eliminated, and the objective factors responsible for the existence and development of a black market in metals would vanish. Soyuzglavmetall would then be able to submit to the Ministry of Ferrous Metallurgy the itemized demand report at the same time the production plans are developed.

These two trends in the modernization of the system would ideally lead to greater use of the production capacities of the rolling mills, balance supply and demand, and economize on the use of metal. Can we expect that these far-reaching plans will be implemented in the foreseeable future?

Like other partial improvements that have taken place in the Soviet economy in recent years, such an event would be only a palliative and, we believe, would not lead to marked results.

Planning in terms of conventional tonnage will be introduced into plant practice only very slowly and without any sort of enthusiasm. Moreover, even at those plants where planning in terms of conventional tonnage is already in effect, planning by the traditional method—that is, in terms of physical tonnage without being expressed in terms of the quality equivalent—continues to operate in parallel. In the statistical reports for these factories, plan fulfillment is shown in terms of both physical tons and conventional tons. It is especially important that data on production of rolled metal in a category breakdown be specified only in physical tons.

Thus the role of the new index is still of little importance. But one can hardly doubt that it will become more important. In fact, the very standardized labor-output ratios according to which physical tons are converted into conventional tons do not yield an effective equivalence between production costs for different types and grades of rolled metal.

The standardized group-derived ratios were developed for groups of rolling mills of the same type. But because of differences in the designs and technical characteristics of these mills, the quality of the raw billet, and a number of other technological features, the productivities of these mills in the manufacturing of the same types of rolled metal differ.

It may even happen that for some factories it is profitable to produce higher-quality and more resource-intensive categories of rolled metal, whereas for others it would be unprofitable to do so, the reason being that for some plants the conversion to conventional tonnage compensates for the increased costs, while for others it does not. In general, a changeover to conventional tonnage would so complicate the planning and accounting process that in our opinion it would make the experiment unworkable.

Computerization of the system seems a more realistic goal, at least at the procedural level. But as of 1982 the software had still not been designed, staff workers had not been trained, and the numerous organizational and procedural issues had not been decided upon. Judging in terms of rates, the training process will be delayed several more years and can hardly be expected to be introduced earlier than the late 1980s.

Optimization of the allocation of orders by type and grade of rolled metal, however, cannot be achieved without optimization of the use of the production capacities of the rolling mills. And if a steel plant is not seriously interested in producing types of rolled metal needed by the customer, then computerization of the consumption plans by itself cannot substantially improve the existing state of affairs.

From what we have said, can we conclude that mismatches and disorder in planning metal consumption and also in the market-like redistribution of metal extend to all branches of the economy equally? No, this would be an overstatement. There are branches of industry that are warped by the metal planning and supply process to a far lesser degree. Defense and shipbuilding, in particular, and the production of pipes, certain types of equipment for nuclear power stations, and some other items have a special status in the Soviet planning and procurement system. Meeting the needs of these branches of industry is a special concern of the State Planning Commission, State Procurement Authority, and the Ministry of Ferrous Metallurgy. Special departments of Soyuzglavmetall keep track of the demands of these branches for different categories and grades of steel. The enterprises in these branches do not become involved in the black market in steel. In a word, we are dealing with a privileged sphere maintained at a far higher degree of order and efficiency, though consuming a relatively small proportion of the steel output.

The limited range of categories of steel and the outdated mechanism of production and consumption planning—rather than the rates of economic growth or insufficient capacities for production of steel—are basically responsible for the unrestricted growth in demand, which in turn creates the illusion of greater and greater shortages.

CHAPTER 2

Qualitative Achievements
of Soviet Steel Production

For almost two decades now improvements in the quality and variety of rolled steel have been both an objective economic necessity and a primary goal of Soviet leadership in ferrous metallurgy. At all levels, from the general secretary to the steelworker, all have proclaimed that the "tonnage fetish" (that is, the pursuit of quantitative indices of production) must be repudiated and that resources and efforts must be redirected to improve the quality of production.

In 1984 V. Antipin, head of the technical administration of the Ministry of Ferrous Metallurgy, said:

> Last year our country produced 153 million metric tons of steel—more than anywhere else in the world. Calculations have shown that further quantitative increases in the production of steel are not economically justified. In order to satisfy more fully the rising demands of the economy, it would be far more rational to follow a different route—to expand the production of the most economic forms of rolled steel, to increase the durability and other consumption characteristics of the metal. In other words, the primary effort should be directed toward the qualitative side of the matter.[1]

Nikolai Sklokin, director of the Institute on the Economy of Ferrous Metallurgy, also stresses the importance and necessity of a reorientation from a quantitative line of development:

The main direction of development in ferrous metallurgy in the eleventh five-year plan (1981–85) will be a radical improvement in the quality and a broader product mix in rolled steel production. The importance of a primarily qualitative line of development in ferrous metallurgy is due to the fact that a further quantitative increase in metal production demands a sharp increase in investment and operational costs, and it will not solve the goal of reducing metal consumption in the national income. Under the existing scales of production, the deficit in metal can only be overcome through a production output that is in complete accord with the parameters of contemporary technology and the rational utilization of this production.[2]

The plan for qualitative improvements embraces all branches of technology, beginning with the production of the original ore and ending with corrosion-resistant plating on the metal. An especially large number of improvements are planned in the area of higher quality and greater variety in the finished rolled metal. Although a comprehensive analysis of the implementation of these ambitious plans cannot be given here, we will try to assess their realization in the principal areas, which include (a) *in steel production,* an increased share of high-quality steel, with a minimization of expenditures of the alloy metals, and an increased proportion of refined steels;* and (b) *in production of rolled metal,* an increased share of sheet in the total production of finished rolled steel, a more diversified product mix in sheet metal, and a higher proportion of heat-tempered rolled steel. As a special goal of particular importance, an increase in the production of high-quality rolled plate has been made a top priority.

Increasing the Share of the Production of Alloyed Steels

Technological progress in machine building, the expansion of plant construction in the northern and northeastern regions of the country, and the rising demands of the energy and military sectors

---

*In the USSR "alloyed steels" refers to all those that include more than 0.2 percent alloying elements (silicon, manganese, chromium, molybdenum, vanadium, etc.). If, however, the main alloying element is manganese or silicon, the steel is not classified as alloyed unless its content exceeds 1.0 percent and 0.6 percent, respectively. The category "low-alloy steels" includes those in which the alloying elements do not exceed the above limits and their aggregate content is less than 3 percent.

of the economy have caused a sharp surge in the demand for alloyed steels that have higher durability characteristics under extreme thermal conditions, that remain stable in hostile environments, and that possess special physical properties (for example, electrotechnical steel). The volume of demand for alloyed and low-alloy steels is determined by the scale of such gigantic undertakings as the construction of the Trans-Siberian Gas Pipeline and nuclear power plants. How successful have the Soviets been in meeting their plan objectives of steel production for these vital economic needs?

In 1980 the plan called for the production of 20 million tons of rolled metal of alloyed and low-alloy steel—that is, about 17 percent of the total production that year (117–20 million tons).[3] This plan, however, was not fulfilled. Indeed, the output of rolled metal in low-alloy steels fell even farther below its target than did the total output in rolled metal: whereas output for rolled metal was 87 percent (102.9 million tons) of the plan, output in low-alloy steels stood at only 62–65 percent of plan objectives.[4] Production of rolled metal of low-alloy steels at the start of the eleventh five-year plan was less than at the start of the tenth, declining from 13.2 million tons in 1976 to 12.4 million in 1981.[5]

The created capacities were sufficient for the production of the planned volume of low-alloy rolled metal. What prevented the output in low-alloy steel from attaining the planned volume? Of the various factors at work, most important was probably the fact that the plants themselves were not interested in the production of a quality rolled metal. Metallurgical plants divide their product mix of rolled metal into "profitable" and "unprofitable"—from their own point of view. Rolled products of low-alloy steel belong to the unprofitable category, since their production consumes more labor and energy, but the enterprise receives no compensation for the higher proportionate expenditures. And more concretely, those who work in the plants derive no material benefit from this kind of production.

Soviet statistical sources do not publish data on the production of steel by type, but give only aggregate data. Nevertheless, by comparing a series of indirect data, we have derived approximate figures for the volume of production in alloyed, low-alloy, and stainless steels for the early 1980s. One source reports that in 1981 the Soviet Union produced 12.4 million tons of rolled metal of low-alloy steel.[6] By taking the magnitude of the metal input coefficient of 1.4, we find that the production of crude low-alloy steel in 1981 was 17 million

TABLE 2.1
Structure of steel types in the USSR (early 1980s)

| | Production | |
Steel grade	Millions of tons	Percent
Carbon	115.5	78.0
Low alloy	17.0	11.5
Alloyed (including stainless)	16.0	10.7
TOTAL	148.5	100.0

TABLE 2.2
Carbon and alloyed crude steel as proportion of total steel production (in percent)[9]

Steel grade	1965	1970	1975	1980s	Early 1990 (plan)
Carbon	81.5	79.7	76.3	78.0	73.0
Alloyed and low alloy	18.5	20.3	23.7	22.0	27.0

tons. Another source indicated that in the early 1980s the aggregate production of alloyed and low-alloy steel in the USSR constituted approximately 22 percent of the total crude steel production—approximately 33 million tons.[7] Since the production of low-alloy steel was 17 million tons, it follows that the production of alloyed steel was 16 million tons. According to one source, the share of stainless steel was about 11 percent.[8] The structure of crude steel production in the USSR in the early 1980s can be seen in Table 2.1. The proportional relationship of carbon and alloyed steels in the total volume of steel production has changed only insignificantly over the course of many years, as Table 2.2 shows. In addition to the data presented in Tables 2.1 and 2.2, we have data on the changes in the share of low-alloy steel in the total production of crude steel: in 1970 the share was 10 percent; in 1980, 11.5 percent; and in 1983, 11.8 percent.[10] In other words, it remained virtually unchanged for this entire period, notwithstanding all the efforts to change its proportion of total output. Taking all this into account, it seems highly unlikely that the Soviets will reach their target goals for 1990. Hence the production of alloyed and low-alloy steels significantly lags behind the planned levels, and the prospects for the foreseeable future can give Soviet leaders no grounds for optimism.

Refinement of Steels

Considerable efforts are being made in Soviet ferrous metallurgy to expand the application of refinement of steel through nonfurnace processing—through vacuum, inert gases, and synthetic slag to achieve a stable high quality in mass production. This nonfurnace processing, which helps to purify the steel from sulphur, oxygen, and nonmetallic elements, is extremely important, moreover, for increasing the effectiveness of its subsequent heat treatment.

Application of these processes, however, has thus far not received wide dissemination. In the early 1980s the refinement of steel by synthetic slags was being practiced only in a few plants (Novolipetsk plant, for instance); likewise, there were only eight vacuum-degassing facilities, of which only three (the Cherepovets, Krasnyi Oktyabr', and Magnitogorsk plants) are sufficiently powerful.[11]

The production of steels that have been subjected to nonfurnace processing was 22 million tons in 1980—15 percent of total production. In 1985 the Soviets planned to use processing by vacuum, inert gases, and synthetic slag for 50 percent of all smelted steel—that is, 75 to 80 million tons. But to judge from the modest level achieved in this area in the early 1980s (22 million tons), realization of this program appears hardly feasible.[12]

Expansion of the Product Assortment

The chief goal in the diversification of product assortment in rolled steel production was to increase the share of sheet metal in the total production of finished rolled steel. In this respect we have the following data at our disposal: the share of flat-rolled steel was 38 percent in 1970, 40 percent in 1975, 41 percent in 1980, and 41 percent in 1985. But by 1985 the plan called for this proportion to increase to 45 percent. If that goal had been achieved, then the output of finished rolled steel in 1985 would have been 50 million tons (45 percent of the total of 109 million tons produced in 1985), not the 44.8 million tons actually produced. A comparison of the dynamics in the growth of finished rolled steel and its main component parts is provided in Table 2.3. As Table 2.3 shows, the production of sheet metal, especially the cold-rolled variety, has grown at a far faster rate than rolled metal production in general. Nevertheless, this higher growth rate is still inadequate. Each year the Soviet

TABLE 2.3
Growth of production of finished rolled steel and flat steel by types
(as percentage of 1960)[13]

	1960	1965	1970	1975	1980	1985
Finished rolled steel (total)	100	141	185	226	236	248
Sheet metal (total)	100	163	217	279	303	318
Plate (over 5 mm thick)	100	152	188	239	—	—
Cold strip and sheet	100	232	338	445	450	626

Union plans for steel mills to introduce a hundred new varieties of rolled product.[14] These plans, however, have not been implemented and remain a dead letter. Here, for instance, is how one leader in the Soviet machine-building industry characterizes the situation on expanding product assortment in rolled steel: "The Ministry of Ferrous Metallurgy each year provides no more than 15 to 17 percent of the new forms of rolled steel required by our industrial branch, and the actual delivery record is still worse. For the tenth five-year plan (1976–80), the enterprises of the Ministry of Heavy Machine-Building received only 43 of the 176 forms of rolled product that it required."[15]

While there are many obstacles to plans for producing new types of rolled metal, the primary one, as suggested above, is the fact that steel plants have no interest in burdening their capacities with the production of ranges that are not economically beneficial to the enterprise. We have already noted this problem in an earlier section of this book, but it should be emphasized once more that, under these circumstances, this means inevitable conflicts with the consumer machine-building plants, for whom the limited product mix in rolled metal means a higher metal input, higher production costs, and in a number of cases the general impossibility of constructing the required machinery.

It is, furthermore, worth noting that Soviet standards for rolled steel assortments do not correspond to the contemporary demands of modern machine building. These standards, to a very substantial degree, are inferior to analogous standards in the industrially developed countries of the West. Thus the Soviet standards include a smaller number of alleviated, thin-walled, and especially complex forms of rolled metal. The subdivision in product assortment for round and square-bar steel, for example, prescribes 2-millimeter intervals; in the United States the comparable figure is 1.6 millimeters. The United States also has stricter tolerances on beams and channel bars (with maximum deviations in width and height), and it sets a smaller minimal thickness of sheet-rolled steel.[16]

Heat Treatment of Rolled Steel

Plans to raise the quality of rolled steel assign a major role to heat and thermomechanical processing, which allows one not only to improve the properties of the metal but also to conserve on the use of alloying elements. In the USSR heat treatment is used, chiefly, for rolled plates from alloyed steel and low-alloy steel. The predominant part of this production is used for the manufacture of large-diameter pipelines, ship construction, and reinforced concrete. (The scale of production of rods and bars for reinforced concrete is not substantial; in 1980 only about 600,000 tons were produced).[17] Heat treatment of rolled metal from ordinary carbon steel, with the aim of using it to replace more expensive alloyed steel, is at an insignificant level. Despite the fact that heat-treating equipment has been installed at many steel mills (thirty-three plants have units for the heat treatment of flat steel product, fourteen for bar metal, and four for rails),[18] the share of heat-processed production remains a small part of total output in finished rolled steel: in 1983 heat-processed steel made up only 8 million tons of rolled steel, or 7.5 percent of total output.[19]

Over the course of many years, Soviet ferrous metallurgy has fallen significantly short of its assigned plans for the production of heat-tempered rolled steel. In the mid-1970s it had already been planned to raise production to 14 million tons. Apparently, recognizing the unfeasibility of such leaps, Gosplan and the Ministry of Ferrous Metallurgy planned to produce only 12 million tons in 1985.[20] But to judge from the fact that only 8 million tons were produced in 1983, even these more modest goals appear unrealistic.

Rolled Plate Production

Among the numerous problems associated with the need to improve quality and to make product mix correspond better to economic and military demands, particular attention must be accorded the fastest possible increase in the production of thick sheet metal from alloyed and low-alloy steel.

The dominant expansion of production of rolled sheet in general, which exceeds the growth of production of rolled sections, is a basic characteristic of the current stage of development of rolled metal production in the USSR. For the period 1975–81, the production of all finished rolled metal increased by 4 percent, rolled sections by 1 percent, and rolled sheet and plate by 9 percent.[21]

Soviet specialized journals have written a great deal about the need to increase production of thin rolled sheet, but they barely mention the difficulties of supplying steel plate. Characteristically, however, the introduction of new capacities in rolled plate production planned for the current five-year period (1981–85) is later aimed primarily at increasing the production of plate and not thin sheet. Evidently, from the standpoint of the State Planning Commission and the Soviet leadership, steel plate is problem number one. It is important to see why they hold that view.

The development of rolled sheet and plate production in the USSR since World War II has gone through three basic stages.

The first was the 1950s. In this phase the Soviet Union rebuilt the steel plants in the south which had been destroyed by the war and also reconstructed several existing plants in the Urals and eastern regions. It was also in this decade that reversing-plate rolling mills with relatively low capacity were put into operation. The output from these mills was intended largely to satisfy the requirements of construction, which had exceptionally high growth rates during this postwar reconstruction and, to a lesser degree, the needs of machine building (which at that point were still relatively moderate). This structure of consumption also determined both the product mix and the quality of sheet metal, for it was rolled plate—of medium thickness (up to 20 millimeters) of ordinary steel grades—which predominated.

The second stage came in the 1960s, when the USSR rapidly developed and constructed huge plants with large steelmaking units. The growing numbers of consumers of rolled sheet who now appeared on the scene included such machine-building branches as the automobile, electrotechnical, and agricultural machinery industries, which require thin rolled sheet with higher-quality characteristics. At the same time, the demand for sheet of medium thickness (8–12 millimeters) also rose because of the expanding production of pipes, which were required for the construction of oil pipelines in the Volga-Ural region, the "Druzhba" oil pipeline, and gas pipelines with relatively low pressure of transported gas of up to 55 atmospheres (in Central Asia–Central Region, Bukhara-Ural, and North Caucasus–Central Region).

To expand the production of thin rolled sheet in the 1960s, three continuous and two semicontinuous wide-strip rolling mills were constructed. The establishment of these mills attenuated the acuteness of the problem with the thin strip and, to a certain degree, with sheet of medium thickness (up to 12–14 millimeters).

It appears that at the end of the 1960s those factors contributing to a higher demand for rolled plate of high quality and large thicknesses became increasingly manifest. The most important causes of the higher demand were the accelerated production of ships and the need to expand production of high-pressure pipes required for gas pipelines in extreme climatic conditions. Old plate rolling mills, many of which had already existed for half a century, could neither provide significant growth in the volume of production nor meet the higher demands on strength properties, sheet geometry, and surface quality.

The problem was partially solved by the modernization of several old mills. In particular, in 1972 the model 4500 plate rolling mill at the Il'ich plant was modernized in order to raise the qualitative characteristics of the special grades of steel it produced, including stainless steel and bimetallic plate.[22] Although the reconstruction at Il'ich was effective, such modernization did not produce the desired effect at the majority of the mills. The only real solution was to construct new mills. One such endeavor was the huge 3600 reversing-plate rolling mill that was put into operation at the Azovstal' plant in 1973.

The modernization of the 4500 mill at the Il'ich plant and the construction of the 3600 mill at Azovstal' opened the third stage in the development of high-quality plate production using modern technology. In 1970 at the Lipetsk plant and in 1975 at the Cherepovets plant, the model 2000 continuous hot rolling mills with a total annual capacity of 11–12 million tons of thin and medium-thickness rolled strip were put into operation.[23] The technological capabilities of the continuous rolling mills at Lipetsk and Cherepovets made it possible to produce strip with thicknesses of 12–16 millimeters and thus to satisfy the demand not only for thin sheet

TABLE 2.4
The consumption of plate in the mid-1970s[24]

	Millions of tons	Percent
Construction	6.3–6.4	28.0
Pipe industry	4.2–4.3	18.5
Machine-building industry (including heavy, energy, transportation, construction, and road-building machinery)	3.7–3.8	16.5
Other users	8.3–8.5	37.0
TOTAL	22.5–23.0	100.0

but in part for sheet of medium thicknesses as well. Although the construction of these two giant mills theoretically should have eased the shortage of thin strip, up to now they have not been supplied with slabs in sufficient quantity to realize their full potential, and the actual volume of production has been significantly below projected output.

Hence by the 1970s, although the Soviets acquired the potential production capacity to overcome the shortage of thin rolled sheet, they encountered an increasingly acute shortage of high-quality plate. That resulted primarily from the rising demand of shipbuilding, military industry, energy and power machinery, and pipe plants, where the requirements for high-quality plate exceeded the production potential by a steadily growing margin. Table 2.4 shows the structure of consumption of plate in the mid-1970s.

At the end of the 1970s the demand for hot-rolled plate increased sharply. According to rough estimates by Donniichermet (the Donetsk Research Institute for the Steel Industry) it amounted to 29–30 million tons in 1980.[25] Although these figures are not precisely comparable with the data in Table 2.4, they do show a sharp increase in the demand for plate after 1975. Of considerable importance, too, is the fact that, according to calculations by Donniichermet, 15 percent of the demand in 1980 (more than 4 million tons) was for plate requiring ultrasonic testing. But only the highest-quality types of rolled sheet and plate undergo ultrasonic testing in the USSR, far less than that required by existing demand. In short, it is clear that the existing plate rolling mills cannot satisfy the rapidly growing demand for high-quality plate. As a result, this urgent need for new plate rolling mills has forced the Soviets to defer all other programs for the development of rolled steel production.

Two goals are apparently being pursued in commissioning this mill. One is to satisfy chiefly the demand for rolled plate of the necessary quality by practically all of the facilities that now produce the large-diameter pipe required for gas pipelines and constructed not only from coiled strips but also from individual sheets (about 50 percent of the total capacity of pipe mills producing pipe for main gas pipelines). The Il'ich reconstruction, however, offers only a temporary solution to the problem, for the development of new gas deposits is shifting to northern latitudes and will require ever greater quantities of rolled plate. Indeed, in the 1980s the USSR plans to build its main gas pipelines with a diameter of 1.420 millimeters, generally with pressures of 75–100 atmospheres from highly cold-resistant steel.[26] Will hard currency and the availability of credit permit the Soviet Union to import pipe of this quality in growing quantities? This is a major question. It seems very likely that the following alternatives will arise: (1) either use coiled strips with continuous mills and make multilayer pipe (as is now done at the Vyksa plant); or (2) continue to expand the production of large-diameter pipe from individual plates (as is now done at the Khartsyzsk plant). But the second tactic would inevitably trigger a new crisis with metal plate. Nonetheless, in the interim the Soviets have established the capability to satisfy the demand of consumers for metal plate in this area.

The second goal is to eliminate the shipments of plates from plate to pipe plants and to shift this production to other consumers. In particular, once the rolling mill at the Il'ich plant commenced operation, the model 3600 rolling mill at the Azovstal' plant could be converted to the production of other products. This mill at Azovstal' deserves particular attention. The grades of steel produced, the capacity to produce heavy plate with a thickness of up to 200 millimeters, the technology for finishing and testing the plates (including heat treatment and ultrasonic testing on the line)—all this shows that output was primarily earmarked for shipbuilding, machinery at nuclear power plants, and military equipment.

By releasing the model 3600 mill from the production of sheet for the pipe industry, it is possible to redirect the mill entirely to help supply sheet and plate for the consumers noted above. The future of this mill is a matter of special concern to the Ministry of Ferrous Metallurgy, for now it is to produce plate of high-quality special steels. To provide the mill with such steel, the Soviets have constructed an electric furnace shop equipped with electric slag smelting facility and modern technology for steel refining.

One can expect the opening of a 2000 plate rolling mill at the Krasnyi Oktyabr' special steels plant in the mid-1980s.[27] One of its consumers will be the military industry: the plant already has a model 2000 plate rolling mill, which, to judge from the plant's specialization, produces plate from stainless and heat-resistant steels. It is very likely that the mill under construction will be analogous to the present mill and will produce the same range of products. At the Izhors Plant for the Construction of Power-Plant Machinery (which is located in Leningrad and, evidently, produces items for military use as well), construction is coming to an end for the gigantic 5000 mill for rolled metal of large-scale thick sheets, which is made from high-alloy steel and used for installations in power plants.[28] Demand is rising sharply, too, in the eastern regions of the USSR, and about 1.5 million tons of plate are currently being shipped to satisfy demand in Siberia.[29] The scale of development of pipeline transportation in Siberia dictates the need to construct a pipe plant in the region: the entire territory of the USSR east of the Urals does not have a single plant producing large-diameter pipe. To satisfy the rapidly growing demand for steel plate in this region, a huge 3600 plate rolling mill is now under construction at a West Siberian plant. The production of such pipes in the east requires a corresponding quantity of high-quality sheet of low-alloy or heat-treated carbon steel, and the 3600 mill of the West Siberian plant is supposed to help alleviate the problem.

But in building these mills Soviet planners are pursuing much broader objectives. Large-diameter pipe can be produced not only from steel plate; coiled steel from continuous rolling mills can also be used, as noted above, to produce multilayer pipe. In the mid-1970s, when the Soviets considered what sort of mill to build at the West Siberian plant, Aleksandr Tselikov (a leading ideologist of Soviet metallurgical machine building) defended the idea of a continuous strip rolling mill as the most productive and requiring the smallest investment.[30] Why, then, did the Soviets decide to build a reversing-plate rolling mill?

One reason was the very capacity of a "modern, continuous wide-strip rolling mill": its requirements for steel are approximately three times greater than that of a plate mill. The West Siberian plant simply does not have such capacities for crude steel production and it would be necessary to expand steel capacities to supply such a mill. But such expansion would drag out over many years, especially in view of the region's weak construction base—a very important factor in Siberia.

The second reason is the existing appetite for steel plate in Siberia today; as noted above, about 1.5 million tons are shipped there from western regions of the country. Steel plate is needed in Siberia today and the demand for it will grow in the near future. That rising demand is a direct result of the development of heavy machine building (energy and power machinery, hoisting-transporting equipment) planned in West Siberia, without which it would be impossible to develop the Kansk-Achinsk fuel-energy complex and carry out other ambitious programs for the industrial development of Siberia.

The Soviet leadership apparently foresees a further expansion of demand for steel plate, notwithstanding the expected opening of the plate rolling mills already under construction.[31] With respect to the long term, there is also a plan to construct a 2800 plate rolling mill at the Orsk-Khalilovsk combine in the Urals.

All the facts examined here attest to the consistent and earnest efforts of the Soviet leadership to solve the problem of steel plate as quickly as possible.

Plan for the Second Half of the 1980s

As is evident from our review of the situation up to the early 1980s, the qualitative level of production in ferrous metallurgy has thus experienced no substantial changes and remains lower than that planned from one five-year plan to the next. Are more substantial improvements to be anticipated in the coming (twelfth) five-year plan for 1986–90?

According to the "Basic Directives for Economic and Social Development of the USSR for 1986–90 and for the Period up to the Year 2000" (which were published in November 1985),[32] the Soviets foresee a production of rolled steel in a total volume of 116–119 million tons in the year 1990. Of this, sheet metal will compose no less than 50 million tons; low-alloy rolled steel, 20–21 million tons; and heat-processed steel, 15–16 million tons. How realistic are such goals and what do they entail?

Above all, we should note that the very appearance of so detailed a breakdown of the production plan in ferrous metallurgy for the coming five-year plan (in which the basic qualitative and quantitative parameters of the five-year plan are fixed) is an extraordinary phenomenon in itself. Its very occurrence testifies to the extremely serious attitude of the new Soviet leadership toward planning in this sector of industry.

Furthermore, it is clear that, in general, the planned level of production of rolled metal is exceptionally modest. Thus the 1980 target was 115–120 million tons, of which 103 were produced; the 1985 target was 117–120 million tons, of which 109 were actually produced.[33] Now, for 1990, an even lower volume—116–119 million tons—is planned, and it seems that, after fifteen years of efforts, this level will be attained at last. One should also note a fact extraordinary for Soviet planning: in the course of three five-year plans the production target for one of the most important sectors of industrial production (and one of the most afflicted by shortfalls) has been frozen at a constant level.

Indeed, the planned increase in production of rolled steel for 1990 (7 million tons) is only half of what had been set for 1985 (14 million tons).[34] We are fully justified to conclude from this that the production in ferrous metallurgy during the twelfth five-year plan has been subordinated to a principle aptly summarized by a favorite Leninist aphorism: "Better fewer, but better."

As noted above, the main directive for an improvement in product assortment concerns an increased share of sheet metal. And just as in the general plan for rolled metal production, the volume set for the production of sheet metal in 1990 does not exceed and is actually less than that planned for 1985 (45 million tons); but by 1990 it is entirely possible that this level will at last be attained. Will this lead to the desired change in the structure of rolled metal in favor of an increased share of sheet metal? This share constituted 40 percent in 1975, 41.5 percent in 1980,[35] and (according to the plan) is to reach a level of 42–43 percent in 1990. The moderation or caution in the planned production of sheet metal possibly is explained by a compensatory improvement in composition—that is, through the production of more complex types of metal.

In the area of qualitative improvement in rolled metal production, moreover, certain advances are planned. This is attested to by the 1990 target for the production of 20–21 million tons of low-alloy steel. If one takes into account that in 1983 14 million tons were produced,[36] the plan for the twelfth five-year plan appears extremely demanding. No less substantial is the planned growth in the production of heat-treated rolled steel. It should be noted that over the course of many years the share of low-alloy steel has never exceeded 11–12 percent of total rolled steel production. To increase this in the span of one five-year plan by 5–6 percent, and to almost double production of heat-treated steel (compared to 1983), is indeed a difficult assignment. But the very fact that this goal has been formulated so concretely and written about in journals increases the probability that it will be attained.

Therefore, in assessing the qualitative advances planned for 1990, it is fair to conclude that these are in no sense revolutionary and that, on the whole, the plan has set exceedingly modest targets. At the same time, the most obvious difference between this plan and past ones is the clear emphasis on an improvement in the quality of steel, a preference for qualitative over quantitative indices.

An improvement in the qualitative characteristics of rolled metal, an assortment of production more attuned to the demands of machine-tool construction in the opinion of the plan's authors, should stimulate a more efficient utilization of metal. That, in turn, will ensure a progressive reduction in the metal intensiveness of the national income and, in the final analysis, will lead, if not to a completer elimination of the metal shortage, then to a substantial alleviation of the problem. For 1986–90, the Soviets plan to save 12–14 million tons of rolled metal consumption.[37] A corresponding goal is apparently planned for machine-tool construction, the construction industry, and other sectors of the economy that use rolled metal.

Nonetheless, and although this may sound trivial, one must state emphatically: all these clever modifications will not yield any real improvements unless there is serious (and not just cosmetic) reform in the economic system and, particularly, unless the planning for the production and consumption of metal is modernized.

CHAPTER 3

Soviet Steel Plants:
Major Descriptive Features

This chapter includes an estimate of the amounts and character of production in steel plants in the USSR. We undertook this analysis because we believe that only by studying the scale and specifics of production at the plant level is it possible to get a vivid picture of the functioning of this branch of industry and to arrive at conclusions independent of those found in Soviet sources.

The Soviet steel industry is a heterogeneous aggregate of enterprises. Many plants in the south and in the Urals have century-long histories, whereas such giants as the Novolipetskii and Cherepovetskii plants were built in the 1960s and 1970s. There is a great difference in the production capacities of enterprises and in the technology employed. Therefore, given the goal of obtaining final results for the steel industry in the USSR as a whole, we must distinguish in this variegated mosaic certain varieties or types of plants and group them according to some sort of criterion.

Criterion for Plant Grouping

The basic idea of this study is not so much to give a photographic representation of current production as to bring out the potential dynamism that is embodied in the productive structure of plants.

And it is precisely this feature—that is, how dynamic enterprises are in their development—which we use as the basis for their differentiation. It should be noted that such an approach is by no means original and was not devised by us. A division of metallurgical plants into three groups has been used by Gosplan and the Ministry of Ferrous Metallurgy since the 1930s.

The first group comprises plants in which major expansion of production is possible by constructing new units like those at new plants.

The second group comprises plants in which reconstruction involves the removal from operation of part of old shops and units and their replacement by new ones, as a result of which production at the plant is temporarily reduced.

The third group comprises plants in which only partial modernization of equipment can be carried out without reconstruction of the enterprise as a whole or, even more so, its expansion.

The first group is in a priority position. Plants in this group receive the lion's share of investment and other resources allocated to the steel industry. The least acceptable variant is the second group, for which it is necessary to reduce production, which is always extremely painful for the leaders of Soviet industry and something they strive not to permit. The role of plants in this group is so great and the level of technology and equipment of many shops lags so far behind today's standards, however, that their reconstruction is unavoidable, although it is delayed by any means possible by the Ministry of Ferrous Metallurgy and Gosplan.

The primary characteristic that distinguishes plants of the first group from the entire heterogeneous conglomerate of enterprises that make up Soviet ferrous metallurgy and that makes their expansion possible is the presence of land for additions of new shops and units. The majority of large plants in the second and third groups are in cramped quarters bounded by residential complexes and can expand capacity only be tearing down old structures and erecting new ones in their place. It is precisely the possibility of spatial expansion that makes plants such as those in Cherepovets, Krivoi Rog, and West Siberia so attractive for investment in their development without harming current production. At the same time, such giants as Magnitogorsk, the Dzerzhinskii plant, and Zaporozhstal', squeezed between housing complexes and rivers, can construct new units only by tearing down old ones; from the standpoint of Soviet planners in the unabating race to increase volume of production, this is the worst variant.

An important feature of the organizational structure of Soviet ferrous metallurgy is the separation of a group of plants for so-called "special steel" and their transformation into an autonomous sub-branch. A special approach is taken and special attention is paid to these plants. They produce only high-quality steels. With the exception of the Cheliabinsk and Serov plants, they have only steel smelting and rolling facilities. Some features of their technology are:

Production of steel in electric furnaces

The presence of refining processes and steel finishing outside the furnace

The production of products in a much larger assortment than at other plants but in small, low-tonnage lots

Plastic working of steel not only in rolling but also in forging-pressing shops

Retaining the grouping described above, we will try to consider the most essential features of the plants in the steel industry.*

Going beyond the bounds of the "ferrous metallurgy" branch, it is also necessary to consider a certain amount of steel produced at relatively small metallurgical enterprises that are part of large machine-building plants. The role of each of the above-mentioned

*The numbers for production of cast iron, steel, and rolled metal at each plant given in this chapter have been obtained by analyzing direct and indirect data from many sources (metallurgical journals, newspapers, regional statistical handbooks, research monographs). Here are a few examples of such analysis. The base numbers for cast-iron production at the ten largest plants in the south (Dneprodzerzhinskiy, Makeyevskiy, Donetskiy, Krivorozhskiy, etc.) were taken from a study of the use of natural gas and oxygen in cast-iron production (*Razvitiye metallurgii v ukrainskoy SSR*, Kiev, Naukova Dumka, 1980, pp. 454, 456). These numbers were adjusted on the basis of information on average daily output (*Metallurgicheskaya i gornorudnaya promyshlennost'*, No. 2, 1978, p. 6) and increases in cast-iron production at these plants in the early 1980s (*Stal'*, No. 8, 1982, p. 70). Steel production numbers at the Amurstal' plant were obtained with the help of information given about the share of steel produced on continuous casting equipment in the total steel output at that plant (*Stal'*, No. 4, 1982, p. 6). Having information on the capacity of this equipment, we were able to estimate the total steel output at this plant. In order to calculate the output of rolled metal at several plants (Zaporoshstal', Kommunarskiy, Rustavskiy, etc.), we have used the data on the average hourly and yearly capacity of equipment (*Metallurgicheskaya i gornorudnaya promyshlennost'*, No. 1, 1976, p. 74; A. Tselikov et al., *Mashiny i agregaty metallurgicheskikh zavodov*, Moscow, Metallurgiya, 1981, p. 21).

TABLE 3.1
Approximate distribution of steel and rolled metal
among various groups of enterprises, 1980[1]

| | Share of group in production (%) | |
Group	Steel	Rolled metal
First	36	38
Second	32	31
Third	17	17
Special steels	11	11
Associated with machine-building plants	4	3
TOTAL	100	100

groups in the production of steel and rolled metal in the USSR is
shown in Table 3.1.

First Group

This group comprises eight plants (Krivoi Rog, Novolipetskii,
Azovstal', Orsko-Khalilovskii, West Siberian, Karagandinskii, Cherepovetskii, and Nizhne-Tagilskii). These plants are the "cutting
edge" of the Soviet steel industry. Their facilities were put into
service mainly in the 1960s and 1970s. At the Cherepovetskii, Krivorozhskii, Azovstal', Karagandinskii, and Nizhne-Tagilskii plants
steel is manufactured in part (and at the Novolipetskii and West
Siberian plants, mainly) in converters, rather than in open-hearth
furnaces, as is the case at most other plants. At the Azovstal', Novolipetskii, Cherepovetskii, and Nizhne-Tagilskii plants steel is produced by continuous casting. Powerful rolling mills can be found at
all the plants in this group. The plants also have a much higher level
of mechanization of labor-intensive processes and use a more advanced technology for finishing the rolled steel. These plants clearly
reflect the dominant tendency in the growth of the Soviet steel
industry: concentration of production through the construction of
ever larger, more powerful blast furnaces, oxygen converters, and
rolling mills.

The dynamism peculiar to the development of these plants in the
past has not been maintained in recent times. No blast furnaces are

being constructed at these plants, except for a 5,500-cubic-meter furnace at the Cherepovetskii plant now under construction. Oxygen-converter shops with three converters each are planned for the Novolipetskii, Azovstal', Cherepovetskii, and West Siberian plants. Two converters are already in operation at each of these plants, though despite the completion of certain facilites, construction of the third converters has been halted. Once the third converters have been constructed, steel production at each of these shops will not grow linearly but rather will jump, roughly doubling to 8–9 million tons per year.[2]

Because the construction of the third converters has been suspended, the growth of the steel production facilities at these plants has slowed down appreciably. And except for the West Siberian plant, where a 3600 plate mill has been constructed, no large rolling mills have been built at any of the plants in this group. Plans for the expansion of the largest plant in this group (Krivorozhskii), whose annual output is to reach 24 million tons of steel and 19 million tons of rolled product, are far from realization.[3]

Thus, although the plants in this group have significant room available for expansion, at the present we observe a falloff in their rate of growth.

To a larger degree than at other plants, at the plants in this group capacities for production of steel do not match those for production of rolled metal. Usually, when a plant is expanded rolling mills are commissioned first, and only then are the steel production capacities adjusted. Usually, considerable time elapses between the commissioning of the rolling mills and commissioning of the crude steel production capacities. During this period, as the capacities of the rolling mills are expanded, supplies of billets produced at their own plants fall increasingly short of the mills' own needs, and correspondingly the mills' dependence on shipments of semifinished product from other plants grows.

In general, intrabranch cooperation (shipments of slabs and other types of semifinished products from one plant to another) is an entirely normal event. But the enormous capacities of the rolling mills constructed at these plants creates a great demand for steel billets. As a result, the rolling mills can operate at normal capacity only where there is explicit correlation between the production of the suppliers and customer need and where there is a reliable transportation system. In the Soviet economic picture, however, these conditions are unattainable, and as a result the rolling mills suffer from considerable downtime. Let us look at an example.

In 1981 over 1 million tons of slabs, mainly contracted for with the Novolipetskii plant, were not delivered to the 2000 rolling mill of the Cherepovetskii plant.[4] The Novolipetskii plant, which now has an overabundance of steel slabs, just a few years ago suffered from shortages of slabs for its own 2000 continuous strip mill, which had operated at 50 percent capacity for some time.

Thus the lag in capacities for the production of crude steel behind the capacities of the rolling mills and interruptions in shipments of billets for the mills from other plants has held back production of rolled metal at plants in this group.

An extremely important feature distinguishes these plants: each of them has an extensive manufacturing site and considerable space for expansion. The old plants are more compact. The ratio of the area of the plant (in hectares) to the annual volume of steel production (in millions of tons) is 142 for the Cherepovetskii plant, 134 for the Novolipetskii plant, 133 for the West Siberian plant, 154 for the Karagandinskii plant, and 143 for the Orsko-Khalilovskii plant. By contrast, this indicator is only 92 for the Magnitogorskii combine and 107 for the Zaporozhstal' plant. Wastefulness in the sense of land occupied is even more apparent by comparison with steel plants of the same capacities in other industrially developed countries. For example, the Novolipetskii plant occupies twice the land area of the Kakogawa Works in Japan, a plant of the same capacity and structure.[5]

The spaciousness of these plants is not, strictly speaking, a matter of technological need. Nor is it a matter of indifference to the layout of the units and to the need for economizing on the use of production capacities. Plant layout is a major element in the design of industrial enterprises in the USSR, and the sections of the General Plan which deal with these sorts of problems are treated as major structural units by planning institutes.

There are other reasons as well. The spacious disposition of steel plants is a policy aimed at accomplishing definite goals, specifically to create:

Extra space for expansion of the shops
Room for storage of vast reserves of raw materials, different semi-finished materials, and spare parts for the equipment

Extra space for the expansion of the finishing sections of the production process (heat treatment, coating, etc.)

In general, extra space is provided at the plants not just expressly to answer technological needs, but also for possible adaptation of production to special categories of output for defense needs.

Novolipetskii

A plant unique in the Soviet steel industry, Novolipetskii has no open-hearth furnaces; instead its entire steel output is melted in converters and electric furnaces and cast by a continuous method. Its main output is in the form of hot-rolled strip produced in coils from low-alloy steel shipped to the pipe plants of the Urals and southern USSR for the production of large-diameter pipe for use in gas pipelines. The plant also produces cold-rolled steel for the electric power industry. A shop for cold rolling of carbon steel with a design capacity of 2.5 million tons of sheet per year, including 800,000 tons of sheet for automobiles, was put into operation at the end of 1980.[6]

Cherepovetskii

This plant constitutes a major center for the development of the steel-consuming branches of industry in the northwest European portion of the USSR, as well as being a basic source of thin sheet for farm machinery plants and pipe and automobile plants.

The capacities of the steel and rolled metal facilities are particularly out of proportion at Cherepovetskii. About 2 million tons of slabs are shipped to the plant from other plants in the branch each year.[7]

The capacities of the new converter shop (two oxygen converters with capacity reaching 350 tons) put into operation as long ago as 1979 are growing at slow rates, though it is clear that once the capacities of the shop have been absorbed, the plant will have the capability of producing up to 12 million tons of steel per year.[8]

Krivorozhskii

This plant is a principal source of small-section product and wire. Its six small-section and wire mills manufacture over 5 million tons of product or nearly half the Soviet Union's output of small-section rolled metal and wire.

Despite the plant's ten oxygen converters, the steel teeming process is carried out according to outdated methods using ingot molds (after which the ingots are fed to reduction mills) rather than by continuous casting. The three powerful blooming mills of the Krivorozhskii plant not only provide billets for its own mills but also supply semifinished product (cogged ingots) to other steel plants.

The Krivorozhskii plant, which is located at the center of a vast raw material deposit, the Krovorozhskii iron-ore basin, has considerable room for further development. Its current developmental plan (or second-line construction) includes the installation of blast furnaces and the construction of a third converter shop with an oxygen converter of capacity up to 350 tons and equipment for continuous steel casting as well as sheet mills.[9] Once these plans have been implemented, the annual production of pig iron at the plant could be increased to 18.5 million tons, the annual production of steel to 24 million tons, and the annual production of rolled metal to 18.6 million tons.[10]

Azovstal'

This plant was destroyed during the occupation of the Ukraine in World War II and was entirely reconstructed in the early 1950s. It now concentrates on the production of large-section metal (beams, channels) and railroad rails manufactured from open-hearth steel. In the mid-1970s, with the opening of a powerful 3600 plate mill and, subsequently, an oxygen-converter shop at the plant, facilities for the production of high-quality plate steel became available. Production of high-quality steel smelted in electric furnaces, as well as refined conversion products—for example, slab ingots weighing up to 20 tons—are manufactured by means of electroslag remelting.[11]

Orsko-Khalilovskii (Urals)

This plant was built during the first decade after World War II. Its output consists of large-section metal and strip for manufacturing pipes for gas pipelines. Despite the comparatively small scale of steel production here, the plant's open-hearth and electric furnaces smelt a broad range of categories of alloy and low-alloy steel.

The plant is continuing to expand, and its output of both section and flat-rolled metal is growing. In 1979 a specialized 800 semicontinuous mill for the production of high-quality strip up to 25 millimeters in thickness was put into operation. There are plans to construct yet another sheet mill at the plant and also to create facilities for additional refinement of steel smelted in electric furnaces.[12]

Nizhne-Tagilskii

This plant is the most modern steel plant in the Urals. In the 1960s and 1970s its productive capacity for pig iron, steel, and rolled metal increased dramatically. A fifth blast furnace 2700 cubic meters in volume was built in the late 1960s. In the late 1970s a fourth oxygen converter was installed, and also constructed were a powerful 1500 blooming mill and a general-purpose rolling section mill for the production of wide-flanged beams with an annual output of 1.6 million tons.[13]

West Siberian

This plant was constructed in the 1960s and 1970s. Together with the Kuznets plant, which is 30 kilometers away, the West Siberian steel plant forms the Soviet Union's largest concentration of steel production facilities east of the Urals, with about 8 percent of all the steel produced in the Soviet Union smelted at the two plants.

All the steel at the plant is smelted in oxygen converters, though as is also the case at the Krivoi Rog plant, continuous casting is not employed here. The plant's principal output consists of medium- and small-section rolled metal and concrete reinforcement wire.

A large-scale 3600 plate mill is currently under construction at the plant. There are plans to build a fourth blast furnace and third converter shop as well. How realistic the long-term plans for the development of the plant are depends on the plans for rebuilding the Kuznetskii plant, with which it is in close cooperation; the amount of time set aside for implementing these plans also depends on the plans for the Kuznetskii plant. Currently, the West Siberian plant shows the most promise (in terms of potential expansion of capacities) of all the steel plants east of the Urals.

To expand the plate, it will be necessary first to create facilities for

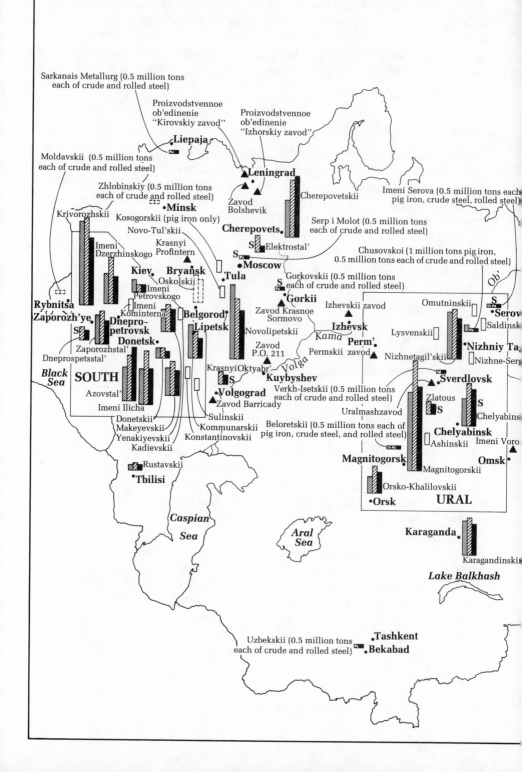

Sarkanais Metallurg (0.5 million tons each of crude and rolled steel)

Proizvodstvennoe ob'edinenie "Kirovskiy zavod"

Proizvodstvennoe ob'edinenie "Izhorskiy zavod"

Moldavskii (0.5 million tons each of crude and rolled steel)

Imeni Serova (0.5 million tons each pig iron, crude steel, rolled steel)

Zhlobinskiy (0.5 million tons each of crude and rolled steel)

•Liepaja

•Minsk

Krivorozhskii

Kosogorskii (pig iron only)

Novo-Tul'skii

Serp i Molot (0.5 million tons each of crude and rolled steel)

Krasnyi Profintern

Imeni Dzerzhinskogo

▲Leningrad

Zavod Bolshevik

Cherepovetskii

Cherepovets.

S Elektrostal'

S Moscow

Chusovskoi (1 million tons pig iron, 0.5 million tons each of crude and rolled steel)

Kiev.

Bryansk

Oskolskii

Imeni Petrovskogo

Tula

Gorkovskii (0.5 million tons each of crude and rolled steel)

Omutninskii

S Serov

Izhevskii zavod

Saldinsk

Rybnitsa

Zaporozh'ye•

Imeni Kominterna

Belgorod•

Gorkii

Lysvenskii

•Nizhniy Ta

Dnepro-petrovsk•

Lipetsk•

Zavod Krasnoe Sormovo

Izhevsk•

Perm'•

Nizhne-Ser

S

Donetsk•

Novolipetskii

Permskii zavod

Nizhnetagil'skii

Zaporozhstal'

Dneprospetsstal'

Zavod P.O. 211

▲Sverdlovsk

Black Sea

SOUTH

KrasnyiOktyabr'

Kuybyshev

Verkh-Isetskii (0.5 million tons each of crude and rolled steel)

Zlatous

S

Chelyabins

Azovstal'

S Volgograd

▲Zavod Barricady

Uralmashzavod

Chelyabinsk

Imeni Voro

Imeni Ilicha

Sulinskii

Beloretskii (0.5 million tons each of pig iron, crude steel, and rolled steel)

Ashinskii

Omsk•

Donetskii

Makeyevskii

Kommunarskii

Yenakiyevskii

Konstantinovskii

Magnitogorsk•

Magnitogorskii

URAL

Kadievskii

Rustavskii

Orsko-Khalilovskii

•Tbilisi

•Orsk

Caspian Sea

Aral Sea

Karaganda.

Karagandinski

Lake Balkhash

Ob'

Kama

Volga

Uzbekskii (0.5 million tons each of crude and rolled steel)

•Tashkent

•Bekabad

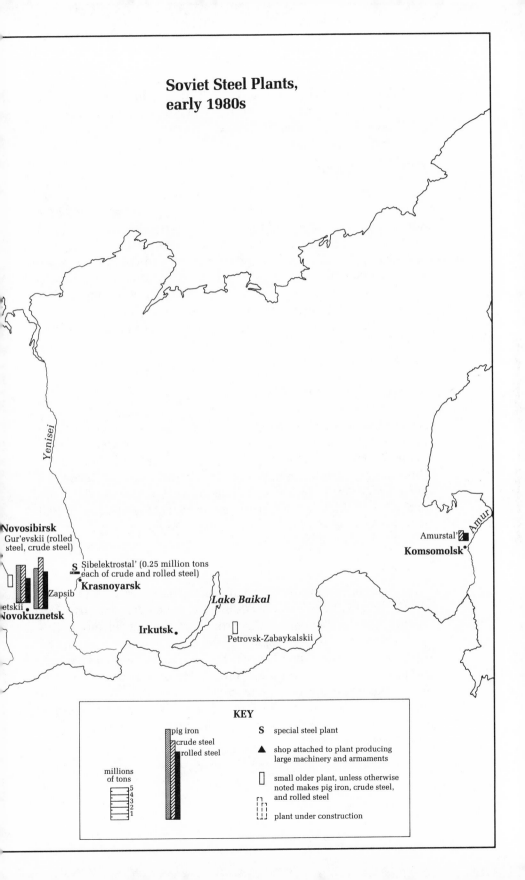

Soviet Steel Plants, early 1980s

Novosibirsk
Gur'evskii (rolled steel, crude steel)

S Sibelektrostal' (0.25 million tons each of crude and rolled steel)
Krasnoyarsk

Zapsib

etskii
Novokuznetsk

Irkutsk

Lake Baikal

Petrovsk-Zabaykalskii

Amurstal'
Komsomolsk

Yenisei

Amur

KEY

pig iron
crude steel
rolled steel

millions of tons
5
4
3
2
1

S special steel plant

▲ shop attached to plant producing large machinery and armaments

small older plant, unless otherwise noted makes pig iron, crude steel, and rolled steel

plant under construction

production of rolled metal, to consist of several sheet mills and shops for manufacturing standardized and cold-stamped consumer goods, along with curved sections.[14]

Karagandinskii

The main steel shops of this plant were built in the 1960s and 1970s. In the 1970s it became the second largest steel plant (after the West Siberian plant) east of the Urals following the construction of two large blast furnaces (2,700 and 3,200 cubic meters in volume) and the opening of a third oxygen converter and cold-rolling sheet shop. The plant's broad range of categories of output includes strip steel for gas and oil pipelines, steel strip for shipbuilding, and in particular tin plate strip, a product in extremely short supply in the Soviet Union; the tin plate strip is manufactured in the reopened shop.[15]

Second Group

This group comprises ten plants, six of which are in the southern USSR (Kommunarskii, Dneprodzherzhinskii, Makeevskii, Yenaki-evskii, Donetskii, and Petrovskii). These six are all old plants, up to a hundred years old, and have been rebuilt and enlarged during the Soviet era. Another four plants (Magnitogorskii, Kuznetskii, Zapo-rozhskii, and Il'ich) were constructed in the 1930s and constituted the main focus of the Soviet steel industry in the prewar period.

Il'ich

The southern plants destroyed during the war years were modern-ized in the 1950s and early 1960s and expanded very rapidly. Dur-ing this time the Il'ich plant was virtually reconstructed, along with its open-hearth furnaces (some up to 900 tons in capacity), the largest in the south. The plant has been expanded with an explicit emphasis placed on sheet metal production and, with the comple-tion of the powerful 3000 plate mill in the current five-year plan (1981–85), became a major source of sheet metal for nearby pipe plants specialized for the production of large-diameter welded pipe for use in gas pipelines.[17]

TABLE 3.2
Soviet steel plants (first group)[16]

| | | | Production (in millions of tons) | | |
| | | Types of steelmaking | Pig | Crude | Rolled |
Plants	Region	processes[a]	iron	steel	steel
1. Krivorozhskii	South[b]	OH, BOF	12.6–12.7	12.7–12.8	9.9–10.0
2. Novolipetskii	Central	BOF, EL	10.8–11.0	9.0	6.7–6.9
3. Azovstal'	South	OH, BOF, EL	5.0–5.2	6.9–7.0	7.9
4. Orsko-Khalilovskii	Urals	OH, EL	2.3	3.8–3.9	3.1–3.2
5. West Siberian	West Siberia	OH, BOF	5.8	7.4	5.2–5.3
6. Karagandinskii	Kazakhstan	OH, BOF	4.9	5.7–5.8	4.4–4.5
7. Cherepovetskii	Northwest	OH, BOF, EL	5.6–5.7	8.3–8.5	9.0[c]
8. Nizhnetagil'skii	Urals	OH, BOF	6.8	7.7	6.2

[a]OH = open hearth; BOF = basic oxygen; EL = electric.
[b]Including Ukraine and Volga.
[c]Including production from own slabs and slabs supplied by other plants.

Kommunarskii

This plant includes both section and sheet metal production facilities. It is important, however, more as a source of high-quality sheet steel for shipbuilding, the pipe industry, and nuclear power stations. Because of the plant's area of specialization, its existing sheet mills could be rebuilt and the capacities of sheet metal production facilities expanded in the future.[18]

Zaporozhstal'

Production of this plant's existing steel smelting shop and set of sheet mills is at near maximal level. According to current plans for the radical reconstruction of the plant, the open-hearth furnaces are to be replaced by oxygen converters. It is, however, highly unlikely that the structure of steel production at the Zaporozhstal' plant will change in the 1980s.[19]

Dneprodzerzhinskii

The Dneprodzerzhinskii plant, among the largest in the south, manufactures an extremely broad range of output, including not only section shapes but also thin sheet, railroad rails, axles for railroad cars, beads, and tabular billets for nearby pipe plants.

The site for modernization at the plant is extremely crowded. The scales of production and breadth of product selection, however, have forced the Ministry of Ferrous Metallurgy to search for ways of providing the plant with adequate quantities of steel and maintaining the efficiency of the plant's already worn out equipment. Thus the plant is in a state of permanent reconstruction, modernization, and repair. Because the steel production facilities, with its small-scale open-hearth furnaces, represent the major bottleneck at the plant, it became necessary first to reconstruct the open-hearth furnaces.

In 1982 a large-scale oxygen converter shop was placed in service as part of two converters with an annual production of 2.8 million tons of steel. One of the oldest open-hearth shops was simultaneously shut down.

The radical reconstruction of the plant, which comprises much old equipment, decrepit structures, an antiquated transportation system, and low-efficiency refining units, has long been a pressing problem, though any decision has been put off to the indefinite future.[20]

Obsolescent equipment, crowded plant sites, and overloading of support services typify the old, relatively small plants (Makeevskii, Yenakievskii, Donetskii, Petrovskii). Reconstruction and modernization of these plants would require such a large investment as to be an inefficient use of capital. Nevertheless, in certain cases reconstruction is under way. Reconstruction has been most extensive at the Donets plant, where a continuous billet mill was installed in the mid-1970s; an electric-steel smelting shop is now under construction.[21]

The Magnitogorskii and Kuznetskii steel plants have much in common, historically speaking. Both were built in the 1930s and were the largest construction projects of the first five-year plans. Both assumed major responsibility for the production of steel during World War II, while the industrial regions of the south were occupied. Equipment that had been evacuated from southern plants was installed at these two plants during this period.

After the war, both continued to expand their capacities over the available areas, which ultimately led to extraordinarily crowded plant sites. At the present time, both plants have virtually exhausted their reserve capacities and are confronted by intractable problems of overall reconstruction requiring billions in capital outlays.

Difficulties caused by the need to maintain the efficiency of equipment worn out during the war years, a shortage of warehouse space, growing disproportions between the capacities of the production shops and support services (power supplies, repair services, transportation), and problems of environmental pollution (the plant is surrounded by residential blocks) have become increasingly significant over the course of time.

Currently the Magnitogorskii plant produces 11 percent of the Soviet Union's output of steel and rolled metal and is the country's largest plant. Virtually every category and size of flat-rolled and section metal cited in Soviet standards can be manufactured at its numerous rolling mills. The plant has accumulated vast experience in the development of new categories of product and, in this sense, is among the country's leading steel plants. Its plant engineers enjoy a high reputation. Many customers prefer the steel produced here because of the plant's reputation, despite its large number of antiquated units.

The Magnitogorskii plant plays a major role in Soviet industry; its operation and further growth are the special concerns of a number of institutes and laboratories. In the 1960s and 1970s there was considerable debate on ways of effectively modernizing the plant.

In 1975 the USSR Council of Ministers adopted a resolution calling for the plant's reconstruction and development. According to the plans, steel production is to be improved (three oxygen converters and ten continuous casters are to be constructed to replace the existing open-hearth furnaces) and antiquated, small-scale blast furnaces and rolling mills are to be replaced by a smaller number of far larger furnaces. The central goal has been basically one of renovation rather than simply increasing productive capacities.[22]

The depletion of the plant's formerly extensive and extremely high-quality raw material base has not encouraged additional growth in its already vast productive capacities. The reconstruction plans call for an increase in steel production capacity of only 6 percent (17.2 million tons per year from 16.0–16.2 million tons). The fact that the plant site is crowded is a further factor militating against the commissioning of new production units.

The reconstruction plan for this vast facility will require an outlay of about 3 billion rubles (in late 1970 prices) and an associated

TABLE 3.3
Soviet steel plants (second group)[25]

Plants	Region	Types of steelmaking processes[a]	Production (in millions of tons)		
			Pig iron	Crude steel	Rolled steel
1. Kommunarskii	South	OH	5.0–5.1	4.2–4.3	2.9–3.1
2. Dneprodzerzhinskii	South	OH, BOF	5.6–5.7	6.8–6.9	4.7–4.8
3. Makeyevskii	South	OH	3.7–3.8	4.5–4.6	3.6–3.7
4. Yenakiyevskii	South	OH, BOF	3.5	4.6–4.7	3.6–3.7
5. Donetskii	South	OH, EL	1.7	1.5[a]	0.9–1.0
6. Petrovskii	South	OH, BOF	2.0–2.1	1.0–1.1	0.9–1.0
7. Magnitogorskii	Urals	OH	11.5	16.0–16.2	12.0
8. Kuznetskii	West Siberia	OH, EL	4.7	4.5[a]	3.5
9. Zaporozhstal'	South	OH	4.5–4.6	4.9–5.0	4.0–4.1
10. Il'ich[b]	South	OH, BOF	5.4–5.5	7.6–7.7	5.4–5.5

[a]New productive capacities are being added at the factory.
[b]Plant also produces steel pipes.

temporary, though significant, drop in output. For these reasons, it seems doubtful that plant reconstruction will commence in the current decade. Funds have already been allocated and spent on partial reconstruction of various units at the plant, particularly the old blast furnaces.

Further development of the Kuznetskii plant has been halted; its volume of output has not increased for ten years now. Because of its antiquated equipment, the steel it produces is of low quality; similarly, the associated costs for labor and electrical power are high. Emission of pollutants into the atmosphere is also higher than elsewhere.[23]

The Kuznetskii plant, no less than the Magnitogorskii plant, requires major reconstruction, the nature and scale of which have yet to be finally decided upon and to this day remain the source of vigorous dispute among experts.

A tentative plan for reconstruction of the plant was developed in 1975. The plan calls for modernization of the plant so as to make possible the production of high-quality steel. The open-hearth furnaces are to be replaced by oxygen converters and electric furnaces and all support services are likewise to be replaced. The main emphasis has been placed on improving the quality indicators and not so much on increasing the annual volume of production, which now amounts to 5.6 million tons of steel and 3.7 million tons of rolled product.

A second version of the plan calls for the construction of electric furnaces exclusively and the elimination of blast furnace production. Other suggestions abound.

Without waiting for final resolution of the major elements of the reconstruction process, the Ministry of Ferrous Metallurgy has already allocated some funds, and the plant has little by little renovated its production facilities. By the late 1970s two electrical furnaces with a total annual output of 400,000 tons of steel had been constructed.

On the whole, then, the reconstruction of the Kuznets plant is an extremely long-term project, and its realization will come after 1990.[24]

Third Group

A total of twenty-three plants may be placed in this, the most numerous group.* The group includes such relatively large plants as Rustavskii, Chusovskoi, and Amurstal', with annual volumes of production of about 1 million tons and more, as well as small plants, such as Konstantinovskii, Komintern, Satkinskii, and Saldinskii, where the output does not exceed 200,000—500,000 tons per year.

Despite the differences in volume of production, age, and technical state of equipment, limited room for expansion and modernization is a problem shared by all the plants in this group. Efforts to renovate the production facilities at these plants are, as a rule, aimed at maintaining existing equipment in working order and are not integrated in nature.

The Rustavskii (Georgian SSR), Sarkanais Metallurg (Lithuanian SSR), and Uzbekskii plants are the only steel plants in the national republics, and therefore are a special concern of the republic administration.

*In addition to factories mentioned in Table 3.4, this group includes the following: Kosogorskii, Komintern, Kadievskii, Kramatorskii, Konstantinovskii, Sulinskii, Satkinskii, Nizhne-Ser'ginskii, Saldinskii, Ashinskii, Lysvenskii, Omutninskii, Gur'evskii, Petrovsk-Zabaykal'skii.

The Uzbek plant, the only plant in all of Central Asia, has even expanded its capabilities for production of steel and rolled metal; an electric steel smelting shop has been constructed, and a new rolling mill has recently been installed.

Of special importance is the Amurstal' plant, located in the far eastern region of the USSR near the Pacific Ocean ports. Constructed during World War II, the plant's output (thick plate and section metal) is earmarked for the shipbuilding and ship-repair yards of the far east, as well as for construction enterprises in the region.

Most of the smallest of the old blast and open-hearth furnaces and primitive rolling mills are concentrated at the old plants in the Urals (Chusovskoi, Satkinskii, Saldinskii, Omutninskii, Verkh-Isetskii, Ashinskii, and others), which were built as long ago as the early 1800s. For some of them, plans have been drawn up for introducing methods of continuous casting of steel so as to ease the extremely hard working conditions and reduce losses in steel production. New small-scale rolling mills have been built at the Verkh-Isetskii, Lys'-venskii, and Omutninskii plants.

The fate of the oldest plants in the Urals has been the subject of considerable debate. These plants have remained open for a long time without any major investments being made for their modernization. Their survival is largely due to their highly skilled work force, which has been put together over the course of many generations in the small cities that have grown up around them. Moreover, some of their output is unique—for example, shapes with complicated cross-sections—and cannot be produced in modern high-efficiency mills because of the small demand for the output.

Plants under Construction

Oskol'skii Electric Steel Plant

A plant for production of high-quality steel has been under construction near the city of Belgorod since the mid-1970s. The plant is to operate using a form of technology entirely new for the USSR: production of iron-rich pellets from ore (thus bypassing the blast-furnace process), followed by smelting of crude steel with an extremely low content of harmful impurities from the pellets in electric furnaces, and, finally, production of rolled metal.

The application of this advanced technology using the rich de-

TABLE 3.4
Soviet steel plants (third group)[26]

Plants	Region	Types of steelmaking processes[a]	Production (in millions of metric tons)		
			Pig iron	Crude steel	Rolled steel
1. Rustavskii[b]	Trans-Caucasus	OH	0.8	1.5	1.2–1.3
2. Beloretskii	Urals	OH	0.4–0.5		
3. Chusovskoi	Urals	OH	1.0–1.1	1.5–1.7	1.7–1.8
4. Verkh-Isetskii[a]	Urals	OH, EL	—		
5. Amurstal'[a]	Far East	OH	—	1.4–1.5	1.0–1.1
6. Sarkanais Metallurgs[a]	Northwest	OH	—	0.5	0.4
7. Uzbekskii[a]	Central Asia	OH, EL	—	0.5[c]	0.4
8. Novo-Tul'skii[d] (Tulachermet)	Central	—	—	—	—

[a] No pig-iron production.
[b] Plant also produces steel pipes.
[c] New capacities are being added at the factory.
[d] Main research and experimental center of Ministry of Ferrous Metallurgy.

posits of the Kursk magnetic anomaly has definite economic advantages. It is also known that alloy steel smelted from iron-rich pellets has higher technological and mechanical properties than steel produced in the usual way. The plans for the Oskol'skii plant utilize Western technology (the MIDREX process), and a contract for delivery of equipment has been concluded with West German firms. Some of the iron-rich pellets produced at the Oskol'skii plant will probably be shipped to steel plants in West Germany.

The production capacities of the plant are to be commissioned in stages. To be constructed at the first stage (through 1985) are facilities for producing 1.7 million tons of iron-rich pellets per year, four 150-ton electric furnaces, together with units for continuous steel casting with an annual output of 1.5 million tons of section billet and a section mill with annual production of 1.2 million tons.

As the plant is further developed, production of iron-rich pellets is to be increased to 3.0–5.4 million tons per year. This in turn will allow 3.5 million tons of steel a year to be produced at this plant. Three more furnaces of the same capacity for increasing production of section billet to 2.4 million tons per year and an additional two section mills are to be constructed.

The last stage of the plan calls for the construction of one more electric steel smelting shop with four 200-ton electric furnaces equipped with units for continuous casting to be used in the production of cast slabs for a 3000 thick-sheet mill with annual output of about 1.6 million tons, also to be built at the plant.

Because of the role to be played by the plant in increasing the production of high-quality steel, construction of the plant will probably be given a green light. Nevertheless, it is highly unlikely that such an enormous project will be completed in the current decade.[27]

Miniplants

The Rybnitskii (Moldavia) and Zhlobinskii (Byelorussia) plants—two small plants with output of 600,000–700,000 tons per year—represent an entirely new phenomenon for the Soviet steel industry from both the technological and economic point of view.* The plants are run through the conversion of scrap or iron-rich pellets followed by continuous casting of the steel in billets and, subsequently, rolling of the steel into small section shapes, reinforcement, strip.[28]

In terms of production technology and equipment, the Zhlobin plant is similar to the Raritan River Steel Plant (New Jersey) constructed in the early 1970s; responsibility for deliveries of equipment has been assumed by the Western firm.

The idea of building miniplants was borrowed from Western, including American, experience and was the subject of lively discussion in the 1970s. The objections of those opposed to the miniplants were based on the deeply ingrown notions common among Soviet planners as to the indisputable economic advantages of increased concentrations of production facilities, a phenomenon that has been especially apparent in the development of the Soviet steel industry. Investment funds have shrunk, however; the capital investment required to achieve a 1-ton increment in steel production

---

*Next to the Amurstal' plant in Komsomol'sk-na-Amure a new miniplant (Dal'nevostochnyy Electrometallurgicheskii—Far Eastern Electro-Metallurgical) is being built. Its annual capacity is projected at 1 million tons of steel sheets. There is also information about construction of yet another minifactory in Petrovsk-Zabaykal'skii in the far east with approximately the same capacity.

has grown sharply at recently built large production capacities; and, finally, construction periods and timetables for commissioning the huge blast furnaces, converters, and rolling mills have grown considerably. Because of these factors, it is no longer possible to assume that economic efficiency can be achieved through larger and larger steel plants.

It is in this light that the attitude of the State Planning Commission and Ministry of Ferrous Metallurgy toward miniplants can be understood. The construction of miniplants requires less capital investment, and the plants can be built far more rapidly than large plants, and thus the demand for a number of categories of metal products can be satisfied far more rapidly. To this we might add that the miniplants operate with scrap, thereby solving the problem of what to do with the growing stores of scrap in major consuming areas.

Large Machine-Construction Plants

Roughly 3 percent of the total output of steel in the USSR is produced outside the steel industry proper, at machine-construction plants.* In general, over 70 percent of all machine-construction enterprises in the USSR produce iron and steel casting for their own needs. At the largest machine-construction plants manufacturing the most important categories of product, complete steelworks, encompassing steel smelting and rolled metal production facilities—not just foundries—have been created. Especially large steel production facilities are in operation at such major machine-construction centers as Leningrad and Sverdlovsk, where open-hearth and electrical furnaces have been installed. The Izhorskii plant, which manufactures equipment for nuclear power stations and, probably, armaments, besides other categories of output, and the Kirovskii plant, which works mainly for the shipbuilding industry, have large-capacity rolling cogging mills in their complement of steel production facilities.

---

*Some large machine-building plants that produce their own steel are: Uralmash (Ural), Kirovskii (Leningrad), Izhorskii (Leningrad), Bol'shevik (Leningrad), Krasnyi Profintern (Bryansk), Krasnoe Sormovo (Gor'kii), Barrikady (Volgograd), Permskii (Perm'), imeni Voroshilova (Omsk), and Izhevskii (Ustinov).

Plants Producing Special Steels

In the Soviet Union, the ten plants whose output consists exclusively of high-quality steel and alloys form a separate subbranch of the steel industry. The emphasis of steel plants on quantitative results at the expense of the quality indicators, the large capacities of manufacturing units that can be efficiently used only in the production of general-purpose output and that are not adapted for manufacturing small lots—these factors together made it necessary as long ago as the 1930s to convert a number of old plants and to construct several new plants designed for the production of relatively small volumes of high-quality steel.

In the postwar period, these plants were placed within an independent organizational structure, now called the Soyuzspetsstal' All-Union Specialty Steel Trust, under the jurisdiction of the Ministry of the Steel Industry. The trust includes the Chelyabinskii, Zlatoustskii, Serovskii, Novosibirskii, Sibelektrostal', Gor'kovskii, Dneprospetsstal', Elektrostal', Serp i Molot, and Krasnyi Oktyabr' plants. Roughly 11 percent of the total steel output in the Soviet Union is produced at these plants. Their output ranges from 100,000–200,000 tons (Sibelektrostal') to as much as 6.7 million tons (Chelyabinskii).[29] It is hardly the case, however, that the entire output of high-quality steel is concentrated in the Soyuzspetsstal' Trust.

Special steels are also produced at a number of other plants under the jurisdiction of the Ministry of the Steel Industry (Lipetskii, Magnitogorskii), as well as at certain large machine-construction plants (in the form of steel casting). Let us be more precise. Plants in the Soyuzspetsstal' Trust are responsible for producing high-quality steel—that is, steel with special physical properties (heat-resistant, corrosion-resistant, or high-speed steel)—and high-quality precision alloys. By contrast, the more common types of high-quality steel (electrical, structural alloy), the demand for which amounts to hundreds of thousands of tons, may also be produced at other plants of the ministry.

Special steel plants may be distinguished by a number of features. First, such plants mainly use electric-arc steel-melting furnaces and apply refining techniques outside the furnace. Pressing and forging equipment is extensively used for shaping low-ductility steels and alloys.

Second, the plants manufacture a great variety of categories of steel, frequently switching from the production of one category to another, and manufacture their output in small lots. At many special steel plants, 35–40 percent of the total output is produced in lots of up to 1 ton.

Third, a highly developed degree of industrial cooperation exists between the special steel plants; this, however, is hampered by the fact that the plants are located at great distances from one another (some of the plants are thousands of kilometers apart). For example, Chelyabinskii and Elektrostal' are large plants that send semifinished product (ingots and roughing billets) to mills at smaller plants. Thus, Serp i Molot receives billets from seven other special steel plants and then processes the billets on its own sorting and strip rolling mills. The Chelyabinskii plant, which smelts about 40 percent of the total steel output of the Soyuzspetsstal' Trust, is the largest supplier of ingots and billets for rolled products. It sends its own steel to the Zlatoustskii, Novosibirskii, and Krasnyi Oktyabr' plants.

Let us now briefly describe the principal individual features of the special steel plants.

Chelyabinskii

The leading plant in the group, Chelyabinskii is regularly being modernized and its output expanded. The converter shop has just been rebuilt, the capacity of the converters having been increased to more than 1 million tons. As a result of the modernization, the annual output of the converter shop can be expected to reach 3 million tons, including 1.5 million tons of alloy steel. In addition, a fifth electric steel shop has been constructed. We believe that the plant's annual output of stainless, ball bearing, electric, and other types of special steel will reach 8–9 million tons by the late 1980s.[30]

The plant possesses a vast collection of cogging, sorting, and plate mills, and so is able to manufacture a broad range of categories of rolled products, including flat-rolled metal made from very fine strips (0.2–0.5 millimeters) of chromium-nickel steel, up to plates 25–30 millimeters thick and bimetal sheets, and round sections 6–200 millimeters in diameter.[31]

Zlatoustskii

The plant nearest the Chelyabinski plant, Zlatoust concentrates on the production of high-quality section metal, including standardized cold-rolled sections. The plant has extensive experience in the production of low-ductility steels and alloys with especially complicated chemical compositions.

Krasnyi Oktyabr' (Volgograd)

The second largest special steel plant in terms of output, Krasnyi Oktyabr' is also being regularly modernized and its output increased. The outdated open-hearth mills are being replaced by powerful electric furnaces. In the 1970s the plant's annual production of steel was increased by roughly 40 percent and now is about 2 million tons.[32] A plate mill for the production of thick plates of stainless steel has just been constructed. The plant produces a broad range of categories of section and flat-rolled metal, including thick sheet and narrow strip down to 40 millimeters in thickness, tubular billet from alloy steel, and stainless and ball bearing steel.[33]

From available information, both the Zlatoust and Krasnyi Oktyabr' plants are important and traditional suppliers of special steel for the production of armaments.

Novosibirskii

This plant does not have its own steel manufacturing facilities and works with billet produced elsewhere. It manufactures narrow steel tape, though it now mainly concentrates on the production of pipe from commercial carbon steel.

Sibelektrostal' (Novosibirsk)

This is a small plant built during the war years. From available information, steel and alloys with complicated chemical compositions to meet extremely critical needs are smelted in the small electric furnaces of this plant.

Serovskii

The Serov plant is specialized for the production of section metal, including standardized cold-rolled steel.

Serp i Molot

An old plant, Serp i Molot has been rebuilt as a small-volume plant located in Moscow and closely linked to the machine-construction enterprises of the capital.

Elektrostal'

Like Serp i Molot, this large plant, located 25–30 miles from Moscow, provides major advantages for the production of new categories of special steels and alloys simply because of its geographical proximity to Moscow, with that city's leading steel industry research facilities.

Dneprospetsstal'

A major source of stainless and ball bearing steel, this plant's special feature is the Soviet Union's most powerful electrostag remelting facility. Because of this facility, as well as its powerful pressing and forging equipment, the plant is able to manufacture special sizes of forgings made from high-quality refined steel.

CHAPTER 4

Capacity Utilization

In 1983, after dropping for four consecutive years, steel production in the USSR jumped by an unprecedented amount (5.3 million tons), reaching a record level of 153 million tons. It would seem that there was nothing to explain so unusual an event in the history of the Soviet steel industry. Nothing, except for one decisive fact: Ivan Kazanets, the minister of the Soviet steel industry, had received an explicit threat from General Secretary Andropov. Had Kazanets not been able to increase steel production, he could expect the same fate that befell Minister of Rail Transport Ivan Pavlovsky, who, along with a number of other ministers, had just been dismissed from office, pensioned into obscurity.

That such a threat was made is clear from the "Letter to I. P. Kazanets, Minister of the Soviet Steel Industry," which was signed by a group of workers and published in *Pravda* in late December 1982 (a month after Andropov's rise to power). In charging the steel industry with having been derelict in its duty, the authors write that because of the shortage of steel,

> teams of workers and even entire workshops are idle for days on end. Worker collectives in existence for many years are now breaking up. Many of the most advanced shops have fallen behind. In turn, we have been unable to make shipments of product to critical start-up industrial and agricultural projects, the Western Siberia Oil and Gas Com-

plex, residential projects and public services. It is incomprehensible to us, Ivan Pvalovich, why management in the steel industry has so little regard for the fulfillment of the state plan and delivery contracts. In the name of workers at the trust's plants, we are turning to you (letters to other levels of the ministry have not improved the state of affairs) not just with a request, but a demand to undertake urgent measures.[1]

Similar letters were printed in Pravda during the Stalin purges in the 1930s; such a letter was a clear signal that the addressee was slated for removal and arrest. Although such letters no longer have such macabre connotations, under Andropov it was an ultimatum: either produce or else. In this instance, either the steel industry would show that it was prepared to fall in line behind Andropov's campaign to impose firm discipline throughout Soviet industry "from top to bottom" ("from the lowest employee right up to the minister") and increase output, or else the highest levels, including many plant managers, would be replaced.

Thus those responsible for the steel industry were confronted with a "crisis situation," not unlike the kind of challenge that would test an army's state of preparedness. In this case much, if not all, available reserves would have to be brought into play to raise the level of utilization of industrial capacity. The result: output jumped to a record level in 1983.

There was also improvement in other sectors of the economy, for example, the transport sector, which eased somewhat the task set for managers in the steel industry. All this demonstrates that reserve capacities are present elsewhere as well. It is also clear that, whenever a critical situation arises, these reserves can be mobilized and production can be increased without drawing on additional resources and without improving the economic system. In short, the existing economic mechanism and existing production capacities are capable of achieving—and in short order—a much greater increase in output than might be expected under ordinary conditions.

Andropov's tightening of the screws, however, could not by itself have produced the 1983 surge in output without the presence of a corresponding material base. Even at the point of a gun the managers of the steel industry could not have increased production by 5.3 million tons in one year if sufficient potential steel production capacity had not been created.

What is the real situation with reserve capacity in the steel industry? Let us consider two aspects of this question: (a) reserves pro-

duced by the economic system itself and (b) reserves of a technological nature.

Reserves Produced by the Economic System

Full Utilization of Plant Capacities

In the USSR, as in the West, it is commonly believed that the
utilization of production capacities in Soviet industry is at an extraordinarily high level. A well-known Soviet economist, Konstantin
Val'tukh, asserted in 1982 that utilization of production capacities
in Soviet industry had reached its maximal level (nearly 100 percent) by the mid-1970s and therefore all available reserves for any
further increase in utilization of existing capacities had been exhausted and production would begin to fall. Consequently, he argued, only through the construction of new capacities (which of
course would entail an increase in capital investment) could output
grow.[2] Val'tukh's main thesis is that the attenuating investment
curve typical of the modern stage of development of the Soviet
economy will have to change, and that a new and expanded investment policy is needed to overcome the economic slump. Vadim
Kirichenko, director of Gosplan's Scientific Institute, has reached
the same conclusion as Val'tukh.[3] The problem, however, is that the
Soviet economy is acutely short of investment capital, and in the
twelfth five-year plan (1986–90) the situation will grow even worse.
Hence both Val'tukh and Kirichenko are rowing against the current
since their demand for a return to high rates of investment runs
contrary to economic realities in the foreseeable future.

Their solution also contradicts present Soviet economic policy.
Adopted by Soviet economists at the insistence of the authorities,
this theory calls for a *slowdown* in the rate of investment and construction of new capacities. According to the "theory," more efficient use of available fixed capital, even with a drop in the rate of
growth of capital investment, will generate an increase in output. It
is, obviously, a convenient theory, since it does not postulate a
change in the adverse investment trend as a precondition necessary
for increasing the rates of economic growth.

But quite apart from the question of investment rates, Soviet
economists are unanimous in their view that there is high utilization of existing capacities, particularly in the steel industry. In

Soviet technical and economic literature one frequently encounters reports that the utilization of production capacity in the steel industry is at the level of 96–98 percent.[4] For example, that view is held by Boris Martynov, head of the division of production capacities of Gosplan, who because of his position would be expected to have a more critical and stricter view of production capacity reserves than virtually anyone else. Yet he, too, has claimed that in the mid-1970s 98 percent of the production capacity for rolled metal was utilized.[5]

If this is what the director of the office responsible for determining and analyzing the production capacities of the entire planning system of the Soviet economy is claiming, then it is clear that he is viewing the concept of production capacity from a standpoint that is in accord with the definition found in the Gosplan procedural guidelines.

The most recent (1980) edition of *Methodological Guidelines for the Preparation of State Plans for the Economic and Social Development of the USSR* contains the following definition of production capacities:

> By the production capacity of an enterprise or production group we understand the *maximal possible* annual or daily output or output per shift or volume of output and volume of refinement of raw materials in the schedule and breakdown as designated for the base year corresponding to the physical output, and for the planning period, the output specified by the plan under the assumption that production equipment and production areas will be fully utilized in light of already implemented (for the base year) and projected (for the planning period) measures for the introduction of advanced manufacturing technology and scientific labor organization. [emphasis added][6]

According to this definition, then, production capacity is nothing other than the potential production. Consequently, Soviet economists (cited above) have concluded that utilization of production potential in industry is at the *maximal possible* level.

Not all Soviet economists, however, hold that view. Iakov Kvasha, an acknowledged authority on Soviet industrial statistics and a leading expert on industrial capacities, wrote in 1970 that "without exception, there are rather significant amounts of reserve production capacity in every sector of Soviet industry."[7] For the steel industry in particular, Kvasha's conclusion has been substantially studied (1968, 1977) by such well-informed specialists as Nikolai

Sklokin, director of the Institute of the Economics of the USSR Steel Industry, and Nikolai Mityaev, professor at the Institute of Steel and Alloys (Moscow).[8]

The Survey

A survey of the productive capacities of steel plants, conducted by the USSR National Scientific Institute of the Steel Industry, provides the most reliable data base at our disposal.[9] The survey was undertaken to establish the extent to which the production capacity, as determined by each plant on its own, conforms to the instructions issued by Gosplan and the Central Statistical Administration on the methods to be used for measuring available production capacities. The survey, which encompassed virtually every plant in the Soviet steel industry, revealed that the *majority* of plants ignored these instructions from above and had artificially *underestimated* their actual production capacity. The principal method for doing this was to make exaggerated—and unwarranted— estimates of the schedule for each unit of production capacity. In other words, they ascribed all losses in productive time (associated with poor organization of the production process) to the scheduled downtimes and, hence, significantly understated the real production capacity.[10]

By artificially underestimating their production capacities, the plants were then able to report to Gosplan and the Central Statistical Administration that they had nearly 100 percent utilization of production capacities. Among the plants that misrepresented production capacity were some of the Soviet Union's largest plants, such as Cherepovetskii, Novolipetskii, Azovstal', Magnitogorskii, Nizhnetagilskii', Chelyabinskii, and Zaporozhstal'. It is important to note, too, that top officials in the steel industry had approved these falsified computations and passed them on to Gosplan and the Central Statistical Administration.

To take a concrete example, let us examine the figures for blast-furnace units. From data supplied by the plants, the total production capacity of 129 blast furnaces amounted to 65.7 million tons. After these figures had been corrected by the institute, however, the total capacity rose to 77.7 million tons—an increase of 18 percent. That meant, in turn, a corresponding change in the rates of utilization of production capacities. Thus whereas the plants had reported utilization to be about 100 percent on the average (and in some plants, such as Cherepovetskii, Novolipetskii, and Azovstal', even over 100 percent), the institute's computations reduced utilization of production capacities of blast furnaces to an average of 84 percent. Thus once the institute had recomputed the production capacity of this industrial sector in accordance with the methods stipulated by Gosplan and the Central Statistical Administration, it found that underutilization amounted to 16 percent—markedly lower than the claim by plants that utilization of production capacity was close to the maximal limit. A similar pattern is seen in the case of open-hearth furnaces, oxygen converters, and rolling mills.

The survey, furthermore, revealed that in their computation of production capacities many plants even incorporated figures less than what in fact was being attained. For instance, the Zaporozhstal' plant set smelting time at 7.25 hours in computing the capacity of the open-hearth furnaces; in fact, however, the previous year about half of all smelting processes took 5–7 hours. Similarly, the Chelyabinskii plant inflated its actual smelting time of 6.0–6.5 hours to an official 7.8 hours.

What is to be concluded from this survey? Obviously, the plants had not calculated production capacities in accordance with the rules prescribed by Gosplan and the Central Statistical Administration. They had lowered their capacities to conform to the annual production plan and hence had correspondingly overstated the level of utilization. Moreover, Gosplan and the Central Statistical Administration had accepted these figures and made them the basis for subsequent planning projections.

While the survey itself applies to the 1960s, it is clear that this pattern is endemic to the Soviet economy. That was attested to as early as the 1930s in M. Barun's classic study *Osnovnoi Kapital promyshlennosti SSR* (Fixed Assets of Soviet Industry):

> We must make every effort to emphasize again and again that, when this or that branch of industry claims in a given year to make nearly full use of its fixed assets and that the resources of the available means of production in some other branch were exhaustively utilized, and that the fixed assets is some branches have placed limits on any further increases in production, we are proceeding of necessity on the basis of the enterprises' own evaluation of the production capacity of their fixed assets. This production capacity is established on the basis of conditions typical of each planning period for the utilization of the

fixed assets of the particular branch of industry (shift ratio, number of work days in the year, machine-hour rate, etc.). Bearing in mind the fact that these conditions for utilization of production assets can in no way be satisfied, and also the fact that it is possible to greatly improve this level of utilization, let us reiterate: in no branch of industry can it be said that the fixed assets have already placed limits on any further increase in production.[11]

To take a more recent study, N. Mityaev came to an analogous conclusion in his 1977 monograph *Osnovnye Proizvodstvennye fondy chernoi metallurgii* (Fixed Production Assets in the Steel Industry).[12] In short, an understatement of production capacities and overstatement of utilization have been fundamental properties of the Soviet economy from the time the Soviet system was first established.

It is hardly possible to assume that Gosplan and the Central Statistical Administration know nothing of the "adjustment" introduced into the computation of production capacity as part of the production plans, that is, the deliberate understatement of production capacities. On the contrary, it is an open secret. Yet that raises an interesting question in its own right: how is one to explain the claim of Gosplan's Martynov, the Soviet Union's leading expert on production capacities, that capacity utilization is at maximum levels?

To understand the contradictions in estimates of the utilization level, it is essential to consider the theoretical underpinnings that underlie the very definition and conception of production capacity.

Theoretical Approaches: Some Conceptual Problems

Whether one is speaking of a market economy or a planned economy, in theory there are dozens of potential definitions of productive capacity. Such a plethora of definition is, as a rule, the case when the essence of economic phenomena has not been fully explored in either a theoretical or practical respect. *Production capacity* is precisely such a category. In the words of Edward Hincks: "Capacity to produce is meaningful but is not measurable."[13] The state of affairs with the definition and measurement of production capacity in American industry was examined in hearings before the U.S. Congress, Joint Economic Committee, Subcommittee on Economic Statistics:

We have often been asked the question, what makes capacity a more difficult concept than other economic terms? The simple answer is that the definition of capacity requires judgement and basic assumptions which vary considerably. Even given a workable definition, capacity figures for the economy as a whole would have to be constructed at present from a variety of sources and data. Many technicians are uneasy about such a lack of precision.[14]

In the American economy the absence of standardized definitions and the unmeasurability of production capacity makes analysis of production difficult and creates problems for government statistics.

For the Soviet planned economy, however, this question is of much greater significance: unless real production potential in each concrete period is known, the entire planning mechanism cannot effectively function but, rather, operates like an engine that has been thrown out of gear. It is, therefore, especially important for the Soviet planners to have reliable and practically applicable definitions and methods of measuring production capacity. The less reliable the data, the less effective the planning and the less effective the control. Efficient use of resources, in fact, becomes positively inconceivable. But due to the very character of the Soviet economy—its bottlenecks, its use of capacity to measure productivity— no institution can function normally without having latent production reserves; concealment of true production potential is intrinsic to the very system. As a result, Gosplan and the ministries lack data on the true production potential of an enterprise and branches of industry and hence cannot control real, not just fictitious, resources. Clearly, knowledge of true production potentials under these specific conditions would give Soviet leaders a powerful lever to wring greater output out of enterprises.

To be sure, all these notations apply an idealized conception of the goals and functions of the centralized planning and management of the Soviet economy. But Soviet experience with developing definitions of production capacity and methods for its practical measurement has not differed from that of American economists.

The official formulation in Gosplan's methodological guidelines, though seemingly inclusive, is simply too superficial to serve as a theoretical basis to determine the production capacity, as the whole experience of falsified—or at least misrepresented—data in the survey plainly shows. How is one to understand "maximal possible"

output of products? Does it mean the maximum possible within the
limits of technological norms for the operation of machinery (considering the necessary standard idle time for repair), or does it mean
the entire time available in the calendar year? What is productivity
per unit of time—that given in the design specifications, or what a
given enterprise actually achieved? What is the meaning of "leading
technology": are Soviet or world standards to be applied here? The
official definition, which fails to answer these and other questions,
leaves a wide range for interpretation.

That has, indeed, been admitted by Soviet specialists. For example, when a group of scholars from the Institute of Economics of the
Ukrainian Academy of Sciences evaluated the practical significance
of official indices for production capacity, they concluded that these
indicators "in essence are not used for planning, for the evaluation
of the production and economic activity of enterprise, or for stimulating the course and effectiveness of production."[15] When they
explained why production capacity could not be used for purposes
of planning and control, the authors limited themselves to vague
explanations, declaring that these indicators are not employed "due
to certain incomplete methodological development."[16]

But why have Soviet economists been content to adhere to an
abstract, nonoperable formulation and to eschew attempts to elabo-
rate a new, more practicable measurement and theoretical base?

Why the Operational Definition Is Not Operational

One reason is the theoretical difficulty of the problem, especially
for Soviet theoreticians. Ideally, to determine the actual production
capacities of the economy, one should adopt an "engineering" interpretation of production capacity, whereby the latter connotes the
maximum volume of production attainable on existing machinery
and equipment (that is, the maximal potential without constraints
on resources in the infrastructure). That approach is especially valuable for military-economic calculations, which seek to determine
production possibilities under extreme situations (when the need
arises for short-term but maximum use of production potential).
Relevant here is the experience of World War II, when enterprises
evacuated to the east and those remaining in unoccupied territory
operated under adverse conditions but produced an extraordinarily
high output.

Such a rigid approach, however, is positively idealistic under the actual conditions of the Soviet economy. Indeed, if Gosplan's operative definition corresponded to the engineering interpretation, it would not give the enterprises and ministries any room to maneuver. The result would be a computation of production capacity sharply higher than current production. But this, as nothing else, would starkly reveal the full scale of inefficiency of the Soviet economy.

The second reason is the fact that Gosplan, the ministries, and especially individual enterprises do not want strict regulations to define and plan production capacities. Enterprises and ministries, without directly flouting the official formulation, in essence transform it by taking the production program for the planned year as the frame of reference. To this they subordinate concrete production conditions and accordingly use the available raw materials, energy, transportation, and manpower resources.

With respect to steel plants, it is necessary to consider as well several other circumstances. Because production units (open-hearth furnaces, converters, rolling mills) are put into operation sequentially and discretely, disproportions can arise between the capacity of a unit installed and that of other units in the enterprise. As a result, when a new production unit (shop) goes into operation, its actual capacity does not correspond to its maximum production potential. Nevertheless, that optimal output is attainable; it is limited only by the potentials of related production units—that is, the other links in the enterprise's unified technological chain. In other words, the capacity of one shop is set depending on the output capabilities of another.

Thus it turns out that the production capacity of a steel plant (like enterprises of other branches of industry) is not an indicator of what can be obtained given the maximum use of all identified reserves for the growth of production as follows from the definition adopted by Gosplan; rather, it is a quantity that characterizes the possibility for producing products in the plan period given that the bottlenecks, losses, shortcomings in the work of the enterprise, and shortfalls in the supply of production resources which existed in the preplan period continue to exist. As Sklokin has confessed, "For production capacity we use the projection of the planning year."[17] This explains why production plans are usually only 1–2 percent lower than production capacity and sometimes even *exceed* 100 percent capacity. But if production capacity is reduced to the level of the production plan, this means that the potential capacity has been interpreted to mean capacity utilization.

Standard Capacities and Their Utilization

Let us try to clarify the concept. Starting with the engineering interpretation, we distinguish between the theoretical (ideal) capacity and the standard (practical) capacity. By theoretical capacity, we understand the maximal potential output under ideal operating conditions with equipment use over the entire available time in a calendar year (24 hours × 365 days) for the equipment lifetime. By the standard capacity, we understand the output produced at maximal efficiency per unit of working time of basic equipment (assuming a designated range and optimal properties of the raw or semifinished materials to be processed), as limited by the level of utilization of the production capacities over time (available time in a calendar year, limited by the designated downtime for maintenance and other technological reasons). Gosplan's definition is close to what we understand as the theoretical capacity. But in planning, compiling plans, and making economic projections, planners always take into consideration the standard production capacity.

A special case of the standard capacity, called *projected capacity*, is widely used in Soviet planning and accounting. The projected capacity is equal to the standard capacity computed in designing plants, workshops, and individual units of manufacturing equipment, but it remains valid only as long as the original equipment (or processes or machinery) are not modernized, rebuilt, or improved. Obviously, once those improvements are made, actual production capacity will increase, and hence the original projected capacity should be reviewed and correspondingly revised.

One often finds reports in the Soviet press that production at some enterprise exceeds production capacity. For example, the journal *Stal'* reported that the Magnitogorsk metallurgical plant, the largest in the USSR, in 1980 exceeded its production capacity for steel by 33 percent and for rolled metal by 22 percent.[18] Of course, the idea of production exceeding production capacity is nonsensical. It can only be explained by the fact that the plant's production capacity for these products set for 1980 manifestly did not correspond to Gosplan's definition, if it is intended to mean the production potential of the given enterprise.

Naturally, the question arises: by how much do the planned magnitudes of production capacity deviate from the true values? Understandably, the data needed to answer this question are not readily available. Still, one can get some idea of the scale of the phenomenon from the following 1980 example. To judge from the published data, capacity utilization of metallurgical plans in the Dnepropetrovsk region (the largest concentration of steel production of the USSR, and possibly in the world, including the Krivorozhskii, Dzerzhinskii, and other plants) averaged 92–95 percent. If compared to normative capacity, however, utilization was only 70–75 percent.[19] As this example suggests, the gap between planned capacity and theoretical capacity (determined for optimal conditions of equipment operation and rhythmical work at an enterprise) amounts to approximately 20 percent. In other words, there is a reserve to increase output by one-fifth of production capacity, and this reserve can be realized by creating normal work conditions that were assumed in the original designs. Such is the real level of the utilization of standard capacity for enterprises in construction materials, the chemical industry, nonferrous metallurgy, light industry, and others.[20]

The Vested Interest in Ignorance

In short, no one seems determined to establish true production capacities. That applies, too, to the steel industry: no one—not the enterprises, the ministries, or Gosplan—has attempted to establish its true productive potential.

Why, then, did authorities undertake the survey of the production capacities of steel plants (described above), which revealed a concealed and intentional understatement of the level of production capacity at most enterprises? The survey was in fact undertaken in 1964, when industry was under a regional rather than branch management (as part of Khrushchev's abortive attempt to raise productivity by abolishing ministries and creating regional economic councils). Since then, however, there have been no such measures, either in the steel industry or in any other branch of industry. But even under the present system, with the same degree of centralization of management of enterprises that exists today, the ministries could—

if they wanted—investigate and establish the computed production capacity at each enterprise. But the point is that they do *not* want to establish potential capacity; a ministry, no less than the steel plants themselves, is interested in maintaining and building up production reserves. If the Institute of Steel Industry were even toying with the idea of a new survey, the ministry would simply forbid it, and thus the accumulation of information so detrimental to its own vested interests. That attitude, indeed, is apparent from the fact that absolutely no conclusions were drawn about increasing production capacities due to hidden reserves. One gets the impression that, after piously noting the importance and necessity of defining, recording, and analyzing the utilization of production capacities, Gosplan, the Central Statistical Administration, and the ministries do not have the slightest desire to obtain an objective picture.

Though one might not expect planners to prefer such ignorance, in fact there is nothing paradoxical here. Indeed, why establish and plan technologically attainable production capacity figures if in practice one cannot eliminate factors that make attaining those indicators impossible? And the fact that these factors cannot be removed within the existing economic system is realized by the leaders of the Soviet economy no less than by Western critics of this system. If production capacities were defined objectively, without considering the real situation—that is, without taking into account the difficulties in supply of raw materials and energy, without considering bottlenecks and disproportions in technology, without considering many other factors of an extratechnological nature, including such important ones as the striving of enterprises to have latent production reserves—the true value of the production potential of the majority of enterprises would be perceptibly higher. But then it would turn out that the utilization of production capacities is not at all on the high level now apparent from Soviet statistics. And it is possible, then, that the utilization of production capacities in the Soviet steel industry would fall to a level close to that of the analogous indicator in the American steel industry in the years of the last recession.

The theoreticians of the Soviet economy are well aware of the need to create a planned reserve of production capacity to ensure the normal functioning of a planned economy and to overcome conflict, oscillations, and haphazard interference. They recognize that without reserve capacity it is impossible to improve output and that "in branches of industry operating with maximal workload, not only are there fewer resources available, but the incentive to replace old products with new ones or with products with better consumer qualities than the older products is not as strong."[21] Nevertheless, in the planning process none of these considerations is taken into account; no allowance is made for them in the methodology for determining potential production capacity and incorporating this into the plan.

Here, as in many other instances, however, reality serves to correct for the inflexibility of the planning process (otherwise it would be impossible for the Soviet economy to function), and the absence of planned reserves of production capacities is more than compensated for by unplanned and unregulated creation and buildup of capacity unaccounted for in government statistics.

Thus it seems obvious that there is significant reserve production capacity in the Soviet steel industry; indeed, it is a reserve that substantially exceeds the figures cited in Soviet publications. Enterprises conceal from the center this real production potential, create a picture of maximum utilization of production capacities, and accumulate latent reserves for production. What form do these reserves take and what is their origin?

Typology of Reserve Production Capacity

From the very start, we have excluded from our discussion reserve capacities due to an absence or falloff in demand. But in branches of heavy industry, this would be the exception. It may be supposed that previously planned reserve capacity, to be used for a rapid expansion of production whenever an extraordinary situation (a major calamity, for example) arises, would become available. But we are convinced that these types of reserves do not exist in such a deterministic form. In the case of the Soviet steel industry, we can be certain of this. In what form do we find the reserve capacities of the steel plants? We distinguish three basic categories.

Basic Structure for Enlarging the Enterprise

Basic structure is created at enterprises that are constructed in stages and thereby are used to expand capacity gradually. This is a widespread phenomenon in the USSR, particularly in planning and construction of large steel plants. Usually, in the second stage lay-

out operations and pipeline construction are designed and implemented, and often manufacturing buildings and sometimes certain
production equipment are erected as well. For example, in the
construction projects for the Karaganda and West Siberian steel
plants specified construction costs in the second stage for stockpiles
of pipelines for auxiliary and service shops (transportation, water
mains, heat and electricity, gas, repairs) amounted to 10–30 percent
of the total cost of these items, and 4–15 percent of the total cost of
the first stage of the project.[22]

Construction times for the first stage of large enterprises usually
amount to seven to eight years, and the "fascination" with basic
structure may be attributed precisely to such lengthy periods; that
is, it may be supposed that the demand for new capacities arises all
at once or very soon after the completion of the first stage of a
construction project. Using the already existing basic structure, it is
possible to construct the second stage somewhat more rapidly, that
is, to increase the additional production capacity more rapidly.

There are certain conditions that must be observed if we are to
subsume basic structure under reserve capacities. To put this reserve capacity into service requires an investment that is somewhat
greater than what has already been "frozen" in the stockpiled fixed
assets. Here we have a special kind of dormant reserve capacity.

Imbalance in Capacities between Successive Stages of Production

This type of imbalance exists at most steel plants and as such
limits (in certain cases, substantially) the utilization of capacity
available for the creation of the final product, that is, the production
capacity of rolling mills. Mismatches between the production capacities of individual units become particularly acute as the iso-
lated capacities of newly commissioned open-hearth furnaces, converters, and rolling mills grow. Installation of huge manufacturing
units may eliminate certain disproportions between plants, but will
create others.

The Ministry of the Steel Industry has tried to even out these types
of disproportions through intrabranch cooperation—that is, shipments of semifinished products from plants suffering from excess
capacity to plants where there are shortages—and in this way keep
adjacent production capacities from being underutilized. Under
these conditions, utilization of the production capacities of many
plants depends on timely shipments of semifinished products from

other plants. The scale of these shipments has become greater and greater (in 1983 about 15 million tons of different types of billets, about 3 million tons of steel ingots, and more than 5 million tons of pig iron), and all this metal is being shipped by rail greater and greater distances.[23] And in view of the crisis state of rail transport, this factor is obviously playing a major role in underutilization of the capacities of many steel plants. Equalization of intraplant disproportions of production capacities, along with the use of construction stockpiles to expand production, constitutes an investment path for placing reserve capacities into service.

Latent Reserve Capacities

Unlike the two preceding categories, in the case of latent reserve capacities there is no need, or nearly no need, for investment. These reserves are in a "fluid" state and are placed into operation through improvements in the planning and procurement system and production management and control, and in the level of material incentives. Under the conditions of the current economic system and habits that have developed over time, no industrial enterprise in the USSR, including steel plants, is capable of functioning normally without latent reserves of the full range of production capacities.

Latent reserves are needed to meet the production plan where there are chronic breakdowns in the delivery of raw material, fuel, and other materials and resources. A plant must have latent reserves that can be readily put into service to fulfill and overfulfill the plans. Finally, reserve capacity is needed to produce a quantity of output that can be used for direct exchange with other enterprises for different types of goods or services in short supply. For all these reasons, a plant must understate its true production capacity and, thereby, build up reserve capacity.

Thus any claim that steel production capacities are utilized at extraordinarily high levels (nearly 100 percent) does not, we believe, correspond to reality. What, then, is the actual discrepancy between the attainable volume of production and the potential capacity of the Soviet steel industry? If we are considering the theoretical (ideal) capacity, then we are dealing with a kind of yardstick more for engineering computations than for determining the potential output under the distinctive conditions of the Soviet economy.

It is quite another matter to compare the attained volume of production and the standard capacity, though there is a practical value in doing so. In view of the unlimited demand for steel typical of the Soviet economy, any falloff from the standard capacity reflects solely breakdowns in the normal (as defined by the technological standards) functioning of the means of production of the steel industry.

The causes of such breakdowns are varied and numerous. Some of them (the intrabranch factors) are long-term in nature—for example, intraplant disproportions; mismatches between the production capacity for pig iron, steel, and rolled product; physical wear and tear and insufficient renovation of equipment; and different technological bottlenecks. Others arise primarily outside the branch and are nontechnological in nature—for example, interruptions in the delivery of particular types of raw materials, fuel, and other resources which in certain cases may be seasonal in nature; and low level of maintenance. Periodically, acute shortages of ore, coke, and scrap iron may be included here.

The major difference between these two groups of causes of underutilization of production capacities from the standard level may be elucidated as follows: whereas the factors in the first group may be overcome only through additional investment for the development of the plants (and therefore it is always problematical whether they can be overcome, nor is there any certainty as to when they may be overcome), for the factors in the second group underutilization of production capacities is associated with elements that are often random in nature, seasonal, and nontechnological, and lie outside the sphere of activity of the steel industry proper. For this reason, no additional investment in this branch of industry is needed to overcome these factors. These types of factors may be overcome largely through improvements in the planning process, procurement, and organizational efforts, and through increasing the level of material incentives.

Particular emphasis must be placed on latent reserve production capacity. Under the true operating conditions of the enterprises, latent reserve capacities are unavoidable. These production capacities are placed into operation depending upon the self-interest of the plants themselves without any reference to plan controls.

Returning once again to the different categories of production capacity, we must bear in mind that, strictly speaking, the standard capacity refers to a definite level of utilization of the productive potential. But this level is unattainable under the true operating

TABLE 4.1
Soviet blast furnaces (as of the early 1980s)[24]

Useful volume (in cubic meters)	Number of blast furnaces	Proportion of total pig-iron output (%)
2,000 or more (built after 1960)	25	37–38
2,000 or more (built after 1930)	74	54–55
Up to 1,000 (built before 1930)	39	6–7
TOTAL	138	97–100

conditions of the Soviet industrial enterprise. The virtually attainable annual volume of production is always less than the standard annual capacity for reasons that may be related to factors in the particular plant or outside the plant. Let us consider the state of affairs with regard to the utilization of capacities in the steel industry at the three basic stages: iron making, steelmaking, and rolling.

Technological Reserves

Iron Making

The 138 blast furnaces of the Soviet steel industry located at 26 large integrated plants and several small enterprises now smelt over 110 million tons of pig iron per year.

The Soviet Union's blast furnaces are extraordinarily varied in terms of volume (productivity), age, and other parameters.

The 5,580-cubic-meter blast furnace now under construction at the Cherepovetskii plant will produce as much pig iron as the twenty furnaces built in the early 1900s at plants in the Urals.[25] Over the past twenty-five years the volumes, hence the capacities, of blast furnaces have rapidly grown through the reconstruction of old furnaces.

Whether the utilization of the capacities of blast furnaces in the Soviet steel industry is increasing or decreasing can be determined from published statistics on the volumetric efficiency* of the blast

---

*Amount of cubic meterage of useful volume per meterage of output per day of operation (in the Russian literature abbreviated KIPO).

furnaces. From the definition of this indicator, it is clear that the lower its value for a particular furnace, the higher the utilization of the capacity of the furnace. In 1982, 106.7 million tons of pig iron were produced at a branchwide average of 0.574, whereas in 1978, when the output of pig iron reached record levels (110.7 million tons), the mean volumetric efficiency amounted to 0.549.[26] If the 1978 volumetric efficiency still held, the 1982 output at already existing blast furnaces would have been 111 million tons of pig iron, or 4.3 million more than was actually produced. But estimates of the potential utilization of the capacity of Soviet blast furnaces made on the basis of the mean-branch volumetric efficiency are insufficiently reliable. Therefore, let us consider what the actual situation might be, using instead the capacity of the blast furnaces, broken down into individual groups of furnaces.

Blast Furnaces with Volume up to 1,000 Cubic Meters
The sixteen largest furnaces in this group have volumes greater than 600 cubic meters, including ten furnaces in the 600–725-cubic-meter range. The volume of the ten furnaces in the old Ural plants is less than 240 cubic meters each.[28]

Because of physical wear and tear and the antiquated design of most of the furnaces in this group, strategies for increasing output (for example, increasing the gas pressure in the hearth or the air-blast temperature above 1,000 degrees Centigrade) cannot be supplied here. Crude ore is used as the raw material at many furnaces in this group. Coke consumption at these furnaces is two to four times higher than at more modern furnaces.[29] On the whole, the cost-benefit indicators of the blast furnaces in this group are the lowest of all the groups, and offer virtually no room for increasing the utilization of their capacities.

Blast Furnaces with Volume in the Range of 1,000–2,000 Cubic Meters
This group of blast furnaces, which is the largest of all the groups, includes several generations of blast furnaces, from the first two 1,180-cubic-meter furnaces put into operation at the Magnitogor-skii plant in 1932; and the 1,033-cubic-meter and 1,386-cubic-meter furnaces typical of the postwar period and constructed through 1958 at most of the plants in the south and the Urals; through the standard modern furnaces with volumes in the range 1,719–1,754

TABLE 4.2
Design productivity of blast furnaces of different volumes[27]

	Useful volume (in cubic meters)						
	1,033	1,386	1,719	2,000	2,700	3,200	5,000
Design productivity	1.0	1.3	1.4	1.6	2.1	2.5	4.0
Millions of tons, KIPO	0.362	0.381	0.427	0.438	0.448	0.452	0.455

TABLE 4.3
Volumetric efficiency of blast furnaces of
different volumes (as of the early 1980s)[32]

Plant	Number of blast furnace	Useful volume (in cubic meters)	KIPO
Cherepovetskii	2	1,033	0.507
Novolipetskii	1	1,060	0.526
Imeny Ilicha	1	1,033	0.484
Kusnetskii	2	1,033	0.517
Magnitogorskii	4	1,180	0.481
Imeny Dzerzinskogo	7	1,719	0.570
Imeny Dzerzinskogo	8	1,719	0.636
Krivoroshskii	1	1,719	0.533
Cherepovetskii	3	2,000	0.448
Novolipetskii	3 and 4	2,000	0.476
Imeny Ilicha	4	2,002	0.524
Krivorozhskii	2	2,000	0.535
Magnitogorskii	9 and 10	2,014	0.402 and 0.448
Krivorozhskii	7	2,000	0.544
West Siberian	2	2,000	—
Kuznetskii	—	2,002	0.548
Cherepovetskii	4	2,700	0.467
Nizhenetagilskii	6	2,700	0.466
Krivorozhskii	8	2,700	0.561
Karagandinskii	3	2,700	0.707
Novolipetskii	5	3,200	0.460
Novolipetskii	6	3,200	0.445
Karagandinskii	4	3,200	—
Kommunarskii	1	3,000	0.708
Krivorozhskii	5	5,000	0.554

cubic meters, installed after 1958.[30] As is clear from Table 4.3, the volumetric efficiency of the relatively small furnaces in this group (volume up to 1,386 cubic meters) did not achieve the levels projected for this size standard furnace (0.362–0.381), though it was significantly better than mean-branch volumetric efficiency in the early 1980s.[31]

In the second half of the 1970s the productivity of blast furnaces at the Cherepovetskii, Novolipetskii, and Magnitogorskii plants (twelve of the eighteen furnaces here belong to this group and have volumes in the range 1,000–1,400 cubic meters) were 15–25 percent higher than the branch average, and in the case of several furnaces as much as 35–40 percent higher, indicating the availability of significant reserve capacity at other plants in this group.[33] A typical example is the 1,180-cubic-meter no. 4 furnace at the Magnitogorskii plant constructed as long ago as the 1930s. This furnace had been the least efficient of all the eight furnaces at the plant, with volumetric efficiency of 0.502.[34] Once the production conditions of the furnace had been optimized, deliveries of high-quality raw materials begun, and a program of standard maintenance organized, the productivity of this old blast furnace increased substantially and its volumetric efficiency attained a level of 0.460.[35] Obviously, the results achieved at this furnace cannot be generalized to all the furnaces in this group, though this example does show that there are significant reserve capacities at the furnaces in this, the most numerous of all the groups, and that these reserve capacities could be put into operation once operating conditions were improved.

Blast Furnaces with Volume above 2,000 Cubic Meters
This group of blast furnaces has the highest cost-benefit indicators, as is clear from two factors. On the one hand, because of the higher cost-benefit indicators of these furnaces, most of which were built in the past twenty years (see Table 4.1), the furnace smelting process can be increased through optimization of the parameters (gas pressure and air-blast temperature). The equipment used in these furnaces is reliable and modern, and there is a high level of automation and mechanization present. On the other hand, the furnaces in this generation were given a higher priority with regard to deliveries of high-quality raw materials, oxygen, and natural gas than were smaller-size furnaces.

Furnaces with volumes in the range 2,000–2,014 cubic meters (of which there are only twelve in all the USSR) have the highest specific productivity.[36] Their highest daily productivity reaches 4,800 tons (1.7 trillion tons per year, which corresponds to the design capacity of this type of furnace).[37] But not all furnaces in this group attain such high indicators. The productivity of some of them (particularly, the three furnaces of the Krivoi Rog plant) are 20–25 percent less.[38]

Thus despite the higher production parameters, there is significant reserve capacity at the furnaces in this group. These reserve capacities could be made use of if the quality of the sinter were improved, the content of the blast furnace air increased. In the opinion of experts, the oxygen content could be increased through the available reserve capacity of existing oxygen units.

Despite the greater attention being devoted to maintenance and support, utilization of the capacities of the Soviet Union's largest blast furnace—the 3,200-cubic-meter furnace at the Novolipetskii have been attained by the Soviet Union's most recently installed blast furnace—the 3,200-cubic-meter furnace at the Novolipetskiy plant. This furnace attained its scheduled capacity (7,100 metric tons per day) relatively quickly.[39] The 2,700-cubic-meter furnace of the Karagandinskii plant is operating at the worst level, since gas is not being used in its operation.[40] The Soviet Union's largest blast furnace—the 5,000-cubic-meter no. 9 furnace at the Krivorozhskii plant—also has low-capacity utilization rates (the scheduled capacity efficiency has yet to exceed 0.85, despite the fact that the furnace was put into operation in 1974).[41]

Judging from published results of an analysis of the operation of blast furnaces at plants in the south, where about half of the Soviet Union's production of pig iron is concentrated, the maximal utilization of capacity exceeds the minimal figures by more than 30 percent in groups of furnaces whose volumes are not too far apart in size.[42] This reflects the difference in the raw materials and technological and managerial conditions of the production process. But such differences also attest to the existence of significant reserve capacities at furnaces with low utilization factors. In fact, studies conducted at plants in the south have demonstrated that the specific productivity (per cubic meter of volume) of the blast furnaces could be increased by more than 20 percent on the average without any additional investment through improvements in the operational management and by observing the manufacturing standards.[43]

Steelmaking

There are three modes of steel production commonly found in the Soviet steel industry: open-hearth furnaces and the tandem hearths that are a further stage of them, oxygen converters, and electric furnaces.

Open-hearth furnaces, which are the oldest mode, are responsible

TABLE 4.4
Steel production in the USSR (millions of tons/percent)[44]

Mode of production	1970	1975	1980	1981
Open hearth	81.9/70.7	79.8/56.4	74.1/50.0	72.5/48.8
Tandem hearth	2.1/ 1.8	11.8/ 8.4	14.6/10.1	15.0/10.1
Basic oxygen	19.9/17.2	34.8/24.6	42.1/28.5	44.0/29.6
Electric	10.7/ 9.3	14.0/ 9.9	15.9/10.7	16.1/10.8
Other	1.2/ 1.0	0.8/ 0.5	0.8/ 0.6	0.8/ 0.6
TOTAL STEEL	115.8	141.3	147.9	148.4

for the production of half of all the steel; converters occupy the second place. Electric furnaces are responsible for a comparatively small fraction of the total output, though they play a special role in the production of high-quality steel and alloys.

As the center of gravity in the industry shifts from the quantitative to the qualitative aspects of the production process, greater and greater attention is being paid to increasing the number of electric furnaces. Table 4.4 shows the changes that have occurred in the structure of the steel industry in the USSR. It clearly shows that production in open-hearth furnaces has fallen and demonstrates how the importance of other technologies has grown.

The increase in the proportion of steel produced in oxygen converters and electric furnaces and the replacement of open-hearth furnaces by converters and electric furnaces is a general policy in the development of Soviet steel production. The overall proportion of steel produced in converters and electric furnaces is to be increased by 46 percent in 1985, and from the current situation this figure seems a realistic goal.[45]

Let us briefly consider the principal features of the development of steelmaking technologies in the USSR over the past two decades and the potential available for increasing the level of utilization of these capacities.

Oxygen Converters

The rapid development of oxygen converter technology, which is now responsible for most of the increase in steel output, is a decisive feature of the contemporary stage of development of steel production in the USSR. Of the total steel production capacity (10.9 million tons) installed in the ninth five-year plan (1976–80), the capacity of the four converters constructed over the course of the plan at the Azovstal' and Cherepovetskiy plants amounted to 8–9 million tons.[46]

Seventy percent of the total capacity (3.7 million tons) installed in 1981–82, or 2.8 million, is provided by just two 250-ton converters at the Dzerzhinskii plant.[47] There are now forty-three oxygen converters in the USSR with capacity in the range 50–350 tons, including thirteen 250–350-ton converters constructed after 1970—that is, all the large modern converters now in operation at steel plants. More than 40 percent of the entire output of converter steel is produced at these large converters.[48]

Converter technology first appeared in the Soviet steel industry in the early 1960s after a decade of experience in the industrially developed countries had demonstrated the technological and economic advantages of oxygen converters as compared to open-hearth furnaces.[49]

The development of the Soviet Union's first generation of small-size (up to 100–130-ton) oxygen converters constructed in the 1960s at a number of plants (Il'ich, Krivorozhskii, Yenakievskii, Novolipetskii, and others) proceeded without encountering any special problems.[50] In the late 1960s larger oxygen converters (the productivity of an oxygen converter increases in direct proportion to its volume) began to be constructed in the USSR, and relatively small-size converters were rebuilt and their volume increased to 160–180 tons. The first two 250-ton large converters were put into service in the 1970s at the Karagandinskii plant.[51] Oxygen converter shops with an annual capacity of 4.0–4.5 million tons, each operating with two 300–350-ton converters, were constructed from 1974 to 1980 at the Novolipetskii, West Siberian, Azovstal', and Cherepovetskii plants.

The utilization of large converters has encountered considerable problems because of technological difficulties and defects in equipment design.[52] Equipment used for continuous steel casting which is linked to the converters in a single production line has in particular tended to hold back the productivity of the converters, because its design still suffers from a number of drawbacks. Thus greater utilization of the capacities of large oxygen converters has become a decisive factor in the growth of steel production. There are a number of technological steps that may be taken to increase the level of utilization of the capacity of oxygen converters; for example, the weight of the melts can be increased, melt time (length of cycle) can be reduced, or the lining life can be increased.

Whether the weight of the melts can be increased depends on the volume of the converters, though this volume is virtually at a maximum already. On the other hand, there is considerable potential for reducing the melt cycle, mainly through reducing the time spent on subsidiary operations. About 30 percent of the total cycle time is consumed in such operations as sampling, waiting for the results of analyses, and temperature measurement. By reducing the length of these operations, the length of the melt cycle can be shortened from 42–44 minutes to 36–38 minutes or 10–14 percent.[53]

But because of imperfections and the unreliability of Russian-produced automatic control systems used to monitor the melting process these steps cannot be taken. Considerable research is under way in the USSR on ways of improving instruments and sensors used in these systems. At the present time, however, only through the use of foreign-made instruments is it possible to improve the reliability of these systems. Thus at the Petrovskii plant converter lifetime and steel quality have grown considerably as a result of the use of imported quantometers in the manufacturing process control system.[54]

Considerable increases in the level of utilization of converter capacity can also be achieved by increasing the lifetime of the lining and by reducing the time spent on preparing the converters for the melting process.

Lining life has increased with the development of oxygen converter technology. In 1967 the mean lining life of 100–160-ton converters was about 180 melts, by 1977 it had grown to more than 500 melts, and by 1980 to 700–900 melts.[55] The furnace lining life for some larger converters is now over 2,000 melts. Refractory in walls that can last longer will make possible more complete utilizations of the annual operational time of converters.

If these technological measures are applied, utilization of the capacity of existing converters could be increased, in the opinion of Soviet experts, by 15–40 percent.[56]

Electric Furnaces

Electric melting has developed at a less dynamic pace than oxygen converters during this period of time, and the proportion of the total steel output produced in electric furnaces has grown slowly.

Even in the early 1970s plans were for raising the output of electric steel to 22–24 million tons by 1980, though the actual volume of production amounted to only 15.9 million tons.[57] The plan to install twenty new electric furnaces in 1975–80 was not met, and the goal of 24 million tons was put off to 1985.[58] The increase in the production of electric steel over the past ten to twelve years has mainly been achieved at large (100- and 200-ton) electric-arc furnaces used to produce steel for castings and ingots and at units for continuous casting of billets. (We will not be considering electric furnaces used for mold casting of steel.) Even in 1972 over 42 percent of the entire output of electric steel was produced in furnaces of this type.[59] Nine such furnaces were constructed in the 1970s, two 200-ton furnaces at the Krasnyi Oktyabr' plant and seven 100-ton furnaces at the Donetskii, Chelyabinskii, Cherepovetskii, and Uzbekskii plants. Since 1982 the 100-ton furnaces have begun to be produced in improved designs (more powerful transformers) whose productivity is 10–20 percent higher than furnaces of this capacity which had been installed in the preceding decade.[60]

Until recently, electric furnaces were mainly designed for production of alloy steel. In the late 1970s about 46 percent of all alloy steel was produced in electric furnaces.[61] The desire to concentrate the production of alloy steel at electric furnaces has been dictated by two considerations:

> The technology of electric steelmaking is more adapted to the production of high-quality alloys.
>
> Such furnaces make more efficient use of left-over alloy steel scrap; by contrast, if this scrap is remelted in open-hearth furnaces, much of the chromium and manganese, and nearly all the vanadium and silicon in the scrap, is usually lost.

In the latter half of the 1970s, however, the worsening situation in iron-ore supplies and the related effort to make greater use of scrap (which will be considered below) forced the management of the steel industry to turn away from electric furnaces as a means of producing exceptionally high-grade alloy steel and alter their plans; instead they would try to increase the production of ordinary carbon steel. In switching over to the production of ordinary carbon steel there is a 15–17 percent increase in the productivity of electric furnaces.[62] Thus though they kept their jobs by achieving high-volume output, the management of the steel industry put off dealing with quality issues, though it is precisely the latter (according to their own claims) which is the problem of highest priority.

Electric furnaces were assigned an especially high proportion of the increase in steel output planned for the 1981–85 period. The bulk of the increase in the output of electric steel in this period was planned for the electric furnaces of the Uzbekskii, Donetskii, Kuznetskii, and Orsko-Khaliliovskii plants.[63] Three of the planned five 100-ton furnaces were put into operation at the Uzbek plant, and two more were planned for 1984.[64] In early 1981 a 100-ton furnace was installed at the Donets plant (a furnace of this size was already in operation there). Four 100-ton furnaces with total annual productivity of 1 million tons will be installed at the Kuznets plant.[65] A 100-ton electric furnace was put into service in 1983 at the Orsko-Khalilov plant. Though the design capacity of these furnaces has yet to be achieved, they undoubtedly played an important role in increasing steel output in the eleventh five-year plan (1981–85).[66] For example, about 17 percent of the total increase in steel production in 1983 was due to the electric furnaces at just one plant (Uzbekskiy). Note, incidentally, that we are speaking of carbon steel, not alloy steel.[67]

During the eleventh five-year plan an electric steel shop equipped with large electric-arc furnaces is to be put into service at the Azovstal' plant and four 150-ton furnaces designed to produce approximately 1.5 million tons annually are to be installed at the Oskol'skii electric steel plant. In addition, several electric furnaces will be included in the Moldavia, Zhlobinskii (Belorussia), and far east (Komsomol'sk na Amur) plants currently under construction. The first furnaces of these miniplants are to be put into service at the end of the eleventh (1981–85) or beginning of the twelfth (1986–90) five-year plan, while the first furnace for the Moldavia plant was constructed in 1985. It is even possible that some of the new electric steel capacity planned for the Oskol'skii plant will be operational in the current (twelfth) five-year plan.

Despite the drop in the proportion of steel produced in open-hearth furnaces, these furnaces will apparently continue to play an important role in steel production in the USSR through the year 2000. But not all the open-hearth furnaces will have the same fate. Of the 325 open-hearth furnaces in operation in 1980, 130 had been in service more than twenty-five years (the standard service life of an open-hearth furnace is twenty years).[68] Some of the already run-down furnaces have been taken out of service, though this step has been taken slowly and with great reluctance.

From the mid-1960s to the late 1970s the total capacity of all the open-hearth furnaces taken out of service amounted to 3.5–4.0 million tons.[69] Open-hearth furnaces will continue to be taken out of service in the 1980s. Some of them—relatively less run-down ones—will apparently be converted into tandem hearths (which we will discuss below), though most of them will continue in operation using the traditional open-hearth technology through the end of the century. These furnaces will be kept in working order through capitalized repairs, and the maximal possible volume of output will be "wrung" out of them. Considerable importance is being placed on increasing the yields of these open-hearth furnaces, as is particularly clear from plans for the installations of a number of plants (Karagandinskii, Uzbekskii, Sulinskii, and others) of horizontal continuous steel-casting units specially adapted for use with open-hearth furnaces.[70]

Tandem Hearths

A number of open-hearth furnaces were rebuilt and converted into tandem hearths as part of the development of steel production in the 1970s. From the available data, over the past decade (1970–1980), thirteen to fourteen tandem hearths each with annual capacity of 1.0–1.5 million tons were put into service.[71] This process of conversion (which involves relatively low expenditures and can be accomplished in relatively brief periods of time, often within the costs and times allocated for capitalized repairs) has made it possible to increase substantially the output of steel at a number of plants and, thereby, compensate for the drop in production typical in the traditional open-hearth technology. At one plant alone (Magnitogorskii), roughly 37 percent of all the steel production output (about 6 million tons) is produced in tandem hearths.[72]

The development of this method of increasing steel production capacity is a departure from the general course of technological policy in steelmaking. Tandem hearths suffer from a number of drawbacks not only by comparison with converters and electric furnaces but also by comparison with ordinary open-hearth furnaces. Tandem hearths require a considerably greater amount of charge per ton of steel produced and, particularly important, (as will be shown below) more pig iron in the charge than do open-hearth furnaces. Greater losses (oxidation) of metal occur in tandem hearths than in open-hearth furnaces.[73] Only a limited range of types of steel can be produced in tandem hearths, which also emit considerably more pollution into the atmosphere than do open-hearth furnaces.[74] But with all these drawbacks, we believe that more open-hearth furnaces will be converted into tandem hearths in the current decade. This will, however, slow down efforts to improve the quality of steel output, though in view of the important advantages gained with the construction of tandem hearths, only in this way will it be possible to make up for the overall drop in open-hearth production.

The Problem of Feed

Of the many problems in the utilization of steel-melting capacity, the problem of feed has been foremost and is increasingly acute. Feed is being delivered at increasingly irregular intervals and the quality of the feed (raw charge) is becoming worse and worse. Let us consider the two sides of this problem separately.

There are at least three factors that hinder efforts to maintain a normal, regular rate of supply of charge for open-hearth furnaces, converters, and electric furnaces: (a) an imbalance between pig iron and steel capacities, (b) consolidation of the capacities of production units, and (c) shorter melt time in converters than in open-hearth furnaces.

Imbalance between Pig Iron and Steel Capacities

This imbalance is found particularly in modern large plants now under construction (Cherepovetskii, West Siberian, etc.).[75] We have touched upon this subject above. At these plants, installation of steel-melting capacities is somewhat in advance of the growth in the capacities of blast furnaces at the particular plant, and as a result supplies of pig iron for steel-melting units have fallen short of demand.

The growing imbalance in production capacities is responsible for the increase in shipments of pig iron from one plant to another, often over great distances. As a result, the steel-melting furnaces' feed rate is now more dependent on the operations of rail transport units, which, as is well known, are in a serious bottleneck.

Consolidation of the Capacities of Production Units

This phenomenon has a dual effect on the rate at which steel-melting units are supplied. First, the larger the steel-melting unit, the more difficult it is to create and maintain reserves of pig iron and other manufacturing materials necessary for sustaining a regular rate of feed.[76] Second, as the individual capacities grow, temporary interruption in the production process because of shutdowns for maintenance or to implement various improvements in the manufacturing units have become more difficult to compensate for. Thus in 1983 a shutdown of just one 5,000-cubic-meter blast furnace (4-million-ton annual capacity) at the Krivoi Rog plant for overhaul made it extraordinarily difficult to meet the steel production plan for the entire group of plants in the south.[77]

Melt Time Shorter in Converters than in Open-Hearth Furnaces

Converter melts last forty to fifty minutes, whereas open-hearth melts are five to seven hours long. Correspondingly, the amount of time needed for all the operations in preparation for the next melt cycle, including the feeding of pig iron, scrap, and other materials, is also shorter. Increasing the rate of the production cycles presupposes greater constraints on the technological conditions, operational management of the production process, and deliveries of semifinished products and raw materials at the times designated. But the actual production conditions do not match the increasing requirements imposed on the technological regime with regard to any of the above points, as is demonstrated by the increase in idle time.

It has become more and more difficult to maintain the required composition of the charge with regard to both of its basic components (pig iron and scrap), and this has caused the *quality* of the feed for steel-melting units to deteriorate. Interruptions in the delivery of pig iron to the steel-melting shops have grown as the problem of coke resources has become acute (depletion of the coke-bearing coal of the Donets basin used to supply the blast furnaces of plants in the south).[78] Switching this group of plants (responsible for about half the entire pig-iron output in the USSR) to the use of coke-bearing coal from the Kuznetskii coal basin in Siberia only complicated matters further because of the growing crisis in rail transport.

With all the problems involved in the production of pig iron, there is yet another factor just as important as the growth in the pig-iron intensity of the steel-melting units: the increase in the consumption of pig iron per ton of steel, a factor that is leading to increased demands for pig iron. The increasing scale of production of converter steel is the main reason for the growth in the rate of consumption of pig iron per ton of steel output.

By comparison with open-hearth technology, converter technology is more pig iron–intensive. The proportion of the charge used for open-hearth furnaces in the form of pig iron amounts to 55–60 percent, whereas in the case of converters it is about 85 percent.[79] Tandem hearths occupy the middle ground; the proportion of their charge in the form of pig iron amounts to roughly 70 percent.[80]

Under these conditions, the replacement of pig iron in the steel-melting charge by scrap is assuming great importance.

The crisis in pig iron supplies could be overcome if:

1. The consumption of pig iron in open-hearth furnaces could be decreased without reducing the productivity of the furnaces, replacing the pig iron with scrap.
2. Existing converters could be adapted to the use of charge with high scrap content.
3. The scrap-refinement sector was able to supply the steel-melting units with required amounts of scrap of suitable quality.

Implementation of this threefold program, which is of great importance for the steel industry, is proceeding extraordinarily slowly, however, and is encountering considerable difficulties.

A high specific consumption of pig iron in the production of steel has been a traditional aspect of the Soviet steel industry. Even in the 1950s and 1960s, when nearly all steel was melted in open-hearth furnaces and converter technology in the USSR was still in an embryonic state, consumption of pig iron per ton of molten steel exceeded 0.7 ton.[81] In view of the growing supplies of scrap in the Soviet Union and the current situation with regard to pig-iron resources, this figure should be reduced to 0.4–0.45 ton in the opinion of Soviet experts.[82]

But to adapt open-hearth furnaces to charge with this low a pig-iron content and anticipating an associated drop in the productivity of these furnaces, planners in the steel industry have suggested that some of the open-hearth furnaces be converted into high-productivity tandem hearths (discussed above) and in this way compensate for the drop in steel production in open-hearth furnaces. But there has yet to occur a noticeable drop in the specific consumption of pig iron in open-hearth production, which now is roughly 0.6 ton per ton of steel.

In the case of oxygen converters, it has been hoped that the proportion of the charge consisting of scrap be increased 35–40 percent from the current figure of 26–28 percent and that the proportion of pig iron be correspondingly reduced.[83] But the realization of this hope has encountered considerable technical difficulties.

In fact, in view of the types of oxygen converters now in operation in the USSR (top-blown converters with gas-intake ducts in the upper portion), if the proportion of scrap in the charge was increased to above 26–28 percent, this would result in heat losses and an increase in melt times, in other words, a drop in productivity.[84] An increase in the proportion of scrap in the charge is possible in a different type of converter (bottom-blown converters, where gas-intake ducts are in the lower portion), and the first two oxygen converters of this type have been constructed at the Dzerzhinskii plant.[85] If these converters justify the hopes placed on them, it is precisely these types of converters that will be constructed in the near future.

There are other methods being developed in the USSR for extracting large quantities of scrap in steel production and in this way economizing on pig iron (for example, preheating the scrap), though none of these strategies has yet to reach the stage of commercial application.[86] Thus there are still problems that must be overcome if scrap is to be substituted for pig iron in oxygen converters. But in addition to technological types of constraints, expanded utilization of scrap has been slowed down if for no other reason than the lack of preparedness for this effort on the part of the entire system of collection, refinement, and sorting of scrap whether at specialized scrap-refining shops or the steel plants themselves.

The productivity of steel-melting units depends, as is well known, on the degree of refinement of the scrap and its rate of charging. In turn, the rate of charging is determined by the mean bulk mass of the scrap. The bulk mass of scrap injected into open-hearth furnaces and oxygen converters has tended to drop at steel plants due to an increase in its lighter-weight fraction (shavings).[87] This trend may be attributed to a number of factors.

First, the proportion of heavyweight scrap (bloom and slab crops) at steel plants has dropped, particularly with the increase in the proportion of continuously cast steel, as well as more economical cutting and patterning of the metal, which is beginning to approach the optimal level.

Second, as the importance of electric steel melting has grown, an increasing proportion of the heavyweight scrap at plants has been sent to electric furnaces. At most plants today, the bulk mass of the scrap amounts to 1.1–1.4 tons per cubic meter; by contrast, the optimal range is 2.0–2.5 tons per cubic meter.[88] An increase in the lightweight fraction of the scrap in the steel-melting charge would result in greater oxidation of metal, greater loss of heat, and an increase in furnace charging time—that is, a drop in the utilization of furnace capacity.[89]

A rate of charging of 350–360 tons per hour, which is required for the normal operation of open-hearth furnaces, can be achieved at a scrap density of 2.0–2.5 tons per cubic meter. But in view of the high proportion of lightweight scrap in the USSR, scrap of this density cannot be obtained using existing methods of scrap refinement.

Therefore, the rate of charging is somewhat less than the normal rate. For example, at the Krivorozhskii plant it is 170 tons per hour (scrap density 1.08 tons per cubic meter); at the Magnitogorskii plant, 130 tons per hour (scrap density 1.14 tons per cubic meter); and at the Zaporozhstal' plant, 135 tons per hour (scrap density 1.18 tons per cubic meter).[90] If we bear in mind that pig iron is cast at a rate of 830–840 tons per hour, it becomes clear why more time is lost with the substitution of poorly refined scrap for pig iron. These adverse results are the reason plants have little desire to replace pig iron with scrap.

Thus the need for high-quality scrap has become a key problem in efforts to increase the utilization of the capacities of steel-melting production. And we must not forget that Soviet management is now devoting considerable effort to the resolution of the problem.

In July 1982 a high-level conference on the subject of scrap was held in Moscow. The upper levels of the management of Soviet industry and the party apparatus took part in the conference, which was headed by Vladimir Dolgikh, secretary of the Central Committee CPSU for Industry and candidate for membership in the Politburo.[91]

The principal journal of the CPSU, *Kommunist*, presented a discussion of the numerous drawbacks and difficulties confronting scrap refinement efforts in its February 1984 issue.[92]

The low technical and managerial level of scrap refinement, the shortage of presses and instruments for scrap cutting and other types of needed equipment, the lack of space set aside at the plants for classifying scrap and storing it (with the frequent interruptions in rail transport, this has tended to paralyze operations at many enterprises)—the weight of all these factors indicates that the problem of scrap utilization will not be solved in the foreseeable future.

Rolling

There are over 350 rolling mills in the USSR. Depending on the function of the particular mill (cogging, sheet, or section), different factors will be of critical importance for the utilization of the mill's production capacity. Thus the weight of the billets and efficiency of systems that serve to control rolling conditions influence substantially the utilization of the operational time of reversing cogging mills.

The level of utilization of the capacities of other types of mills (continuous section mills and mills producing rolled metal in complicated shapes) depends largely on the mill's range of product. Utilization of the capacity of a sheet mill depends to a great extent on the type of steel to be rolled (carbon or alloy) and the temperature conditions maintained in the rolling process (under controlled or ordinary temperature conditions).

Thus if a thick plate of low-alloy steel is to be rolled under controlled temperature conditions, the mill's productivity may drop by 20–25 percent.[93]

In general, the hourly productivity of rolling mills varies widely; for most section mills, the maximum hourly productivity is two to three times the minimal productivity.

Utilization of the capacities of rolling mills depends to a far greater degree than the preceding production stages (blast furnace and steel melting) on the range of output required by the mill's customer. Less certainty, therefore, attaches to estimates of the reserve capacity of rolling mills.

Let us consider the level of utilization of the capacities of the basic types of rolling mills in the USSR: cogging, sheet, and section mills.

Cogging Mills

At most Soviet plants, slabbing and blooming are still the basic means of obtaining steel billets. No more than 12 percent of the steel produced is cast using continuous methods.[94] Of the twenty-four blooming and four slabbing mills in operation in the early 1980s, fifteen of the blooming mills and one of the slabbing mills were in operation twenty-five years or more.[95] The annual output of the most modern cogging mills (thirteen out of twenty-eight mills) amounts to 4.0–6.5 million tons, whereas the annual output of the other mills is 1.5–4.0 million tons.[96] There are mills so antiquated as to be no longer worth modernizing, though there are also mills whose output could be significantly increased were they to be modernized. Thus the annual output of the rebuilt slabbing mill at the Magnitogorsk plant grew by 56 percent and is now 7.2 million tons (the highest of all cogging mills in the USSR).[97]

The level of utilization of the capacities of many cogging mills in the USSR can be increased mainly through a reduction in routine downtime caused by lack of metal and frequent shutdowns for repairs.[98] There are also definite opportunities for cutting down on the time spent on each rolling cycle and on the total number of cycles, and also increasing the dimensions (weight) of the slabs, which is another means of increasing the utilization of the capacities of cogging mills.[99]

Sheet Mills

As noted earlier, the main purpose in altering the production structure of the rolling mills is to increase the proportion of rolling output produced in the form of flat-rolled metal, a proportion that, according to plans, is to increase to 43 percent by 1985.[100] Growing demands for rolled metal with particular quality characteristics on the part of such end users as the automotive industry, main pipeline construction, the shipbuilding industry, and nuclear power stations have forced the management of the steel industry to apply an extraordinary amount of effort to renovating all the flat-rolled metal mills in the USSR.

Over the past fifteen to seventeen years, capacity for the production of hot-rolled sheet has grown by roughly 15 million tons, and for cold-rolled sheet by 5.0–5.5 million tons.[101] As already noted, these capacities were created basically through the installation of large continuous strip rolling mills. Because of disproportions at a number of plants between steel-making capacity and the capacity of the flat-rolled metal mills, however, the level of utilization of the latter is not high enough. Thus the 2000 continuous strip rolling mills at the Novolipetsk and Cherepovets plants have projected annual capacities of 6.0–6.5 million tons each, though because of a lack of metal their annual output is below 4 million tons at present.[102]

Section Mills

The highly nonuniform structure of the more than 150 section and rolled wire mills in the Soviet Union includes dozens of antiquated mills, mills that are already outdated though still producing output of a more or less satisfactory quality, and fully modern continuous and semicontinuous high-productivity mills. It is at the latter mills that we find the bulk of the reserves for increasing the utilization of the capacities of section metal mills. Virtually the entire growth in the output of bar stock in the 1970s was due to new continuous mills installed at the Krivoi Rog, West Siberia, and Chelyabinsk plants; the productivity of these mills is more than five times that of older mills.[103]

The production of section metal is faced with two conflicting goals. On the one hand, the economy is increasingly requiring an ever greater range of output; on the other, the broader the range of output, the lower the level of utilization of the mill capacities.

The number of different types of section metal produced in the USSR has grown at a faster pace than the actual volume of output of the section metal (expressed in tons), which in and of itself is a positive trend, since it will lead to a reduction in metal consumption.[104] But a greater range in types of output produced will lead to more frequent overhauling of the mill stands and changing of the mill rollers—that is, to an increase in mill downtime.[105]

This has a direct effect on the utilization of the capacities of high-productivity continuous mills whose capacities are used most completely in rolling large batches of standard shapes. Geography plays no small role here; the section mills of the plants—of which there is only one per region (Petrovsk in the Baikal region and eastern Siberia; Sarkanais Metallurg in Lithuania; Amurstal' in the far east; Uzbek in Central Asia; etc.)—produce the widest range of product, and the utilization of their capacities is correspondingly lower than at mills of plants located at major centers of steel production (Urals, the south) which have the highest degree of specialization and, consequently, less downtime for overhauling and roll changing— that is, higher utilization of capacities.[106]

On the whole, section mills in the USSR are suffering greater and greater downtime as a result of increases in the range of output they produce. Downtime on the average amounts to 1500–1600 hours annually or 18 percent of one-year calendar time.[107] The downtime due to roll changing and overhauling is about 40 percent of the total routine downtime.[108] Thus the specialization of the section mills is an important prerequisite for increasing the utilization of the capacities of these mills.

In many cases, however, the high-productivity specialized mills that have already been constructed are standing idle due to a lack of orders that would correspond to their capacities. Thus, in 1983 the high-productivity universal beam mill of the Nizhnetagil plant did not have sufficient orders for wide-flange beams to be fully utilized. A new section mill at the Amurstal' plant and a number of mills at other plants are faced with similar problems.[109] The advantages of specialization, therefore, are not being made use of.

That the capacities of all the different types of rolling mills is not being utilized at a high enough level is largely attributable to the lengthy downtime for repairs needed because of the low reliability of the equipment and the poor organization of maintenance operations. Most rolling mills stand idle because of repairs a far greater length of time than is allowed for by the plan standards. At many plants in the south the length of time spent on maintenance of the rolling mills is 80 percent greater than the standard time.[110]

Another reason for the extraordinarily lengthy downtime common to all rolling mills is the irregular rate of delivery of semi-finished product (billets), which may be attributed both to external factors (transportation problems for plants that use the billets) and to internal factors (lack of coordination between the different "flows" of metal in the steel melting–rolled metal system).[111] Downtime due to the first group of factors is especially high at the Soyuzspetsstal' association of plants, since the degree of interplant cooperation has been developed to a particularly high level with regard to billets.

The case of the 3600 rolling mill constructed in the mid-1970s at the Azovstal' plant is typical in this regard. The mill was not supplied with ingots from the plant itself. In order to keep it charged, it was necessary to obtain ingots from many plants as far away as the Urals and West Siberia and transport them over great distances to Azovstal'. Once an oxygen converter shop had been installed at the plant in the mid-1970s, the plant then began to suffer from surpluses of ingots, more than 1 million tons of which were shipped 1,000 kilometers to the Cherepovets plant in order to feed the newly constructed large rolling mill there.[112]

A number of rolling mills, including blooming mills, are used at only 75–85 percent capacity due to interruptions in the supply of metal from their own steel-melting shops.[113]

The relationship between interdependent units in the production process has become stronger with the growth of individual capacities at steel plants and the strengthening of their technological links (for example, steel-melting furnace–continuous casting machine–rolling mill). Under these conditions, continuous casters are playing an increasingly important role in the utilization of the capacities of rolling mills. They constitute a bottleneck in this system, so that when operating unreliably they have an adverse affect on the utilization of the capacities of the rolling mills, particularly sheet mills (75–80 percent of all continuous casters have been installed in conjunction with sheet mills).[114]

We have arrived at the conclusion that, at all stages of steel production, the utilization of the capacities of the steel industry is substantially lower than is customarily assumed. According to our estimates, it is at most 75–80 percent.

Thus there are considerable reserves available for increasing steel production within the range of standard capacities of the existing system of production. Furthermore, once conditions appear that would cause these reserves to be placed into operation, the Soviet steel industry would be able to greatly increase output rapidly.

"Old" and "New" Capacities and Their Role in Growth of Output

In any particular period, an increase in production is achieved both through startup of new production capacities and through a higher level of utilization of old capacities present at the start of the period.

Was there a slowdown in the rate at which new steel production capacities were placed in service during the late 1970s, a period

TABLE 4.5
Increases in steel production and installation of new production
capacities in postwar five-year plans[116]

Five-year plan	New capacity	Increase in output	Increase in output less new capacity	Ratio of new capacity to increase in output
			(in millions of tons)	
1946–50	8.9	15.1	6.2	0.59
1951–55	8.9	17.9	9.0	0.50
1956–60	13.1	20.0	6.9	0.65
1961–65	15.6	25.7	10.1	0.61
1966–70	18.1	24.9	6.8	0.73
1971–75	10.9	25.4	14.5	0.43
1976–80	14.3	6.6	−7.7	2.20

characterized by a falloff in production? It is remarkable that at the same time that the increase in steel production in the 1976–80 period fell nearly 75 percent from the 1971–75 period, there was a 30 percent increase in new steel production capacity.[115] Consequently, the drop in production was related not to a slowdown in the development of the production potential of this branch of industry, but to a decrease in the level of utilization of this production potential.

Table 4.5 shows the dynamic relationship between increases in steel production and the rate at which steel production capacities were placed in service.

Through the mid-1970s, increases in output in Soviet steelmaking typically ran well ahead of the installation of new capacities, as the result of both the greater utilization of existing production capacities and improvements in these capacities.

Between 1946 and 1975, 75 million tons of new steel production capacity were put into service, whereas the increase in production amounted to 129 million tons.[117] The increase of 54 million tons was achieved through a speedup in the production process and improvements in existing open-hearth furnaces, converters, and electric furnaces, rather than through the installation of new capacities as a result of the construction of new steel production units and capital reconstruction of old units.

But in that case what happened in the tenth (1976–80) five-year plan? Why did the increase in output fall so sharply and why was there a change in the long-term trend for increases in output to

Table 4.6
Structure of increases in steel production in ninth and tenth five-year plans[118]

Five-year plan	New production capacity	Increase in output					
		Total		Capacities operational prior to start of five-year plan		Capacities installed during plan	
		Millions of tons	%	Millions of tons	%	Millions of tons	%
Ninth (1971–75)	10.9	25.4	100	16.5	65	8.9	35
Tenth (1976–80)	14.3	6.6	100	2.8	42	3.8	58

exceed newly installed production capacity? Let us see how the structure of production increases evolved in the tenth five-year plan by comparison with the preceding five-year plan (1971–75).

From Table 4.6 it is clear that the roles of "old" and "new" capacities in the increase in production changed places; whereas in the ninth five-year plan the greater proportion of the increase occurred at old capacities, in the tenth five-year plan it was due to newly installed capacities. The increase in output in the tenth five-year plan is attributable to a far lesser extent to all the production facilities present at the start of the period, and to a far greater extent to steelmaking furnaces installed during the period. It is also clear from Table 4.6 that newly installed capacities were utilized at a remarkably low level.

It is especially noteworthy that the greatest difference between the increment in output and the increment in newly installed capacity in the postwar years (14.5 million tons) occurred at a time preceding a sharp drop in production. In this period (1971–75) the greater portion of the increment in output (65 percent) was attributable to excessive use of old capacities rather than operation of the newly installed capacities. But the greater utilization of equipment was not accompanied by a corresponding compensation in equipment wear. Conversely, contrary to all logic, the rate of replacement and decommissioning of worn out equipment fell and equipment maintenance deteriorated.

The consequence of this way of dealing with the fixed assets of the steel industry at every level—from extraction and ore and coke benefaction to blast furnace, steelmaking, and rolled steel production—was felt in a drop in efficiency and a sharp increase in equipment downtime in the latter half (particularly the late) 1970s. Thus in the ninth five-year plan (1971–75) equipment wear accelerated and the stock of worn out fixed assets in the steel industry began to grow; both these factors played a large role in the drop of the output of these fixed assets in the succeeding period.

The low level of utilization of capacities newly installed in the tenth five-year plan in turn could be attributed to the growing technical difficulties associated with the adoption of newer and more complicated equipment. In the late 1970s the state of affairs with regard to supplies of ore, coke, and scrap became acute. We will be considering all these problems in greater detail in subsequent chapters.

Thus the pattern in the late 1970s and early 1980s was that the production potential of the steel industry grew, but the level of utilization of this potential dropped.

From our analysis of steel production in the ninth and tenth five-year plans we are led to the following conclusions. First, the drop in the growth in steel output in the tenth five-year plan, an event unprecedented in the history of the Soviet steel industry, occurred mainly because of the extraordinarily low level of utilization of both old capacities and capacities installed in the course of the plan. Second, as is implied by the first conclusion, in the eleventh five-year plan (1981–85) appreciable undeveloped capacities have come into operation which, it would seem, will make a major contribution to the growth in output.

It seems reasonable to conclude that the explosive growth in steel production in 1983 occurred as a result of a buildup of capacities installed in the late 1970s and early 1980s and undeveloped capacities (unutilized productivity), and that the spark that set off this growth was the threatening situation that confronted the management of the steel industry in the Andropov period.

The Use of Capacities in Soviet Industry in the 1970s

The branch of industry we have been studying is part of the vast organism of Soviet industry and it functions in accordance with the

TABLE 4.7
Distribution of branches in terms of level of utilization of capacity as a
percentage of the total number of branches[120]

Year	Level of utilization of capacity (%)			
	Less than 85	85–93	Greater than 93	Greater than 97
1975	16.8	33.6	49.6	21.7
1976	15.3	41.9	42.8	18.1
1977	14.4	44.1	41.5	16.9
1978	19.6	33.3	47.1	17.1
1979	31.3	41.7	27.0	6.1
1980	32.4	38.9	28.7	6.5

laws governing its vital activity. Therefore, in order to achieve a
deeper understanding of the causes and nature of the metamorpho-
sis that occurred in the second half of the 1970s, as demonstrated in
Tables 4.5 and 4.6, let us change the scope of our analysis and take a
look at the industrial situation in the USSR as a whole. We wish to
discover the dynamics underlying the utilization of the capacities of
the steel industry, viewed against the backdrop of Soviet industry as
a whole and a number of its leading integrated branches.

The utilization of capacities in industry in the USSR as a whole
was excessive* in the first half of the 1970s—as in the case of
the steel industry—and declined noticeably in the second half. In
1971–75 utilization of capacities for all industry on the average increased from 90 percent to 91.5 percent. The percentage of branches
in which the utilization of capacities exceeded 93 percent grew from
57 percent to 71 percent, and those in which utilization of capacities
exceeded 97 percent, from 15 percent to 22 percent. The picture
changed dramatically, however, in the 1976–80 period. In 1980 the
average utilization of capacities throughout all industry dropped to
87 percent.[119] The dynamics underlying the distribution of branches
of industry by level of utilization of capacity in number of branches
are given in Tables 4.7 and 4.8.

The number of branches with utilization of capacity below 85
percent nearly doubled from 1975 to 1980, and the percentage of all
branches with level of utilization above 93 percent dropped from
49.6 percent to 28.7 percent. The downward trend in utilization of
capacity became especially strong toward the end of the period.

*Within the framework of the practice of measuring productive capacities ac-
cepted by the planning system (as discussed above).

TABLE 4.8
Variation in level of utilization of capacity in integrated economic branches*
(in percent)[121]

Branch	1976	1977	1978	1979	1980
Steel industry	2.2	0	−0.3	−1.7	−3.0
Machine-building industry	0.4	0.8	−0.2	−1.4	−2.8
Building-materials industry	−0.4	−3.0	−4.3	−6.3	−5.6
Coal industry	−4.3	−3.2	−5.5	−10.5	−9.9
Forestry products	0.1	−1.1	−3.1	−7.6	−7.1
Consumer-goods industry	0	1.1	2.2	1.4	1.9

*1975 = 100.

This process reached beyond the steel industry and embraced machine building, the chemical industry, and other branches. The drop in the level of utilization of capacities in the machine-building industry was felt particularly strongly in all of Soviet industry, including the steel industry. In addition, the rates of growth of capital investment in this branch of the economy dropped markedly.

But even more dramatic was the drop in utilization of newly installed capacities for most types of industrial output in the 1976–80 period.

Indeed, the ratio of increments in output to net increments in capacity took a sharp turn for the worse in the second half of the 1970s as compared to the first half. As Table 4.9 shows, there were only two categories in which this relationship improved in the period 1976–80; in all others it deteriorated or remained unchanged. Indeed, in eight of seventeen categories the increment in output amounted to less than half the increment in productive capacity.

In the coal industry, from 1975 to 1980, productive capacity increased 90.4 million tons, but yearly output increased only 15 million tons over that period. In the chemical industry, a 9.7-million-ton increment in capacity for the production of sulfuric acid over the same period resulted in an increase of only 4.4 million tons in annual production. In the case of soda ash, the comparable figures were 505,000 and 88,000 tons; and for mineral fertilizers, 39.3 and 13.8 million tons. In the machine-tool industry, introduction of productive capacity for an additional 12,500 machine tools was matched by an absolute 15,000-unit drop in production.[123]

The reasons for the increase in unused productive potential are

TABLE 4.9
Ratio of increments in output to increments in capacity in Soviet industry,
1971–80[122]

Products	1971–75	1976–80
Pig iron	1.32	0.71
Steel	2.29	0.49
Rolled ferrous metals	1.47	0.58
Steel pipes	1.51	1.16
Sulfuric acid	0.75	0.45
Mineral fertilizer	0.91	0.35
Plastics and synthetic resins	1.19	0.53
Fibers and chemical fibers	0.95	0.95
Automobile tires	1.31	0.65
Turbines	0.48	0.46
Automobiles (including buses)	1.07	0.96
Excavators	1.22	0.22
Cellulose	0.81	0.33
Paper	2.02	0.26
Cement	1.29	0.27
Knitted underwear and outer garments	1.18	3.20
Leather footwear	0.28	2.13

many and varied. They include languishing of the raw-material industries and inadequacies of transport conditioned by the growing distance between where the raw materials are produced and where they are used; irregularities in fuel deliveries; and finally, an overall breakdown in control over the economy. More specifically, the delays reflect the following concrete factors: technologically interconnected stages of production processes are not put into operation simultaneously, and auxiliary facilities (particularly repair shops) are usually opened later than the production operations they are meant to service.

The interbranch imbalance in capacities present throughout Soviet industry has been a general factor in the drop in the utilization of capacities in the late 1970s. Simple logic would suggest that the greater the interbranch balance of capacities, other conditions being equal, the higher the level of utilization of these capacities and the more likely that new capacities will help to eliminate and prevent the appearance of bottlenecks in the industrial structure. And conversely, the growing imbalance will lead to a drop in the utilization of capacities, and thus installation of new capacities will create additional bottlenecks in industry.

According to the data of Boris Lavrovskii of the Institute of Economics and Industrial Management (Novosibirsk), the growing interbranch imbalance has played a major role in the drop in the utilization of capacities in Soviet industry in the late 1970s.[124] According to Lavrovskii's estimates, this factor was responsible for nearly 60 percent of the drop in the utilization of capacities in this period throughout all industry on the average.

The steel industry was one of the branches in which the interbranch imbalance in capacities was felt most acutely. The pattern of utilization of capacities in the steel industry is typical of most branches of Soviet industry, and the reasons for the drop in the production must be found primarily in the general trend of industrial development in the USSR.

The greater imbalance in industrial capacities reflects the increasingly acute faults in the Soviet economic system in the latter half of the 1970s; most important are the hypertrophied departmentalization in management and the growing inability of the rigidly centralized planning system to distribute resources in accordance with the needs of proportional development of the economy.

These general factors became exacerbated in the eleventh five-year plan (1981–85), and there is therefore every reason to assume that the imbalance in industrial capacities will not improve in the current (twelfth) five-year plan.

CHAPTER 5

Iron-Ore Resources
and Their Utilization

In Chapter 4 I came to the conclusion that the existing capacities in the Soviet steel industry permit a substantial expansion in the production of steel. If one disregards the general economic and political factors outside this sector (errors in planning, ineffective economic incentive, etc.), and if one concentrates on those causes of the underutilization of production capacities which emanate from the metallurgical sector itself, then the problem of an inadequate supply of iron ore stands at the very top of the list.

In this chapter we shall analyze the problems involved in the production of the main raw material component—iron ore. Attention is given here to dimensions of iron-ore resources according to their regional distribution; particular attention is given to Siberia, a region that is projected as a potential center of a new metallurgical base of the USSR. The following analysis aims to explain why Soviet metallurgical plants, notwithstanding sufficient resources of raw iron ore, nevertheless suffer supply shortages for production.

To elucidate the problem, this chapter examines the difficulties that the Soviets face in the mining and preparation of iron ores. Given the possibility that demand for iron ore may decline through the intensive substitution of scrap for pig iron in the charge of the steel blast furnaces (and the consequent potential for a shift in iron-ore production from a quantitative to a qualitative basis), this study examines as well the situation in regard to scrap resources and their utilization.

In sum, on the basis of the technical and economic analysis of all basic stages in iron-ore production, this chapter presents our findings on the lack of real possibilities for improving the conditions under which iron-ore production operates in the foreseeable future—that is, until the end of the 1980s. Hence this research shows that there are no grounds to expect an improvement in the supply of iron ore for metallurgical plants before the end of the present decade.

The situation in the iron-ore branch is typical of the entire mining-extraction industry in the USSR. The causes of the crisis in the iron-ore branch, as well as the opportunities for ending it, cannot be understood outside the context of the development of the whole mineral-resource sector of the Soviet economy.

Self-Supply of Mineral Resources and Their Price

Pattern of an Industrially Developed Country and Soviet Deviation from It

The scale of extraction and processing of fuel and mineral resources determines, to a very large degree, the structure of investment, the geography of industrial distribution and its proportions, the development of new territories, environmental conditions, and other socioeconomic parameters of development in the country.

The USSR is the sole industrially developed country of the world that satisfies almost all its demand for raw materials and fuel through the exploitation of its own mineral resources. This policy of relying on domestic supplies (adopted by the Soviet leadership from the outset of the regime) not only has important advantages but is also fraught with a host of serious negative consequences for the Soviet economy.

The immanent predominance of the mineral and raw material sector (in its material and energy base) in the Soviet economy is the consequence of the objective factors at the time of initial industrialization. But this became one of the primary drags on economic growth in the 1970s and 1980s. As with many other aspects of the Soviet economy, the development of this sector in the USSR followed a model that is distinct from what one finds elsewhere in the world. In general, it is typical for industrially advanced countries to exhibit the following dynamic for the internal consumption of energy and raw materials: a sharp jump in the initial period of industrialization, followed by exponential growth rates, succeeded in turn by slower growth, then by a stabilization in consumption and in some instances even by a decline. That pattern reflects the specific processes at work in industrialization—structural advances in the economy that ensue from progress in technology and machinery as well as the redistribution of functions between countries that are more or less industrially developed (the more advanced become consumers of fuel and raw material resources, the less advanced become the suppliers).

Though that is only a general pattern and admits some exceptions, it is the process normally observed throughout the industrialized countries of the world. Hence among industrially advanced countries that possess a significant volume of fuel and raw material reserves, it has been typical for them to reduce their exports of these resources over the course of time. Significant deviations from this general trend include the expansion of fuel exports by Great Britain and Norway in the 1970s which resulted from the development of oil reserves in the North Sea. Another exception is Australia, which was late in exploiting its mineral resources and for the time being continues to increase the export of these raw materials. But these are exceptions to the general rule. The reduced export of raw materials—even when these are still abundant, as in the case of Canada—reflects the normal pattern of changing comparative advantages of developing countries. It becomes more profitable to export processed and manufactured goods, and hence this activity is more attractive to investment capital than is extractive industry. Ecological problems also play an important role in this.

In light of the above, it was fully justified on economic grounds for the USSR to have extremely high growth rates for the production of energy and raw materials in the early stages of its industrialization. The Soviet reliance on its own mineral and raw material base was caused by several factors: by the enormous volume of its reserves, by a self-imposed isolation from the world economy (explained by "hostile encirclement," that is, essentially by the regime's foreign policy), and also by exceptionally favorable conditions for the exploitation of mineral reserves through the use of cheap labor. To this should be added the massive number of prisoners in Gulag, where under the most difficult climatic conditions they developed mineral and raw material resources at minimal cost for their support and for the infrastructure.

If the processes of development are examined at the broadest, most general level, one must conclude that—at least by the second half of the 1960s—the Soviet economy had reached a level of industrial maturity at which manufacturing should have begun to displace the production of raw materials and fuels. That, however, did not occur.

The growth of production in raw materials and fuels in the USSR has, since World War II, significantly exceeded average rates found elsewhere in the world. The Soviet economy also experienced a general increase in its demand for these resources, partly for internal use and partly for export. In the 1980s the USSR became the leading country of the world in the production of raw material resources; it produces 26 percent of the world's output of raw materials and fuel[1] and obtains this from areas that, to a significant degree, are located in undeveloped territories with extremely adverse climatic conditions.

Thus arises the contrast between economic processes in advanced Western countries and in the USSR. The industrially developed countries increasingly tap the rich and little processed mineral and raw material resources of developing countries; as a result, they can eliminate the burden of producing their own raw materials and fuels at great expense and direct their investment toward the practical application of discoveries in science and technology. By contrast, the economy of the USSR has become mired ever more deeply in producing raw materials and fuels, both for its own use and for export. Meanwhile, the conditions for the extraction of these raw materials have steadily deteriorated, with corresponding changes in the economic indices on the capital expenditures necessary for each unit of incremental growth in output. Moreover, these expenditures increasingly go not to bring an expansion in production, but simply to sustain present levels. Thus in the early 1980s only 5 percent of the expenditures in the petroleum industry went for its growth; by the mid-1980s the entire capital investment in this sector served simply to sustain production at current levels, with no additional production whatsoever.[3]

TABLE 5.1
The dynamics of extraction of basic mineral resources[2]

	1901–20	1921–40	1941–60	1961–80	Total from 1901
Coal					
Billions of tons					
world	21.8	25.7	35.5	58.5	141.5
USSR	0.4	1.4	4.7	12.6	19.1
USSR as % of world	0.2	5.0	13.0	22	13.5
Percent of total extraction for 1901–80					
world	15.4	18.2	25.1	41.3	100.0
USSR	2.1	7.3	24.6	66.0	100.0
Oil					
Billions of tons					
world	1.1	3.4	11.7	44.5	60.7
USSR	0.2	0.35	1.1	7.55	9.2
USSR as % of world	18.0	10.0	9.0	17	15.0
Percent of total extraction for 1901–80					
world	1.8	5.6	19.3	73.3	100.0
USSR	2.2	3.8	12.0	82.0	100.0
Gas					
Trillions of cubic meters					
world	0.3	1.0	4.8	21.0	27.1
USSR	—	0.02	0.21	4.41	4.64
USSR as % of world	—	0.2	4.0	21.0	17.0
Percent of total extraction for 1901–80					
world	1.1	3.7	17.7	77.5	100.0
USSR	—	0.5	4.5	95.0	100.0
Iron Ore					
Billions of tons					
world	2.9	3.3	5.9	14.5	26.6
USSR	0.1	0.25	0.98	3.87	5.2
USSR as % of world	3.0	8.0	17.0	27.0	19.5
Percent of total extraction for 1901–80					
world	10.9	12.4	22.2	54.5	100
USSR	1.9	4.8	18.8	74.5	100

Economic and Ecological Consequences of the Superexpansion of the Mining-Extraction Sector

The policy of self-sufficiency in raw materials and fuels has generated a growth in the mining-extractive sector of the economy, and this has meant an exponential increase in the demand for resources necessary to its maintenance and development. Thus machine-building capacities are increasingly burdened with the production of machinery and equipment for the mining industry. The hypertrophic development of the mining sector of the economy consumes approximately 40 percent of all industrial capital investment, and the share of industrial fixed capital given to mining represents 30 percent.[4] As shares of the total volume of industrial output, the production of extractive and primary industries has tended to increase, while the output of the manufacturing industries has declined. The ratio between these two components of industrial output was 36 to 64 in 1960 and 19 to 81 in 1985 (in current prices).[5]

To sustain and accelerate this growth rate in the extractive sector it has been necessary to divert ever greater proportions of capital resources away from manufacturing. Crucial here is the fact that in the USSR the extraction of raw materials and fuel places a far higher demand on capital than does manufacturing. At the beginning of the 1980s capital investment to increase production capacity by 1 million rubles cost 4 million rubles in the case of extractive industries, but just 0.7 million in the case of manufacturing industries. Extraction costs have been growing rapidly and are expected to continue to do so.[6]

Prominent Soviet specialist Aleksandr Arbatov has characterized the situation in the following way:

> A further increase in the tempos for extracting and processing raw materials is leading to a disproportionately large increase of expenditures, but in a number of cases this is physically impossible. It must be granted that the USSR has embarked upon a period of its development when the existing structure for supplying the economy with mineral resources, based on large-scale production from its own mineral and raw-material base, is an important factor in retarding economic growth.[7]

But economic problems hardly exhaust the negative effects of the Soviet policy of self-sufficiency. To these must be added the irreversible impact upon the environment. The construction of mining enterprises and open-pit mines occupies a large amount of land and, moreover, in many cases displaces fertile lands valuable for agricultural utilization. The land area allocated for the construction of a single mining enterprise encompasses a territory ranging in size from 4,000 to 10,000 hectares. Furthermore, additional vast areas must be set aside for the construction of the accompanying infrastructure required by each enterprise. For example, significant losses of fertile land in the center of the European part of the USSR have resulted from the development there of the iron-ore basin of the Kursk Magnetic Anomaly (see "The Center of European Russia," below). On the average, in each five-year period 10,000 to 14,000 hectares in this densely populated area have been diverted from agriculture to open-pit mines and spoil dumps. In the Ukraine, which has exceedingly fertile land, 1,800 to 2,000 hectares are turned over each year for exploitation by the mining sector.[8]

According to Soviet law, lands that have been disturbed by mining must be reclaimed for agricultural cultivation. Such reclamation, however, by no means makes it possible to return all such land to agricultural utilization; at least one-half of the land area is occupied by quarries, communications installations, dumps, and is permanently lost. As a result of the growth of open-pit mining for iron ore alone it is expected that the amount of land lost to spoil dumps will be 100–150 square kilometers per year, and that the development of open-pit mining will increase the amount of land expended for each ton of ore by 25–40 percent in each five-year period.[9]

A further ecological problem is the heavy demand on water supplies. As a rule, the enrichment of low-grade ores requires a significant expenditure of water. In the central and southern regions of the European part of the USSR a shortage of fresh water already exists and is intensifying. With each year, however, the mining of relatively low-grade iron ore is increasing, and it is enriched through wet magnetic separation—an enrichment technology that is extremely water-consumptive.

Disproportionate Expansion of Mining-Extractive Sector as a Consequence of the "Mania for Superhigh Tempos"

Generally speaking, the process of developing mineral and fuels reserves proceeds under the interaction of two diametrically opposed tendencies. On the one hand, the cost is rising because of a natural deterioration in the quality of raw materials as well as the mining and technical conditions under which these are extracted. On the other hand, economic efficiency has risen through improvements in the technology and machinery for extraction and, in some cases, through price increases in raw materials and fuels. But the exhaustion of resource reserves will inevitably ensue—unless there are radical changes to modernize the technology for extracting and processing the raw materials—and make extraction of a given reserve an inefficient use of resources. As a result, the extraction industry must abandon that reserve and move on to another. The relocation to new deposits that offer a sufficiently high level of output efficiency, however, entails other expenditures (for the creation of infrastructure and transportation), which therefore diminish the rate of return from the new undertaking.

Because the number of explored and known mineral deposits is limited and, in terms of exploitation, their number is declining, the economic efficiency of exploiting the USSR's own raw material base has in general declined. As a result, that country's economy must choose the optimal policy mix from among the following:

1. It can continue the large-scale extraction operations, with steady increases in expenditures to sustain this sector.

2. It can adapt the technology of its consumption to new conditions to raise the efficiency of resources and fuel utilization.

3. It can use other sources of raw materials (waste products, secondary resources, substitutes, imports).

4. It can undertake fundamental structural changes in the economy to reduce the dependence on raw material and fuel supplies.

The necessity of confronting these choices was clearly recognized by Soviet economists as far back as the mid-1960s, when a number of leading scholars discussed the issue in various publications. Beginning with the propositions that the Soviet economy has a highly industrialized structure and that the military backwardness of the country has already been overcome, they argued that it is essential to make a fundamental shift in the structure of economic sectors and to embark on a planned reduction in economic growth in order to optimize the correlation between investment and consumption. Moreover, they had in mind an increase in the level of consumption. That was the chief thesis in the writing of Serafim Pervushin, Abram Notkin, Iakov Kvasha, and Solomon Kheinman—authors of the programmatic monograph *Proizvodstvo, nakoplenie, potreblenie* (Production, Accumulation and Consumption), published in 1965.[10] In support of their position, the authors—who all belonged to the elite of Soviet economists—adduced the following arguments:

1. It is time to dispense with the "mania for superhigh tempos," which leads to "overloading and disorder in the economy."

2. To achieve a high long-run rate of growth, the optimal short-run growth rate must be consistent with the potential capacity of the raw material and resource base of the country.

3. Tempos that exceed optimal levels and the predominant development of heavy industry cause a disruption of proportions between the extractive sector of industry and manufacturing and lead to an excessive development of the sector of extracting raw materials and fuels. Moreover, "the rich deposits of ores and mineral fuels that lie close to the surface are being progressively exhausted and it becomes necessary to go deeper and deeper, to process deposits with poorer quantities of useful elements, to search for mineral beds farther and farther from inhabited areas, and to make enormous outlays for its enrichment."[11]

Their conclusion from the above arguments was: "All this makes one stop and consider how justified it is to increase the share allocated to extractive industries and, in particular, to find an answer to this question by comparing the structure of economic sectors in the USSR and the United States."[12]

In examining the experience of the United States, one author (Iakov Kvasha) came to the conclusion that investments in the extractive industry were much smaller in the United States than in the USSR. The United States had increasingly tended to satisfy its demand for raw materials and fuels by means of import, a policy that at once brought greater economic benefit and also enabled the country to protect its environment. Still, he noted, even if the American experience here was highly attractive, "it is nonetheless backed by a long history and an enormous volume in capital export. One has to keep that in mind, *when it is suggested that mineral resources be imported from countries with rich resources as one means to cut capital expenditures on the extractive sector*" (emphasis mine).[13] As the last quotation indicates, Kvasha took issue with those who proposed to shift the Soviet economy, in part, to the import of mineral and raw material resources—that is, to follow the American model—so as to reallocate more investment to manufacturing and hence to modernize and raise the industrial potential of the Soviet economy. In brief, then, by the 1960s Soviet economists had begun to consider the question of whether the Soviet Union should continue its policy of self-sufficiency in raw material and energy resources or reorient its economy toward import of these from the mineral-rich countries of the Third World. It was already clear, even in the mid-1960s, that there was a growing disproportion between the lower and higher stages of industry, that the opportunity cost of the policy was very high. The Soviet Union was paying a high price for its self-sufficiency and independence in raw materials and fuels, and it was necessary to make changes in the structure of industrial branches. Yet Kvasha, one of the most perceptive and thoughtful economists of the time, warned that if such a change were made without having created the necessary material base, it would lead to grave economic consequences. But to create this base, it was essential to reduce—not spontaneously, but in a planned manner—the growth rates of the economy.

One can conclude that, in order to attain a high long-run rate of growth the short-run planned growth rates must be greatly reduced in order to carry through to vital structural changes. But none of this theorizing had any impact on the real course of planning. Throughout the 1970s and 1980s, the mineral and raw material extractive branch of the economy continued to expand, and its share of investments and other resources rose as well. At the same time, the technical and economic indices for extraction sharply declined: the capital expenditures per unit of output swiftly rose and labor productivity fell. Growth in extraction could only be achieved by ever increasing expenditures of labor and capital. Development of technology proceeded, for the most part, along the path of increasing capacities and quantitative parameters, without fundamental improvements in the methods of extraction or the machinery and equipment. The rising costs of extraction and of machinery and equipment are so significant that the increased capacities could not compensate and cover the additional outlays. This applies to several things, such as the correlation between the depth of the bore hole and the rising cost of extraction in the natural gas industry and the cost of coal mining as a result of applying contemporary extraction complexes. Table 5.2 demonstrates the state of affairs in the fuel industry. It should be noted that one cannot put too much faith in the absolute figures found in official statistics; still, they do reflect the general trend.

The technological level of extraction and enrichment of raw materials and fuel is rising at such an insignificant rate that additional inputs of labor and capital—no matter how great they might be—would give diminishing return.

TABLE 5.2
Economic indices for the Soviet fuel industry, 1980–85 (in percent)[14]

	Total soviet industry	Heavy industry	Machine building	Fuel industry
Rate of growth in fixed capital	+38.0*	+39.0	+42.0	+52.0
Rate of growth in volume of output	+20.0	+23.0	+36.0	+6.0
Labor productivity	+17.0	+19.0	+29.0	−0.6
Change in expenditure per unit of output	−0.3	−0.5	−1.8	+2.8

*The positive (+) sign indicates an increase in expenditure; the negative (−) sign indicates a reduction in expenditure.

Future Domestic Demand for Raw Materials and Fuel

To what degree are opportunities used to reduce the internal consumption of raw materials and fuels? The experience of industrially developed nations of the West, especially in the period of acute energy crisis, demonstrated clearly how much could be achieved to economize on fuel consumption. There is no question but that the Soviet economy has enormous opportunities to reduce its consumption of minerals and raw materials. The losses incurred in transportation alone are enormous. In general, it is well known that the Soviet economy is distinguished by extreme waste in the utilization of natural resources both in the production and nonproduction spheres. The problem of resource saving has long been one of the most important and most widely discussed in the Soviet press. Moreover, over the course of the last few decades, the Central Committee and the Council of Ministers have adopted many resolutions on the problem.[15] Nevertheless, achievements in this sphere—right up to the present time—have been insignificant.

Take, for example, the problem of energy resources. One can, without exaggerating, say that the USSR has had an "energy crisis" for several decades and that, indeed, this crisis continues to become more and more acute. For example, at a conference of the Central Committee in April 1987, Lev Zaikov (a member of the Politburo) referred to "serious interruptions in energy supply for many enterprises."[16] The factors leading to the wasteful expenditure of energy resources are manifold and characteristic of the whole economic system. Thus to take one aspect of the technological sphere, the shortcomings of the truck and automobile stock constitute a significant problem. The use of diesel engines for trucks and buses would alone bring a savings of 20 million tons of oil. Still, despite the desperate need to expand production of fuel-conserving diesel engines, only 23 percent of truck motors and 1 percent of bus motors currently being produced are diesels.[17]

Enormous possibilities to reduce expenditures of a fuel extracted at such great cost are found in an optimalization of the structure for power delivery. Electrical energy is by far the most efficient means, as well as the one most adapted to contemporary technology. It is striking that in relative terms the growth rate of consumption of electrical energy has declined: whereas in 1950–70 the annual growth rates for the use of electrical energy exceeded by 80 percent the growth rates for consumption of fuel-energy resources as a whole, in 1971–75 that figure declined to 35 percent, and in 1976–80 it declined still further, to 15–20 percent. By contrast, in industrially developed countries this figure has, over an extended period of time, remained at the level of 70–100 percent. The share of electrical energy in total end-use consumption of energy did not exceed 11–14 percent in the USSR in the mid-1970s. To achieve optimal use of mineral fuel resources, it is essential that electrical energy be given an increasing role as an energy delivery system.[18]

Extremely unsatisfactory use has also been made of possibilities to replace the extraction of raw material and fuel with the production of these from waste products, formed as by-products both during the extraction of the main raw material at a given deposit and during the process of their reworking and consumption. Only an insignificant share of the demand of the Soviet economy for raw materials is satisfied by the production of resources in this manner.

From the above it follows that to reorient the Soviet economy onto the path of resources conservation, time and extremely great investments will be needed. Moreover, the effect from all this will not become apparent for a considerable while.

Is there a serious possibility that the Soviet Union will in fact reduce its level of domestic extraction and shift to a significant increase in the level of fuel and raw material imports? This approach to solving the country's economic problems remains, as before, outside the field of vision of Soviet leaders. Characteristic in this regard is the statement by the minister of Non-Ferrous Metallurgy, Petr Lomako: "The main direction in solving the problem of minerals and raw materials remains, *of course*, the successful exploration, discovery and exploitation of [our own] deposits" (emphasis mine).[19] Aleksandr Arbatov, cited above, also asserts that "the predominant utilization of raw materials from external sources cannot become a major alternative for us insofar as an adequate economic potential has not been created for a sharp expansion of international economic exchange in the necessary direction."[20]

Thus from that perspective the only real prospect is for a continuing attempt to satisfy the growing demand by expanding the scale of extraction of raw materials and fuel. But this orientation means choosing "a path of development that is high in resource consumption and a trajectory of exponential growth of expenditures even if the growth rate for the volume of useful minerals extracted is reduced or stabilized."[21]

In his first programmatic statement on economic problems in June 1985, M. S. Gorbachev noted that one of the main causes of the serious economic situation is due to the fact that "we did not demonstrate, at the right time, resoluteness in changing our structural policy." In speaking further of "problems in modifying the policy on investments and structure," Gorbachev declared: "The greatest acute problem is the relationship between capital investments in resource-extractive, processing, and consuming sectors."[22] One should expect that the new Soviet leadership will at last "demonstrate resoluteness" and actively set about optimizing the distribution of resources among the different sectors of the economy. The intention to reign in the escalating growth of investments in the mineral and raw-material sector was obvious. Nevertheless, this in fact did not transpire. Despite all the impressive verbiage, the new leadership is exhibiting the very same indecisiveness as its predecessors on this issue. In characterizing the situation, Arbatov wrote in January 1987:

> Although a series of steps have been outlined to deal with the situation, the real state of affair has for the time being changed but little. Apparently, the main cause of the slow restructuring is an inappropriate investment policy. To a significant degree, it continues to follow the existing structure of production, directing means proportionately to previous expenditures and thereby sustaining the existing structural proportions. Evidence of this, for example, is found in the increase of capital investments in the fuel sector.[23]

However clearly Soviet leaders might recognize the ruinous consequences for the economy if the fuel and raw material sector continues to expand, they cannot embark on a reduction of investments
here—given the country's energy crisis and given the fact that export of this output saves the country from starvation and permits the
acquisition of much-needed Western technology. Hence Gorbachev's good intentions—to balance the industrial sector—have
come to nought.

What explains the reluctance of all the post-Stalin Soviet leaders
to respond to the powerful arguments of their economists? One
possibility is that they are simply not convinced that the opportunity costs of the traditional policy are as high as the critics assert.
A second possibility is that an increased dependence on imports of
fuel and raw materials is unacceptable for strategic reasons. A third
is that it is politically impossible for a Soviet leadership deliberately
to retreat from the traditional drive for high short-run growth rates,
even at the cost of lower long-run growth.

It is hard to evaluate the significance of each of these possibilities.
On the basis of the public statements of the current leadership,
however, I believe that they (unlike Brezhnev's government) understand perfectly the opportunity cost of the traditional way. Precisely
because of that, it is evident that it is the strategic and political
factors that predominate in Soviet policy, even under the extremely
pressing circumstances of today.

Self-Sufficiency in Iron Ore

The full meaning of this complex, contradictory set of advantages
and disadvantages is manifest in the case of raw materials for metallurgical production.

On the one hand, the Soviet Union stands first in the world in the
production of iron ore and not only provides for its own needs but
also exports a significant part of its production.

As the data show, it was precisely in the final twenty-year period
that the USSR, in response to the increased demand for steel production, made a substantial leap forward in the production of iron
ore. These data demonstrate an unquestionable success in the
achievement of an economic goal that had been set from the very
beginning of the Soviet state. Such massive results in the development of iron-ore extraction were attained through intensified min-

ing of older deposits (which had been brought into production earlier) and through significant efforts to discover and develop new deposits.

Soviet autarkic policy—that is, the desire to rely solely on domestic supplies in iron ore—has certain objective grounds for its justification. Apart from military strategic considerations, this policy derives from two key factors.

1. The concentration of iron-ore deposits (discovered and partially developed), which can mostly be exploited through open-pit mining, are located in the areas where the main metallurgical production enterprises are concentrated.

2. The demand for iron ore in the USSR is so great that only the development of domestic mining can suffice to satisfy it. Import of raw materials is alien to Soviet trade policies, which is characterized by an expansion in the export of raw materials and fuels and by the import of advanced technology and agricultural products. Indeed, even as matters now stand hard currency does not suffice for these purposes.

On the other hand, the Soviet Union, in choosing to depend solely on its own resources, forces itself to make enormous expenditures to maintain and expand these production levels. Moreover, it is increasingly obliged to exploit inferior-grade ores (as older, richer deposits are exhausted) and to work deposits that are difficult to exploit and have ores of lower quality. Production costs for iron ore are rising steadily, and the investment costs for further increases in iron-ore tonnage have risen sharply (twofold in the last ten years).[24]

Thus the full opportunity cost of the marginal ton of pig iron has long exceeded the cost of producing it with imported iron ore. The USSR is paying a very high price for complete self-sufficiency in its raw iron ore. The United States, like the USSR, has immense reserves of iron ore at its disposal, but the riches of these have already been largely exhausted. In contrast to the USSR, however, the United States—for a variety of economic reasons, such as low prices and relatively lower transportation costs—has shifted to a steady expansion of the importation of iron ore and to the conservation of its own deposits.

Expanding imports of iron ore is also characteristic of the other industrially advanced countries. In contrast to the USSR, which has tended to exploit iron ore of increasingly inferior grade, ferrous metallurgy in the United States, England, Japan, Italy, France, and the Federal Republic of Germany—thanks to the import of richer and richer ores, which are imported regardless of the distances involved in oceanic transport—utilize higher and higher grades of raw iron ore. At the same time that the iron content in the ores used by these countries rose significantly, in the USSR the analogous index fell for the period of 1950–80 by 15 percent. In 1974 one of the leading Soviet scholars in the area of metallurgy, academician Aleksandr Tselikov, wrote that "with each passing year it becomes necessary to utilize ores that are poorer and less accessible."[25] In the period that has elapsed since Tselikov made that statement, such tendencies have become still more salient.

Thus the objective conditions that favor the development of the domestic base of raw materials and the strategy of autarky have come to mean that Soviet ferrous metallurgy utilizes an ore that is almost half as rich as that used by advanced Western countries, and that to obtain this ore it must make expenditures that are significantly greater and are constantly rising.

In the following section of this chapter we shall examine the iron-ore reserves in the USSR and the basic problems that impede their extraction and enrichment. In assessing the potential demand for iron ore, it is also important to examine the real situation with regard to scrap as an alternative form of raw material for steel smelting; the demand for pig iron (and hence iron ore) will depend directly on the degree to which scrap can be utilized in metallurgical production.

Iron-Ore Resources of the USSR

Despite the enormous amount of iron ore now being mined in the USSR, the existing usable (marketable) reserves make it possible to give a highly optimistic assessment on the supply of raw iron ore. That supply, moreover, suffices not only to sustain the present level of extraction, but also to raise it. The territory of the USSR, which embraces a large segment of the earth's crust (one-sixth of the land area of the globe), is characterized by an extreme heterogeneity in geological structures. This crust contains enormous deposits of iron ore; the volume of these deposits have been explored and calculated only in part. The Soviet Union accords great significance to the prospecting and exploration of iron-ore resources, which of course

TABLE 5.3
Distribution of iron-ore reserves according to ore type and iron content[28]

Ore type	Usable reserves (billions of tons)	Percent of total	Average iron content (%)
Martensitic-hematite	8.9	14	57.4
Magnetite	10.8	17	39.5
Limonite	5.6	9	37.2
Ferric quartzites	31.1	48	34.2
Siderite, iron, chromium, nickel	1.0	2	32–33
Titanium-magnetite	6.3	10	16.6
TOTAL	63.7	100	

corresponds to its urgent concerns about the development of ferrous metallurgy. The results of such work are impressive: the usable reserves of iron ore for the USSR as a whole have increased from 5.2 billion tons in 1946 to 78.1 billion tons in 1980—that is, an increase of more than fifteenfold.[26]

The USSR has twenty major deposits, which constitute about 80 percent of all iron-ore reserves in the country. The remainder are dispersed in more than 280 smaller deposits, most of which lack sufficient resources to justify establishing a metallurgical plant there. Of the total quantity of reserves, approximately 15 percent have rich ores that contain an average of 55 percent iron or more and do not require enrichment according to Soviet standards. About 67 percent of all orders are enriched by a simple technological process, and 18 percent require complex methods of enrichment.[27] Iron-ore reserves in the USSR are distributed according to type and iron content, as shown in Table 5.3.

The predominant tendency in Soviet ferrous metallurgy is toward enlargement of capacity in blast furnaces, open-hearth furnaces, and the basic-oxygen process, and toward an increase in the production capacity of metallurgical plants as a whole. As a result, this has caused an orientation toward large concentrations of iron-ore deposits. Such deposits make it possible to establish enormous iron-ore enterprises, primarily through open-pit mining, and with an expected term of exploitation fixed at no less than fifty years.

The chief concentrations of production of iron ores in the USSR today are the deposits of the Krivoi Rog Basin, the Kursk Magnetic Anomaly, the northwest part of European Russia, and the Kustanai

Oblast of Kazakhstan. Characteristic in the territorial distribution of iron ore in the USSR is its separation from main deposits of metallurgical fuel: the predominant reserves in iron ore are located in the western regions of the country, the coking coal is found chiefly in the eastern regions. In noting this asymmetry, we have in mind usable reserves.

As far as potential reserves are concerned, there is reason to suppose that the eastern regions of the USSR are no less rich in iron ore than the western regions. It should be kept in mind that exploration of useful mineral deposits in the eastern regions, and especially in Siberia, is as yet only in its initial stages. The geologic structure and mineral deposits of European Russia have been explored several times more intensively than in the case of Siberia. The economic development of the country concentrated growth in industry and especially machine building in the western regions of European Russia—the traditional industrial core of Russia. The eastern regions served as a source of raw materials and fuels; in these regions it was primarily the extraction of those useful minerals not found in the western regions that developed.

It is entirely natural that all efforts were directed toward the development of an iron-ore base in the main metallurgical centers— in the south, center, and Urals, which in turn were integrally tied to the main centers of metal consumption. But if the economic strategy were directed toward the autonomous, harmonic development of the economy in the eastern regions, then the potential resources of iron ore would not represent a barrier to the establishment here of a powerful metallurgical industry.

The uneven distribution of explored iron-ore resources in the USSR creates problems in supplying these resources to metallurgical plants, a difficulty that is aggravated by the critical conditions prevailing in rail transport. More than 70 percent of all industrial reserves of iron ore are concentrated in the European part of the USSR; metallurgical plants here are reliably provided with a raw materials base for a long time to come. But because the growth in capacities for steel production is occurring, and for the rest of the 1980s will occur, in the European part of the USSR, the gap between the current production of commodity iron ore and the growing demand for it by the metallurgical producers is obvious and will become even wider. Therefore the problem is not in having sufficient ore reserves, but in putting these new deposits into industrial production, in the expansion and the acceleration of their exploitation.

The metallurgy of the Urals, which produces more than a quarter of all pig iron in the USSR, has insufficient local iron-ore resources at its disposal. Specifically, it has 13 percent of the usable reserves of the USSR, and only 7 percent if one calculates strictly on the basis of iron content.[29] This deficiency is especially marked in the metallurgical plants of the southern Urals, where iron-ore resources were exhausted in earlier periods through intensive exploitation. The sole local potential for new resources here is limited to ores found in deposits far below the surface. Hence the demands of the metallurgical plants in the southern Urals are satisfied, and in the foreseeable future will evidently be satisfied, through the magnetite deposits in the neighboring areas of northern Kazakhstan. At present, 10–14 million tons of iron ore per year are still being transported to the southern Urals from the Kursk Magnetic Anomaly. It is to be expected that in the near future, as the capacity for mining and enrichment of iron ores in the Kacharskii deposit in northern Kazakhstan is established, the delivery of iron ore from the Kursk Magnetic Anomaly to the Urals will cease.

The iron-ore base of Siberia, in terms of the volume of usable reserves, is capable of satisfying the demand for the amount of pig iron that is planned for production in Siberia itself up to 1990. It can also cover the possible increase in demand for iron ore which may arise from the proposed construction of the first set of metallurgical plants in eastern Siberia.[30] In general, the iron-ore base of Siberia is characterized by territorial dispersion into many relatively small deposits, which are suitable for exploitation chiefly through underground mining and which demand very significant capital expenditures to put them into production. A reliable iron-ore base for the creation of a potentially new large-scale metallurgical enterprise in eastern Siberia (Yakutiya) can be provided by the deposits of the rich magnetite ores in the southern Aldan iron-ore region, and also the deposits of the Charo-Tokkinsk ore regions, which are located 120–150 kilometers north of the Baikal-Amur Railway Line and are presently under exploration.

The chief goal of geological prospecting for iron-ore reserves in the 1980s is the preparation of an ore resource base for the construction of new metallurgical plants in eastern Siberia, and also for the expansion of the iron-ore resources for the Urals and northern Kazakhstan.

Let us now examine more closely the characteristic features of the iron-ore bases of the major economic regions of the USSR.

The North of European Russia

The usable iron-ore reserves in this region contain 2.5 billion tons, of which 2.14 billion tons are found in three main deposits: Olenegorsk, Kovdor, and Kostomukshsk (the largest of the three). All three are exploited through open-pit mining.

The Olenegorsk and Kovdor deposits, located in Murmansk Oblast, serve as the iron-ore base for the Cherepovets metallurgical plant, which is located 1,500 kilometers from the mines and operates as the chief producer of steel in this region. Moreover, a gigantic new blast furnace is expected, and when it is put into operation this plant will indeed be one of the largest in the USSR for the production of pig iron. As noted above, both deposits are exploited through open-pit mines. In terms of iron content, the magnetite ore of both deposits is low-grade (32 percent iron composition), but it is successfully enriched and the result is a high-grade concentrate.[31]

The Kostomukshsk deposit in the Karelian ASSR has ferric quartzites, and the reserves under exploitation consist of 1.1 billion tons of ore. It should become the base for the production of pellets, and it is planned to raise the capacity for production of these to 10 billion tons by the mid-1980s.[32]

The Center of European Russia

The usable iron-ore reserves of this region comprise about 17 billion tons and are concentrated within the parameters of the Kursk Magnetic Anomaly—one of the greatest, if not indeed the greatest, iron-ore basins of the world. The rich marensitic-hematite and martensite-siderite ores make up 35 percent of the usable ore deposits here. The quality of the Kursk ores is extraordinarily high. In terms of metallurgical value, they are superior to the ores of the Krivoi Rog Basin. Their iron content reaches 69 percent (the average is 59.5 percent). One shortcoming of these rich ores is the high sulphur content in a number of the deposits (up to 0.1–0.6 percent), which requires that they be agglomerated.[33]

The deposits of the Kursk Magnetic Anomaly are also distinguished by the unique, exceedingly complicated conditions of the deposits. Over the beds of iron ore lies a thick (30–650 meters) cover of heavily waterlogged sedimentary rock, which makes both prospecting and industrial exploitation extremely difficult. Mining ore under such adverse hydrogeological conditions is a complex task, which can only be solved by utilizing specialized, expensive machinery and technology, and hence by means of significant capital investment.

The Oskol electrometallurgical plant operates on the basis of the Kursk Magnetic Anomaly, and the ores from this ore district supply a number of other plants in the center, the Urals, and Siberia.

The Kursk Magnetic Anomaly occupies an extraordinarily favorable economic-geographic position: between the Donets coal basin (with its excellent coking coals) and the chief metal-producing regions. This is also a region with a well-developed infrastructure and high population density (Kursk, Belgorod, and Orel oblasts).

The South of European Russia (Ukraine)

This region holds a leading place in usable iron-ore reserves in the USSR (approximately 32 percent of all such reserves). There are seventy-seven deposits here, most of which are in the Great Krivoi Rog Basin (the Great Krivbass), which produces more than 90 percent of all iron ore in the southern USSR. The Krivoi Rog Basin is the greatest supplier of iron ore for ferrous metallurgy in the USSR. Its high-quality, rich ore with high iron content is sent to all the metallurgical plants of the south and to central European Russia, and it also provides the main component of ores sold for export. The usable reserves comprise about 18 billion tons. The ores of this basin are divided into three commercial categories of ferruginous quartzites or taconite ores: (1) the naturally rich martensite-hematite and magnetite with an iron content of over 46 percent; (2) magnetites, with an iron content of over 10 percent; and, (3) hematites (with an iron content of over 28 percent). A striking fact about the Krivoi Rog ores is that a significant portion of them (21 percent) can be used directly in metallurgical production without any enrichment.

The Krivoi Rog Basin, to a greater degree than any other large iron-ore basins of the USSR, relies on underground mining for extraction of the iron ore.[34] Of the forty iron-ore mines in the USSR, twenty-two are located in the southern iron-ore basin. And it is precisely here, in this underground extraction of the ore, that so many of the problems of the Great Krivoi Rog Basin arise. The essence of these problems is that the depth of the shafts is rapidly increasing (a matter discussed in further detail below), but as the shafts go deeper, the ore platform (the frontal area under exploitation) shrinks, the productivity of labor declines, and the production costs rise significantly. For the period 1976–80 alone, the extraction of ore in the majority of Krivbass shafts reached 100 meters and more, and at the present time some have gone as deep as 1,500 meters. It is, therefore, becoming more and more difficult to sustain the necessary conditions for extraction, from the point of both technology and labor safety. As a result, production in these mines is declining each year by 1.0–1.5 million tons. Thus whereas in 1975 underground mining yielded 44 million tons, in 1980 production amounted to only 37 million tons.[35]

Urals

Usable iron-ore reserves in the Urals are dispersed into many small deposits and altogether comprise 15.3 billion tons—that is, 14 percent of Soviet iron-ore reserves. The Urals are the oldest iron-producing center of Russia and have been the object of intensive exploitation ever since the early eighteenth century. The main mass of known reserves consists of ores that are of relatively low quality but are easily mined. Indicative of the low quality is the fact that only 2.4 percent of the known reserves can be utilized without further enrichment. Moreover, most of these deposits are characterized by a complex structure and extremely heterogeneous composition.

The largest deposits of iron ores in the Urals are found in Kachkanarsk. Its usable reserves of titanic-magnetite ore consist of more than 6 billion tons—that is, more than 70 percent of all reserves in the Urals. The ores of this deposit consist of 16–17 percent iron and are the poorest of all ores mined in the USSR.[36] The economic expediency of the industrial utilization of these ores derives from the size of the reserves, the relative facility of their extraction, and the presence of vanadium in the ore. In the recent past one of the most important deposits in the Urals has been Magnitogorsk, which had exceptionally rich ore and which intensively exploited this for more than forty years. Representing the iron-ore base of the Magnitogorsk Metallurgic Plant (the largest plant in the USSR), these reserves have now been almost totally exhausted.

An important characteristic of the iron-ore base of the Urals is the fact that, while comprising only 13 percent of the utilized reserves in the USSR, it produces 25 percent of all pig iron. That, of course, corroborates the observation about the extremely intensive rate of exploitation of almost all the Urals deposits.

Kazakhstan

The usable iron-ore reserves in Kazakhstan represent 53 percent (7.6 billion tons) of the total usable reserves in the Asiatic part of the USSR. The overwhelming majority (7.1 billion tons, or 93 percent) is concentrated in the region east of the Urals—the Kustanai Oblast. The iron-ore resources of Kazakhstan are, in general, represented by two types of ores; somewhat less than half is composed of magnetite ores that are easily mined and require no enrichment (with 45–60 percent iron content), and somewhat over half is composed of limonite that is difficult to extract and has an iron content of 35 percent.[37]

The largest deposits of the first type are found in Sokolovskii, Sarbaiskii, and Kacharskii. These deposits are, in general, exploited through open-pit mining. The Sokolovskii and Sarbaiskii deposits produce 30–35 million tons of raw ore per annum, and this production goes primarily to the metallurgical plants of the Urals—Magnitogorsk, Orsko-Khalilovskii, Nizhnetagil'skii—and also to the Karaganda plant in Kazakhstan itself. In the early 1980s plans were laid to increase the production at the Kacharskii deposits to 20 million tons per annum.[38] Among the deposits of this type it is also important to note Atasu, whose rich ores (50–60 percent iron content) go primarily to the Karaganda plant. In general, the main production of iron ores in this region is oriented toward filling the shortages in iron ore of the Ural plants, a problem that has intensified as the old areas of exploitation have been gradually exhausted.

The largest depository of the second type of ore—limonite that is difficult to extract and has a lower iron content—is found in Lisakovsk and Ayatsk. Their ores require expensive methods of enrichment. Nevertheless, their extraction is worthwhile, since they are located relatively close to coking coals of the Karaganda Basin. This deposit can, to a significant degree, be exploited through open-pit mining. At the present time, exploitation of the Lisakovsk deposit is in its initial stages, and the annual production capacity already stands at 36 million tons. As to the Ayatsk deposit, the complexity and high enrichment costs of its ores have caused it to go unexploited and to be left in a state of conservation.

Siberia[39]

A characteristic feature of the distribution of iron-ore resources in Siberia is their territorial separation from the centers of metallurgical production. All pig-iron production in Siberia is concentrated in its western part, whereas only 20 percent of usable Siberian iron-ore reserves are to be found in this part of Siberia; the remaining 80 percent is found in the eastern part of Siberia. As a result, the demand for iron ore by the two main Siberian metallurgical plants (the Novo-Kuznetsk and West Siberian plants), which produce all the pig iron and 90 percent of all steel in Siberia, is met less and less through local deposits and must rely increasingly on ores from distant areas. As the tempo of growth in mining from local deposits declines, the share of remote ores will steadily increase as a proportion of the raw materials used in Siberian blast furnaces; in recent years this has reached more than 50 percent.[40]

Amid conditions of extraordinary overloading of the transcontinental railway system between east and west and the railway system of Siberia, the mounting dependence of Siberian metallurgical plants on distant ores has a profoundly negative impact on the orderly rhythm in their production.

The greatest significance of the Siberian mines presently being exploited belongs to Korshunov in eastern Siberia and several deposits in Gornaya Shoriya and in the Sayanskii mountains. They are all located in eastern Siberia and supply ores for the West Siberian and Kuznetsk plants, which are located 1,600 kilometers away. The Korshunovsk deposit is the largest in Siberia for the extraction of iron ore (approximately 20 million tons per annum). Its magnetite ores, which are extracted through open-pit mines, contain 24–45 percent iron. This deposit belongs to the Angaro-Ilimsk iron-ore basin, whose reserves were estimated at 600 million tons in 1975.[41]

As assessment of the iron-ore reserves of Siberia is much less reliable than assessments of the western regions of the USSR and Kazakhstan, given the lesser degree of geological exploration in its vast and unconquered terrain. In the 1970s geological prospecting here was sharply intensified in areas adjacent to the Baikal-Amur Railway Line and in areas where oil, gas, and coal deposits were being exploited. This contributed to exploration of iron-ore deposits found in these territories. The new, if incomplete, data on iron-ore resources in Siberia differed substantially from earlier data in 1975 which are customarily cited by Soviet sources. Just how different these data were can be gleaned from the following comparison: if the 1975 assessment posited the iron-ore reserves of eastern Siberia at 3.6 billion tons, in Aldan iron-ore province (which is adjacent to the Baikal-Amur line) geologists have recently raised this estimate to 8 billion tons.[42]

It seems that one should expect growth in the volume of iron ore mined in Siberia in the near future and a corresponding increase in its share of total reserves in the USSR.

In contrast to the iron-ore base of the western regions, which are oriented toward the satisfaction of demands of the metallurgical industry already established here (and which therefore have clear quantitative and qualitative indices for its development), the iron-ore production of Siberia as yet has no such clearly defined goals. The reason is that the future ferrous metallurgy of Siberia is hazy and remains mired in seemingly endless discussion. And it is precisely this circumstance that determines the contradictions in various assessments of the Siberian reserves in iron ore.

Insofar as the progress of ferrous metallurgy in the eastern part of the USSR represents an absolute precondition for accelerated industrial growth in Siberia, the development and expansion of iron-ore mineworks on its territory acquires constantly growing significance.

As data from 1975 and later years show, Siberia's share of usable iron-ore reserves is 10–11 percent and this is approximately its share in the production of steel.[43] Hence from the perspective of total volume of reserves, Soviet metallurgy should be provided with sufficient iron ore. But the problem is that these deposits are either relatively small in size or difficult to exploit (distant from existing rail lines and in undeveloped areas). These circumstances serve to retard the development of iron-ore production in Siberia.

The dispersion of iron-ore reserves in numerous relatively small deposits and the generally undeveloped state of the territories where they are located provide some of the most cogent arguments against the construction of new metallurgical plants in Siberia. But the appearance of the Baikal-Amur Railway Line in areas close to new substantial deposits with high-grade iron ore erodes the persuasiveness of such arguments. It is important to examine, if only briefly, the possibilities for an expansion of the iron-ore base of Siberia against the background of this prospective development of metallurgical production there.

At the present time, ferrous metallurgy in Siberia is concentrated in its southwestern part. East of Baikal there are only two relatively small reprocessing plants as well as one relatively small plant in the Soviet far east. The entire central part of Siberia, embracing the vast territories of Krasnoyarsk district and Irkutsk Oblast, in effect have no metallurgical production. At the same time, Angaro-Yensey region—the central part of this territory—stands as a center of investment activity not only for Siberia but also for the whole Soviet Union. Hence it is here that one finds accelerated industrial development. This region represents not only a center for rapid growth in the consumption of steel but also has favorable conditions for the development of its production. The basic, most inexpensive fuel and energy resources—coal and electrical energy—are concentrated here. This region also has over half of the iron-ore reserves of Siberia, and these are the most geologically suitable for production. The potential reserves are also enormous. Available, too, are various other raw materials required for metallurgical production.

In short, the Angaro-Yenisey district should be regarded as the primary contender for the possible development of ferrous metallurgy in Siberia. Hence one should expect an expansion in the usable iron-ore reserves in this area.

Great possibilities for the development of ferrous metallurgy can also be discerned in a territory that intersects and overlaps southern

Yakutiya, Irkutsk Oblast, and Chita Oblast, all in connection with the construction of the Baikal-Amur Railway Line there. Usable reserves that have been explored in the Aldan iron-ore province, as noted above, contain about 8 billion tons. The most thoroughly explored is the Tarynnakh deposit (about 2.5 billion tons), where the predominant ores are the easily mined magnetite and ferric quartzites. In terms of quality, the ores in these deposits are better than those found in Krivoi Rog Basin and the Kursk Magnetic Anomaly.[44] The deposits of the Aldan iron-ore province are located only 35–150 kilometers from the Baikal-Amur Railway Line. The rich iron ores of the Aldan province, together with the vast reserves of high-quality coking coal located within 80–100 kilometers, and with the presence here of all forms of supplementary raw materials (dolomite, limestone, etc.)—all this creates uniquely favorable conditions for the establishment of large metallurgical production. One should also regard these deposits as a potential source of iron-ore exports.

Besides the usable reserves that were prospected by 1956 in western Siberia (Tomsk Oblast), an iron-ore province called the West Siberian iron-ore basin has been discovered and found to contain virtually unlimited potential reserves of limonite. But the location of this ore deep within sedimentary rock, the necessity of enriching the ore through complex processes, and above all the undeveloped infrastructure of the region and its severe climactic conditions push prospects for the development of these reserves into the indefinite future. But the most southern deposit of this basin (Bakchar), located 190 kilometers from Tomsk and containing (according to preliminary assessments) 100–120 billion tons of raw ores with an iron content of 30–40 percent, has some chance of eliciting more intensive exploration and production of some segments (those close to oil and gas deposits are already being exploited) in the foreseeable future.[45] The reason for this is the current construction of an oil-gas complex in this district, which will create a more favorable infrastructure and transportation network to facilitate development of the contiguous iron-ore reserves.

Thus the potential reserves of raw iron ore are virtually unlimited in Siberia. The rising demand for metal here will give increasing urgency to the question of creating new capacities for steel production in the eastern parts of Siberia. That, in turn, will give new

TABLE 5.4
Iron-ore mining in the USSR, 1960–81[46]

	1960	1965	1970	1975	1980	1981
Raw ore production						
Total	142.1	241.0	354.1	440.5	482.0	502.0
Underground mining						
millions of tons	73.3	83.0	73.6	77.3	73.0	74.3
percent of total	51.6	34.4	20.8	17.5	15.1	14.8
Open-pit mining						
millions of tons	68.8	158.0	280.5	363.2	409.0	427.7
percent of total	48.4	65.6	79.2	82.5	84.9	85.2
Commercial ores						
millions of tons	105.6	153.5	197.3	234.9	244.7	242.4
Iron content percentage						
Of commercial ores	54.3	56.3	58.8	59.3	58.9	59.4
Of raw ores	44.5	—	37.3	36.3	34.7	—

impetus to more vigorous exploration of Siberian deposits of iron ore.

Problems of Iron-Ore Mining

In the late 1970s the Soviet Union experienced a sharp slowdown in its growth rates for iron-ore extraction. A concise picture of these production patterns since 1960 is given in Table 5.4, which shows both the production volume and its division according to open-pit and underground mining methods.

Open-Pit Mining and the Increasing Concentration of Production

Although this tendency toward declining growth rates in the production of commercial iron ore first became evident in the late 1970s (see Table 5.4), it became still more marked in the early 1980s. Thus whereas the average annual growth rate in the 1960s was 6.4 percent and in the 1970s had declined to 2.2 percent, in the first four years of the 1980s (1981–84) it had plummeted to 0.2 percent.[47]

In the last two decades the iron-ore production of the USSR has been characterized by an expansion of the scope of open-pit mining in large deposits. At present 85 percent of the raw iron mined in the USSR is obtained through open-pit mining. Considering that the iron content in raw ore obtained through underground mining is higher, however, the share of commercial ore from open-pit mining and underground mining is 74 percent and 26 percent, respectively. This method has advantages over underground mining: it allows greater concentration of production, higher tempos of progress in machinery development and utilization, greater possibilities for complex mechanization of mining, and consequently a higher labor productivity. Hence in the late 1970s labor productivity in large open-pit mines reached 40 tons of raw iron ore per labor shift, whereas the comparable figure for underground mining was only 24 tons. Underground mining must be maintained and developed because in a series of iron-ore deposits (including one of the largest of the USSR, Krivoi Rog Basin), the richest ores are buried at considerable depths below the surface. For the period 1960–80 the volume of iron ore extracted by open-pit mining grew sixfold, but the growth tempo in recent years has been significantly reduced.[48]

The process of concentrating metallurgical production and the construction of powerful and superpowerful blast furnaces and gigantic plants oriented Soviet iron-ore mining toward the establishment of powerful ore-enrichment combines. These combines include open-pit mines and underground shaft mines, enrichment complexes and agglomeration plants, and in some instances plants to produce sinter and pellets. For the period 1960–80 the average capacity of an iron-ore enterprise—primarily as a result of the tendency to construct such combines—rose from 1.35 to 6.8 million tons of commercial ore (an increase of 4.2 times). At the same time, the general quantity of iron-ore enterprises for this period shrank from 124 to 100, even while the mining of iron ore rose by 3.4 times. In terms of total volume, 80 percent of the extraction through open-pit mining occurred in fifteen open-pit mines, each of which has a capacity of 10 million tons of raw ore per year; by comparison, 75 percent of the total ore extracted through underground mining was concentrated in nineteen large mines, each of which has an annual capacity of over 2 million tons. Hence thirty-four iron-ore enterprises of the one hundred in operation provide more than three-fourths of the entire raw iron ore mined in the USSR. Some mining combines with open-pit mines attained a capacity of 40–50 million tons of raw ore per year.[49] The largest mining and processing combines include the following:

    1. Southern European Russia—Yuzhnyi, Novo-Krivorozhskii, Tsentral'nyi, Severenyi, Inguletskii, and Dneprovskii
    2. Kursk Magnetic Anomaly—Mikhailovskii, Lebedinskii, Gubkinskii
    3. Northern European Russia—Kovdorskii and Olenegorskii
    4. Kazakhstan—Sokolovsko-Sarbaiskii, Lisakovskii, and Kacharskii (The latter is still under construction.)
    5. Siberia—Korshunovskii (in eastern Siberia)

To these iron-ore extraction and processing combines of the greatest capacity two others were added in the early 1980s: the Stoilenskii mining-enrichment combine in the Kursk Magnetic Anomaly and the Kostomukshskii combine in the northern European part of the USSR.

As far as underground mining is concerned, at present the Soviet Union has forty underground iron-ore mines with an annual production of 2 million tons of raw ore per year. But dominant here are seventeen large mines with an annual production of 2–5 million tons per annum, and these alone account for 70 percent of all iron ore mined in the USSR.[50]

The economic superiority of iron-ore extraction through open-pit mines is apparent. For example, in the Krivoi Rog Basin the production cost of iron from open-pit mines is 2.3 times less than that obtained from underground mines (with iron content at constant levels). Capital investment for each additional ton of ore—with identical iron content—is 24 percent higher for underground mines than for open-pit mines. The time required to construct production capacities is two to three times less for open-pit mines than for underground mines.[51]

The increasing concentration of iron-ore production and the expansion of capacities for open-pit mining, it would seem, should lead to a growth in iron-ore production and diminished expenditures on unit production costs for incremental growth. But in fact just the opposite is occurring. Capital expenditures for production growth (for each additional ton of iron ore) rose threefold in the period between 1960 and 1980.[52] How does one account for this situation?

Open-Pit and Underground Mines:
Great Depths and the Consequences

Iron-ore production is a basic component of ferrous metallurgy. Its operation is regulated by the Ministry of Ferrous Metallurgy and hence strictly depends on the rhythm and peculiarities of metallurgical production, with all its disproportions. The unlimited demand for steel and constant pressure on metallurgical plants is relayed to iron-mining enterprises and creates conditions there that simply preclude adherence to an intelligent, coherent strategy for the exploitation of underground and open-pit mines. To that must be added the quantitative and qualitative discrepancy between the machinery and equipment available for mining, the dimensions of the mining tasks, and the physical characteristics of the materials to be worked in the mining.

These general factors, which lead to a maximum intensification of extraction under conditions of inadequate machinery and equipment, result in an excessive, irrational deepening of mines that are not reinforced by the necessary expansion of surface area for normal, efficient operation. On the average, open-pit mines for iron ore in the USSR become deeper each year at the rate of 5–12 meters per annum.[53] In a series of mines in the Krivoi Rog Basin each year the open-pit mines have become deeper at the rate of 30 meters per annum, and this has gone on for many years. As a result, in a relatively short span of time the majority of open-pit mines in the southern European part of the USSR have reached a depth of 200 meters or more. For the five-year period 1975–80 alone, the depth of open-pit mines in Sokolovskii and Sarbaiskii mines in Kazakhstan increased from 240–300 meters.[54] For the period 1976–80 the number of large-capacity open-pit mines (those producing 10 million tons of mining material per annum) which operated at less than 200 meters depth had declined by 26 percent, and their share of total production by open-pit mining declined from 74 to 58 percent. For this same period the number of open-pit mines operating at 200 meters or more had significantly increased, and their share of the iron ore mined rose by more than 50 percent.[55]

This tendency toward deeper and deeper mine operation has some adverse consequences. As the mines go from higher to lower strata in open-pit mining, the proportion of useful ores in the iron-ore beds declines. For example, in the Sokolov open-pit mine in

Kazakhstan, the extension of the mine from 200 to 300 meters has been accompanied by a decline in the average iron content of the ore from 34.3 percent to 29.7 percent.[56] The reduced proportion of iron in the ore has meant that to sustain the existing level of iron production and especially to increase it, it is necessary to process more and more raw ore. An increase in rock spoil per unit of production has increased the volume of mining, the demand on machinery and equipment, and an increase of expenditures on the extraction and enrichment of the ore.

The average iron content in raw ore declined between 1961 and 1982 by almost 13 percent (see Table 5.4). For this same period, the volume of raw ore extracted per ton of commercial ore rose by more than 43 percent (from 1.39 to 1.92 tons). Of the 1.3 billion tons of raw mass mined in 1977, raw ore constituted only 37 percent, commercial ore stood at 19 percent, and the iron content of the commercial ore was 11 percent. For the production of 1 ton of commercial ore in 1977, it was necessary to mine 5 tons of material; by 1982 this figure had risen to 8 tons.[57] An important distinguishing consequence of the deeper mining tendency in open-pit and underground methods is the increase in the share of hard rock waste that is encountered in extracting the iron. In the early 1980s it represented 70 percent of the entire volume of material being mined.[58]

There are still other problems that accompany deeper mining practices. One is the decreasing productivity of truck transport, excavators, and other forms of mining machinery. Moreover, as the mines go deeper, the geometric parameters of working zones in the open-pit mines are reduced, and that in turn causes a deterioration in conditions for both labor and the utilization of machinery and equipment. The result is declining productivity and higher production costs for the iron ore. Finally, one should not overlook the ecological costs of deeper mine operation, which is especially destructive in the European part of the USSR, where the open-pit mines of the Kursk Magnetic Anomaly and Krivoi Rog Basin (and their infrastructure) steadily encroach on the fertile land in southern Russia and the Ukraine and take this land out of agricultural production.

Violation of the Relationship between
Mining Depth and Surface

How does one explain the continuing tendency to mine more and more deeply, despite all the negative consequences discussed above? The general cause is disregard of the proportions between depth of mining operation and the expansion of the surface area. For the normal development of an open--pit mine, it is necessary for surface operations to surpass downward tendencies in mining. The problem in the Soviet Union is that this principle is violated: surface work lags far behind work to make the mine deeper and deeper.

This lagging in surface extension—that is, inadequate preparations to clear the overburden and expand the surface area of the mining operation—is the fundamental factor preventing normal exploitation of ore deposits, retarding the growth of ore production, and reducing its economic efficiency. Normal exploitation of a deposit through open-pit mining presupposes an optimal correlation between the depth of the mine and preparation of the perimeter for its expansion (a correlation that is definite for each concrete situation). That preparation must be undertaken before the mine has reached the depth allowed for its given surface area; if the mine exceeds that depth, the result is a smaller frontal area of mine operation and declining content of useful iron content in the ore extracted. All this makes further exploitation less efficient.

It is obvious that the available production resources must be distributed in such a way as to achieve the required proportion between current production (extraction of the ore) and further surface expansion (removal of overburden to prepare for enlargement of the mine). In practice, however, exploitation and development of iron-ore deposits in the USSR (and, it may be assumed, this applies to other mining operations as well) violate this proportion. The available production resources—labor and machinery—are directed above all toward current production and only to a small degree to preparatory work for perimeter expansion. At work here are such factors as the insufficient supply of machinery, its improper utilization, and the discordance between the mine's exploitation parameters and the physical characteristics of the material being mined. One should also note, in particular, the pressure of constantly rising goals set by central planners, for this factor deprives managers of mining and processing enterprises of maneuvering room. They cannot divert working machinery from current production to prepare for extension on the perimeter. The negative impact of these factors is especially intensified because of the tendency for a thickening of the overburden in many of the ore deposits now under exploitation. In a series of open-pit mines in the Kursk Magnetic Anomaly, for example, the depth of the overburden has risen in recent years from 70 to 110–130 meters, and it is predicted that it will increase to 160 meters.[59]

Typical of this practice is one of the largest open-pit mines in the southern part of the USSR: the mining operation Dneprovskii, which (according to the plan for 1985) is to have a capacity for 34 million tons of raw ore production per annum. The development of the open-pit mine has been stalled by the disproportionately slow tempo of work to remove more overburden and to expand the mine's perimeter. Over the course of the nine years that the mine has been in operation, work on its surface expansion has been fulfilled at no more than 65–68 percent of that required for the proper correlation. The director of the Dneprovskii mining and processing enterprise declared that "under conditions of an inadequate volume of work on surface expansion, the danger has arisen that the poorly developed working front will exhaust the mine." The main cause of this condition, as the director's words suggest, is a lack of the high-productive machinery that the plan had prescribed (excavators, dump trucks, locomotives, etc.).[60] Although we shall give further attention to the problem of machinery and equipment, here it is important to stress such an essential factor as the reduction of the "ore front," and that this is a direct consequence of the failure to observe the proper correlation between surface area and depth in the mine. In general, between 1970 and 1980 the ore front of open-pit mines in the USSR shrank from 57.5 percent to 27.2 percent of the general area of the mines—that is, it decreased by more than half.[61] As a result, the working platform of the open-pit mine was reduced, the maneuvering of extractive and transport machinery became more difficult, and in the end this meant a decline in productivity of the mine.

Such is the situation at operating open-pit mines. But if examined in terms of the total volume of iron-ore production, can the construction of new capacities compensate for the declining growth of production at operating capacities?

The establishment and development of new capacities is in fact being realized at an extremely low rate. The reasons for this are many: the inadequate tempo of surface work to remove overburden; the belated delivery of machinery and equipment; and more generally, factors that are characteristic of all construction processes in the USSR—poor organization and insufficiency of material support and resources.

An example of this is provided by the construction of one of the largest open-pit mines in the Kursk Magnetic Anomaly (Stoilenskii), which was recently put into operation. Surface excavation here was performed at only one-fifth of the rate that had been projected by the construction plans and that were necessary for putting the mine into operation according to the prescribed time schedule. As a result, surface expansion was not performed until the eighth year of the construction, which in turn caused a delay in the completion of the work.[62]

As a result of the protracted terms for construction, which are often caused by insufficient investment, the time required for putting mines at iron-ore deposits into operation has grown sharply in recent years. In turn, delays in the exploitation of new capacities have forced the Ministry of Ferrous Metallurgy to put pressure on the existing mines and and to violate all technological norms for efficient exploitation. The rise of production, from the ministry's perspective, is to be achieved at any cost; it pays no heed to the problems this will create for the future. In the mining sector this kind of thinking—which is typical of the Soviet economy generally—has especially deleterious consequences, since the timely preparation of the body of a useful mineral to compensate for an exhausted stratum is a necessary condition for supporting production and its growth.

The situation is still more dramatic in the case of underground mining of iron ore. One-half of all ore extracted through underground mining in the USSR comes from the shafts of Krivoi Rog Basin. Hence the circumstances that have arisen there have a decisive impact on the general situation and also offer a typical example of the problem in Soviet mining. For the decade 1970–80 the volume of ore from underground mines in the Krivoi Rog Basin declined by 25 percent.[63] The extraction of rich ores continues to decline by 1.0–1.5 million tons per annum. At the largest shaft in the basin (the Dzerzhinskii mine), the volume of production declined from 10–11 million tons in 1970 to 3–4 million tons in 1985.[64]

In an effort to find ways to prevent such declines in production, studies are also being made of the possibility of mining ore deposits at great depths (1,500 meters and more). It is highly unlikely, however, that such methods have much chance of being realized: it is too capital-intensive and, technologically, very complicated. To mine the rich iron ores in the shafts of the Krivoi Rog Basin at such depths, it would be necessary to make a radical reconstruction of the shafts, which according to estimates by Soviet experts, would demand more than 1 billion rubles of capital expenditure.[65]

It appears to be more realistic to save the situation by tapping the lower-grade ores (magnetite quartzites), which are deposited along the perimeter of the existing shafts. In the opinion of experts, extraction of such ores will grow, and their share in total production of the Krivoi Rog Basin through underground mining will increase and steadily displace the rich ores.[66] Apparently, in this way the Soviets will try to compensate for the decline of rich ores in the shafts of this basin, which remains for now the chief iron-ore base of the USSR. This of course will demand substantial investment and the resolution of a series of technological problems. Nevertheless, this is less complex and expensive than the proposal to make the shafts deeper to obtain the richer ore.

From this situation, it follows that the support of the achieved volume of iron-ore production and, even more so, increases in such production depends in the most direct way on the possibilities for the iron-ore mining industry to raise the tempos of surface extension. The minister of Ferrous Metallurgy, Ivan Kazanets, declared in his report to a meeting of iron-ore specialists in 1982: "The successful fulfillment of the plan for the production of commercial ore will be determined, above all, by fulfillment of the plan for surface excavation to expand the mines."[67] The growing volume of such surface work means a sharp increase in the volume of mining material which must be handled. Thus for the five-year period of 1981–85 the planned volume of production of iron ore can be fulfilled only under the condition that the volume of work for mine expansion increases to 44 percent over the previous five-year period, and the annual volume of material handled for this period must increase by 39 percent.[68]

It is, however, perfectly obvious that the existing level of supply in machinery and equipment—both in a quantitative and qualitative sense—does not correspond to such monumental goals. The projected dimensions of work can be performed only if the supply of machinery increases not only through higher delivery rates for existing serial production but also through the introduction of new, more productive technology. Thus the goal really is to raise the level of utilization of existing machinery and to supply new, highly productive equipment and machinery.

TABLE 5.5
Coefficients of utilization of calendar time in the
operation of mining-transportation machinery[69]

Equipment	1970	1975	1979
Drilling rig	0.30	0.34	0.33
Excavators	0.62	0.50	0.49
Locomotives	0.68	0.70	0.67
Dump trucks	0.62	0.63	0.54
Conveyers	0.76	0.74	0.76

Mining Machinery and Equipment

The machinery now being used in open-pit mines consists of excavators to extract the mining mass, truck transport (loaded from the excavator), and transporters of the mining mass to reloading stations at the upper levels of the mine, to which railway lines come. Here the mined material is loaded by excavators onto special freight cars, which transport the ore outside the mine. As the open-pit mine goes deeper and the dimensions of production are expanded, this system becomes less and less efficient. Especially great difficulties arise in regard to the transport equipment. This section examines how the existing machinery is utilized, how iron-ore mining enterprises are supplied with equipment within the framework of traditional technology, and how new technology is developed and applied. Table 5.5 gives us an idea of how machinery and equipment are used in the open-pit mines.

As Table 5.5 shows, four of the five categories of extraction and transportation machinery listed here show a decline in the utilization of capacity in the second half of the 1970s. According to data for 1984, the situation did not improve in the beginning of the 1980s.[70]

There are many reasons for this: a disregard for the norms of exploitation, unsatisfactory conditions of working platforms and roadways, tardy preparation of working fronts in the open-pit mines, and low indicators for the shift system in the utilization of equipment (that is, machinery is left idle) because of shortages in and low qualifications of the work force—that is, poor organization of work through the fault of the iron-ore enterprises themselves. The low level of utilization of equipment is also closely linked to its exhaustion. Thus of 1,046 excavators operating in open-pit mines of the USSR in the early 1980s, approximately 45 percent were in need of replacement.[71]

Another important cause of these problems is poor maintenance of the machinery. This is a separate question, to which we shall return later and which we shall examine in the context of the repair and maintenance problems of ferrous metallurgy more generally. Here we shall point out only the lack of spare parts. The demand for spare parts for excavators in iron-ore mining, for example, was satisfied at the rate of only 30–50 percent in the early 1980s.[72] Shortcomings in maintenance and repair services are especially apparent when they cause a decline in the use of powerful rotor complexes (utilized in the removal of loose overburden). This is particularly true of the rotor complexes operating at the largest open-pit mines of the Kursk Magnetic Anomaly—the Mikhailovskii and Stoilenskii mines.[73]

Matters stand no better in regard to the supply of iron-ore mining enterprises with new machinery. Soviet machine building is simply not in a condition to satisfy the increasing needs for modern technology and machines. Thus in 1980 only 42.6 percent of the demand on ordinary excavators (with a bucket displacement of 4 cubic meters and more); for dump trucks only 30 percent of the demand was satisfied; and for locomotives only 33.3 percent of the demand was met.[74] In the 1970s open-pit iron-ore mines were provided chiefly with excavators having a bucket capacity of 5–8 cubic kilometers; by the early 1980s they represented 78 percent of all excavators utilized in iron-ore mining.[75] But such excavators are not appropriate for working hard rock; for that, machines with a greater capacity and power are needed. This kind of excavator model has been created in the USSR, but it is being produced at a very slow rate. No less important is the supply of open-pit mines with dump trucks having a much greater load capacity than those currently used. The chief producer of large dump trucks is the Byelorussian Truck Plant (BELAZ). Table 5.6 shows the structure of production for dump trucks that it has manufactured for iron-mining enterprises:

TABLE 5.6
Exploitation indices for large dump trucks of BELAZ[76]

Load capacity (in tons)	Number (as % of 1980 production)	Volume of transport (%)
27	28.0	20.4
40	67.9	70.3
75	4.1	9.3

More than 90 percent of the transport of mined materials is performed by trucks with a load capacity of 27 and 40 tons, at a time when the iron-ore enterprises need dump trucks with a far greater capacity.

It should, however, be noted that the USSR is taking steps to design and produce more powerful dump trucks. In the early 1980s BELAZ began the serial production of dump trucks with a load capacity of 110 tons, and industrial experimentation was also begun to test models of dump trucks with a load capacity of 180 tons. But the production of the 110-ton model and the development of the 180-ton model have been accompanied by such problems of an organizational, technological, and supply nature that it is unrealistic to expect any kind of significant increase in their production before the end of the 1980s.[77] The acute demand for powerful dump trucks (with a load capacity up to 120 tons) cannot in the foreseeable future be satisfied by the Soviet automotive and truck construction industry. In part the problem will, evidently, be resolved through imports.[78]

Utilization of excavators with a larger capacity is held back by the absence of dump trucks of corresponding load capacity. But at large open-pit mines the growth in productivity can be attained only by providing them with powerful excavators; some part of this demand in the USSR can only be met by means of imported machinery. The need for powerful excavators not only for iron-ore mining but also in other sectors, especially for use in open-pit coal mines, is becoming exceedingly acute. Hopes for a reduction in demand in these depends on putting into operation the Krasnoyarsk plant for heavy excavators. This factory began to be built in the beginning of the last decade, but production in any kind of meaningful volume will commence only in the last half of the 1980s. If one takes into account that it will be the sole plant producing excavators not only for Siberia but for the entire Asiatic part of the USSR, with the enormous dimensions of its mining operations (in addition to the iron-ore mines, there are also coal mines in Yakutiya, the Kansko-Achinskii complex, etc.), then one must conclude that even at maximum development of this plant's capacity its production cannot satisfy the demands of the iron-ore industry.

The projected dimensions of mining operations can be realized only on condition of intensive renewal of the machinery and equipment, and this renewal must be not only quantitative but also qualitative in character. Important in this regard is the transition to more efficient technology for open-pit mining, which would make it possible to intensify mining at deeper levels and to handle the enormous volume of overburden. Such a technology, which has been termed "cyclical-flow technology," is based on a partial replacement of dump trucks with conveyers in the transport of mined materials. Before being placed on the conveyer, the raw materials must be broken into small pieces through mobile crushing machines that are directly integrated into the whole system.

It is also possible for there to be other combinations of truck transport, railway transport, and conveyers, which will create a more efficient system for open-pit mining. The application of such systems has substantial advantages compared to the traditional technology. But their application requires significant investments for their creation as well as for the reconstruction of open-pit mines to adapt mine operations for their use. It takes five to eight years to transfer an open-pit mine to this technology. The creation of complexes of cyclical-flow technology is cost-efficient only if used together with powerful types of crushing machines, conveyers, and other machines that have been specially adapted for use in open-pit mines. The Soviet machine-building industry, however, is simply not capable of producing this equipment in the requisite numbers. As a result, modernization of technology in iron-ore mining is being realized at a very slow pace. In the early 1980s the share of cyclical-flow technology in open-pit mining was only 10 to 11 percent. The Soviet economic plan intended to increase this quotient to one-third by 1985, but it is highly unlikely that this goal will be realized.[79]

Many problems also arise in the use of railway transport in open-pit iron-ore mines. They are, basically, connected with the laying of rail ties to deeper levels as the open-pit mines themselves go to lower and lower levels. Moreover, the slope and curvature of the tracks increases, and that in turn means greater load and stress on the locomotives, which operate in many open-pit mines—in particular, in the immense open-pit mines of the Krivoi Rog Basin. For that reason these mines are being reequipped with electric locomotives, which are far more reliable in deep open-pit mines.[80] This task is made more difficult by the inadequate load capacity of the special freight cars and their outmoded form of construction. Freight cars with a load capacity of 180 tons, which corresponds to contemporary conditions for ore transport, made up only 5 percent of the entire stock of freight cars in open-pit mines in 1980.[81]

To sum up, the chief reasons for the sharp decline in the tempo of growth for iron-ore production are: (1) in the drive for uninterrupted, maximum increase in output, Soviet mining enterprises have excessively intensified the extractions in existing open-pit and underground mines and violated the fundamental technological norms for their effective exploitation; and (2) there has been a lag in supply of machinery and equipment both in a quantitative and, still more important, in a qualitative sense.

The declining iron content in the ore mined, under conditions of the rising demand for production, and the rising demands on its quality, have increased the pressure on ore processing—the technological buffer zone between ore extraction and its use in blast-furnace production. In the next section we shall see how successful the Soviets have been in compensating for the decline in ore grades by means of its enrichment.

Problems in Iron-Ore Processing for Metallurgical Production

Ore Enrichment

Expanding utilization of low-grade ores naturally increases the importance of ore enrichment, that is, its preparation for use in blast-furnace smelting. Increasing the iron content in the blast-furnace charge—one of the most important conditions for increasing its productivity—is achieved by the development of enrichment processes, that is, improvement of the technology of enrichment processes and expanding the degree to which this is applied. The economic effectiveness of expenditures on enrichment, manifested in the intensification of blast-furnace smelting and in improving the quality of pig iron, are an axiom in the metallurgical industry. The experience of Soviet blast furnaces shows that raising the iron content in the charge by 1 percent raises its productivity by 2.0–2.5 percent and reduces the specific expenditure on coke by at least 2 percent.[82]

Hence the role of ore enrichment and its absolute priority in development, especially given the increasing reduction in the useful component in ores being mined in the USSR, are perfectly obvious. To determine how successfully enrichment processes function, one should consider the following indicators:

1. The average iron content utilized in ore prepared for use in blast furnaces

TABLE 5.7
Development and results of iron-ore enrichment in the USSR[83]

| | Actual | | | Plan |
	1970	1975	1980	1980
Total raw ore mined (millions of tons)	354.1	440.3	482.0	556.0
Raw ores sent for enrichment (millions of tons)	280.8	359.4	424.7	481.0
percent of total mined	79.3	81.6	88.2	
Production of commercial ore (millions of tons)	197.3	234.9	244.7	274.6
Production of ore concentrate (millions of tons)	120.8	151.0	176.2	201.5
Concentrate as % of commercial ore	62.0	65.1	72.0	
Iron content percentages				
total raw ore	37.3	36.3	34.7	
commercial ore	58.8	59.3	58.9	
concentrates	61.8	62.4	62.3	
Concentrate with iron content over 65%				
total production (millions of tons)	40.3	75.0	72.5	106.0
percent of total concentrate	33.4	49.6	41.2	

2. The share of concentrates in the ore prepared for smelting
3. The iron content of concentrates
4. The production of concentrates with a high iron content (defined as 65 percent by Soviet standards) and its share of total concentrate production

The dynamic development in all these areas is charted in Table 5.7.

The data in Table 5.7 enable one to draw the following conclusions about the supply of Soviet ferrous metallurgy with iron ore.

The Quantitative Aspect

In general, for the decade of the 1970s, growth occurred in all forms of ore production. The tempo between the first and second half of the 1970s, however, was fundamentally different: in the second half it was substantially lower than in the first. A circumstance of particular importance is the significant underfulfillment of plan objectives in the ninth five-year plan (1976–80) for the production of ores and concentrates, including that of the highest grade. Consequently, the mining industry failed to supply ferrous metallurgy with iron ore in the planned volume.

The Qualitative Aspect

The iron content of ore sent for blast-furnace production declined in the second half of the 1970s. Consequently, the quality of the iron ore received by ferrous metallurgical plants in this period worsened. The level of enrichment depends heavily on the degree of uniformity of the iron ores sent for processing. The more carefully the chemical, granular, and mineralogical composition of the ores is controlled, the more effective the process of enrichment; the degree of iron extraction is higher and the consistency of product quality in the enriched iron-ore concentrate is higher. These are all extremely important conditions for economic efficiency in the blast-furnace and steel-smelting processes. The way ore composition is standardized is through repeated crushing, sorting, and blending together of the fractions. The machinery available in the USSR, however, does not permit this processing to be performed at the proper level. As a consequence, the iron content in ore deliveries can vary as much as +1−−2.0 percent (by contrast, this figure is only +0.2 percent in Japan and +0.25 percent in the United States).[84] The problem of neutralizing the ore composition is aggravated by the fact that each metallurgical plant in the Soviet Union receives its ores from different deposits, and the diversity in ore content is continually increasing.

The increasing demand for ore enrichment and the corresponding increase in the burden on enrichment plants is not met by an increase in the supply of machinery and equipment. The equipment in enrichment enterprises is in a state of extreme exhaustion and is poorly maintained because of the shortage of spare parts. The machine construction for enrichment enterprises is lagging farther and farther behind the development of enrichment production; in 1976–80 only 70 percent of the total demand for enrichment and crushing machinery was produced. Moreover, the quality of the machinery that was produced, as well as its productivity, does not correspond to contemporary standards.[85]

In 1981–85 the economic plan called for a 20 percent increase in the production of enriched ore. According to the calculations of the Academy of Sciences, fulfillment of this plan by 1985 would require a 200 percent increase in the production of machinery for enrichment plants.[86] To secure such an increase in production, it would be necessary to increase by 300 percent the existing capacities for the production of enrichment machinery. All this, of course, is simply unrealistic. Enrichment of lower-grade types of ore demands the production of new forms of enrichment machinery, but a significant proportion of such machinery is not even manufactured in the

USSR. Specialized plants for the production of enrichment machinery have not been constructed in the USSR over the course of a long period.

Therefore, the enrichment division of the iron and steel industry is not coping with the task of supplying the blast-furnace state with raw materials of the requisite quality. Its capacities and equipment simply do not correspond to the assigned task. It is not in a condition to process the massive and increasing volume of ore being sent for enrichment, which is of steadily declining iron content and is inadequately prepared (that is, insufficiently standardized in its composition) for the very process of enrichment.

In the above discussion of the causes for the increasing quantitative and qualitative demands for ore enrichment, one important factor that lies outside objective matters was omitted: the deliberate degradation of ore quality, which creates a significant supplementary burden for the enrichment sector. The essence of this phenomenon is that the mining enterprise has no vested interest in selective mining of ore—that is, ore with better qualitative characteristics. On the contrary, it is interested in the very opposite. Apropos of this problem, one of the leading Soviet specialists in the field of ore deposit exploitation, A. Yanshin, wrote: "In the race for the notorious gross output, the leaders of mining enterprises permit the excavation of poor ores along with rich ones. The result is the so-called 'impoverishment' of rich ores, that is, they are polluted with useless rock and the iron content in them is artificially lowered."[87]

The natural attempt of mining enterprises to exploit an existing mixture of rich and poor ores, which is not only simpler but also in many respects more economical, evokes no opposition from the higher organizations responsible for supervising them. Moreover, their interests apparently coincide here. An index of the ministry's activity—along with the production of pig iron, steel, and rolled metal—is also the volume of iron ore production. The production of iron ore stands, in Soviet planning and Soviet statistics, as one of the basic forms of industrial production, according to which the achievements of the USSR in this area are judged. In an effort to demonstrate these achievements, both the Ministry of Ferrous Metallurgy and Gosplan seek to create an optimistic picture of production in iron ore. And this induces them to close their eyes to the "impoverishment" of ores in the course of the mining process.

At the present time, in almost all the iron-ore deposits of the

Urals, Kazakhstan, and Siberia, geologists give a gross assessment of the geological, economic, and technical characteristics of the ore; that is, they calculate the average of reserves and the average of iron content for rich ores and poor ores together.[88] Previously, these were distinguished from each other and calculated separately. That change in approach to the assessment of reserves could only have been done by order of the Ministry of Ferrous Metallurgy and Gosplan.

The peculiarity of the situation rests in the fact that the Ministry is simultaneously interested in improving the quality of iron-ore concentrates for blast-furnace production *and* in increasing the production of iron ore, with priority given to the quantitative indicators over qualitative ones. It is possible to reconcile this contradiction only at the stage of enrichment, but the burden placed on this sector simply exceeds its real capacities. Lacking the possibility to provide enrichment enterprises with equipment in the proper scale to accord with its demands, failing to invest sufficiently in the support of existing or creation of new capacities for enrichment, the Ministry and Gosplan are not alleviating the burden placed on this sector but, on the contrary, have made it significantly worse. At the same time, the leadership of ferrous metallurgy overemphasizes the problems connected with equipment, the inadequate development of enrichment machinery (which, however, does correspond to reality)—in a word, all that does not pertain to their responsibility. Hence they completely conceal internal factors, among them one of the most important, the deliberate policy of degrading high-quality ore with others of inferior quality.

Agglomeration

A special problem is presented by the final stage of preparing the ores in the metallurgical process—sintering and pelleting.

The technological characteristics of the relatively low-grade ores (chiefly magnetite quartzites), whose share in Soviet iron-ore mining is steadily increasing, require a finer crushing procedure in the enrichment process. At the same time, the finer the crushing of the enriched concentrate in this process, the more difficult becomes its transportation and use in the blast-furnace process. Therefore expansion of the dimensions of the extraction of low-grade iron ores in the USSR and, accordingly, the increasing dimension of its enrichment have demanded a corresponding development in the final stage of ore preparation—conversion of the iron-ore concentrate into sinter and pellets.

In 1980 the share of raw materials sintered and pelleted constituted more than 90 percent of the ores used in the blast-furnace charges in the USSR, and in the judgment of experts this will increase still more.[89]

In the 1960s and 1970s the Soviet Union intensively developed the traditional technology for ore agglomeration—sintering. The massive use of sinter in blast-furnace smelting led to a significant increase in the productivity of furnaces (14–16 percent), to a reduction in the use of coke per ton of pig iron (13–14 percent), and therefore to a reduction in the production costs for pig iron.[90]

By the end of the 1960s the experience of industrially advanced countries in the intensification of blast-furnace production through use of a higher-quality product of enrichment—the pellet—raised the question of the necessity of such production for Soviet ferrous metallurgy. But transition to this higher qualitative stage for preparing raw iron ore proceeded far less successfully. The program planned for the replacement of sinters with pellets on a broad scale in the blast-furnace charge was not fulfilled.

Although, as Table 5.8 demonstrates, a significant increase in pellet production was attained in the 1970s, their share in blast-furnace charges had still not exceeded 30 percent in the early 1980s. In the industrially advanced countries, by contrast, the proportion was far higher.[91] Consequently, Soviet ferrous metallurgy is far from finished utilizing the possibilities of higher production of pig iron presented by the substitution of pellets for sinter. The production of pellets occupies the center of attention of the leadership in Soviet ferrous metallurgy. At the outset of the 1980s about one-half of all metallurgical plants used pellets in blast-furnace smelting, including such larger ones as Magnitogorsk, Krivoi Rog, Novolipetsk, and Cherepovets. Experience in the application of pellets in Soviet plants, however, has brought disillusioning results because of their low quality (above all, their inadequate physical solidity, which has adversely affected the stability of processes in blast-furnace smelting). For the same reason, the effect of the application of this advanced form of iron-ore material has been diminished sharply.

The necessity of raising the quality pertains not only to pellets but also, in no less measure, to sinter, which remains the primary form

TABLE 5.8
Production of iron-ore sinter and pellet in the USSR (in tons)[93]

	1950	1955	1960	1965	1970	1975	1980
Sinter	12.0	33.8	65.1	111.4	138.2	151.0	154.4
Pellet	—	—	—	0.3	10.6	27.2	50.4
TOTAL	12.0	33.8	65.1	111.7	148.8	178.2	204.8

of iron-ore agglomerate prepared for blast-furnace production (see Table 5.8). The majority of Soviet agglomeration plants are constructed according to outmoded schemata, which do not allow for the necessary neutralization of the charge, the cooling and crushing of the agglomerate. One of the leaders of Soviet ferrous metallurgy, V. Vanchikov, characterized the condition of agglomerate production in this way: "Agglomeration plants in many metallurgical plants are in a dilapidated condition, the time schedules for the repair of machinery are systematically violated, the technological regime of production is violated, and the quality of the agglomerate is inferior."[92]

Replacement of Pig Iron with Scrap

How will the iron-ore situation develop in the future? Should one anticipate an improvement or will the dynamics delineated here intensify and make the supply of iron-ore materials more and more difficult to come by for metallurgical plants?

One should not expect an expansion of capacities for the extraction and, more important, the enrichment of iron ore, an accelerated renewal of machinery for this sector, since like ferrous metallurgy in general, and indeed the entire Soviet economy, this sector will continue to operate under conditions of severely limited investment in the foreseeable future (till the end of the 1980s). This pertains as well to industries that produce machines and equipment for the mining and enrichment of iron ores. (Problems of investment will be treated below.)

Can one expect an amelioration of the tense situation with ores as a result of reduced demand? This depends on changes in the demand for pig iron, which in turn depend on: (a) changes in demand for steel; or (b) the degree of replacement of pig iron with scrap in steel-smelting production.

Based on the conclusions presented in this book, there is clearly no reason to expect a reduction in the demand for steel in the Soviet economy.

As far as the replacement of pig iron with scrap is concerned, it would be worthwhile to examine this in detail, although it has already been partially discussed (see Chapter 3). That discussion concerned the technological aspects of the scrap problem; here we shall briefly analyze the situation with regard to the use of scrap from an economic perspective.

The effectiveness of replacing pig iron with scrap should be viewed from a much broader economic perspective, not just from the point of view of alleviating the excessive burden on iron-ore production. Such a substitution has the following advantages:

> Reduction of dependence of ferrous metallurgy on the raw mineral basis and saving of irreplaceable reserves of high-quality ores (1 ton of scrap permits the conservation of 3.8 tons of raw iron ore and other ores that are difficult to mine)
>
> The conservation of energy resources (1 ton of scrap conserves 1.5 tons of coking coal)
>
> Reduction of the enormous capital investments to sustain and develop the iron-ore industry, which is especially important at present, given the contemporary decline in investment in the Soviet economy and the necessity of diverting investments from primary industries to high technology (a subject that will be examined in greater detail in Chapter 6)
>
> Reduction of the negative ecological consequences of metallurgical production (the use of scrap in lieu of pig iron will substantially reduce—by several fold—discharges into the atmosphere and water pollution)
>
> Some compensation for the increased price of iron-ore raw materials, related to natural factors and regional advances (in the 1960s and 1970s the average annual tempos for increased costs of raw ores were 3.7 percent under conditions of open-pit mining and 4.2 percent for underground mining)[94]
>
> Reduction of labor expenditures (use of scrap instead of pig iron saves 25–28 man-hours for the smelting of 1 ton of steel)
>
> Reduction of the excessive burdens on the already crisis-laden system of railway transportation (the delivery of scrap requires far less transportation services than that required for iron ore)

> The creation of greater possibilities for a more flexible territorial
> distribution of capacities for steel-smelting production independently
> of direct ties to an iron-ore base and deposits of coking coals

Notwithstanding all these advantages for growth tempos, however, use of scrap in the USSR declined from 22 percent in the first half of the 1970s to 5–6 percent in the second half of that decade.[95]

Utilization of scrap depends on several factors: (a) the availability of this resource; (b) the technological structure of steel smelting; and (c) the vested interest of enterprises and the Ministry of Ferrous Metallurgy in replacement of pig iron with scrap.

Creation of scrap resources, to begin with, depends on a series of factors. In the judgment of Soviet experts, in the not too distant future the USSR will lead the world in terms of the scale of its metal resources, which by the end of the 1970s equaled about 1.5 billion tons.[96] This gives us some notion of the potential resources of scrap. The wasteful expenditure of metal and the enormous tailings during its processing also contribute to the growth of this resource. But on the other hand, the low tempo for the depreciation and replacement of machinery and equipment retards the accumulation of scrap. For the period 1970–80, the scrap resources of the USSR showed virtually no growth (a mere 0.7 percent).[97] According to the calculations of Soviet experts, the tempo of growth of scrap resources in the 1980s will be the same as it was in the preceding decade. Thus from the point of view of resources, there is no reason to count on an acceleration in the replacement of pig iron with scrap.

Moreover, over the course of the 1960s and 1970s the expenditure of scrap per ton of charge in steel-smelting production tended to decline, while the expenditure of pig iron tended to increase, which to a significant degree is connected with the accelerated development of the basic-oxygen process of steel production, which is oriented toward higher pig-iron consumption. According to the assessment of Soviet experts, in the 1980s the expenditure of scrap per ton of charge will not rise. It is possible that there will be some decline in the share of pig iron in the steel-smelting charge, but not so much as a consequence of its replacement with scrap, as a consequence of the increased utilization of metallized pellets in the charge of electric steel-smelting production (the Novo-Oskol'skii plant, which has 150–200-ton electric furnaces). From the point of view of reducing the demand for iron ore, however, increasing the share of metallized pellets will yield nothing, since this represents nothing other than a specially processed form of iron-ore concentrate.

For the decades 1960–80 the annual tempos of growth in steel production and scrap resources composed, respectively, 4.5 percent and 4.1 percent.[98] In other words, the growth tempo for scrap resources remained behind the growth tempo in steel production. This correlation has remained, apparently, in the 1980s. The problem of scrap consists not only in insufficient growth of its resources, but also in its low quality. The quality of scrap used in steel-smelting production is steadily declining. This is reflected in the increasing role of scrap requiring preparation, and in the increase in its impurities with nonferrous metals and other debris. Thus for 1970–80, the share of scrap requiring processing rose from 63 percent to 66 percent, the content of nonferrous metals in it rose from 14 percent to 22 percent, and the waste content increased from 1.8 percent to 2.1 percent.[99]

In Chapter 3 we examined the dependence of scrap consumption on the correlation of open-hearth, basic-oxygen process, and electric steel-smelting technology in steel-smelting production. Under the technological structure for steel smelting that exists in the early 1980s, 65 percent of the scrap consumption goes for open-hearth production, 15 percent for basic-oxygen process, and 20 percent for electric steel-smelting production.[100]

According to the conceptions of development of Soviet ferrous metallurgy, plans are being laid to change the correlation between open-hearth and basic-oxygen process technologies in favor of the latter. Insofar as the open-hearth method of steel smelting consumes twice as much scrap for 1 ton of steel, this change (if it occurs) will lead to a substantial reduction in scrap consumption. Although a surpassing growth in electric steel smelting (which most heavily consumes scrap) is also planned, its share in the total production of steel became relatively small (13–15 percent), and some expansion will not substantially affect the consumption of scrap, given the effect exerted by the growth of the basic-oxygen process technology. The relation of the ministry and Gosplan to expanding the potential use of scrap is graphically demonstrated in the allocation of investments in this sector: it receives only 1.5 percent[101] (according to other sources, 0.2 percent)[102] of the investment allocated for the development of metallurgy—and this at a time when 30 percent is directed toward expansion of the iron-ore base.[103]

In the expanded utilization of scrap in lieu of pig iron, the metallurgical plants themselves have no vested interest, which is explained by the inadequately low price of scrap. The average ratio between the price of scrap and the production cost of pig iron before 1982 was 0.77, and after the price reform of 1982 it declined to 0.6. But this difference is not sufficient to stimulate plants to replace pig iron with scrap. By comparison, in the industrially advanced states of the West the analogous ratio does not exceed 0.5 and tends to decline.[104]

The gap between prices of scrap and pig iron in the USSR does not secure a reduction in production costs of steel through a higher utilization of scrap in the charge. Moreover, in a series of cases the production costs of steel even increase through the expanded use of fuel in the smelting of scrap in open-hearth production. But the chief negative consequence of the expanded content of scrap in the charge is the prolonged time required for smelting of the steel, which negatively affects all forms of production expenditures (wages, depreciation, etc.).[105] One should not regard this as an abnormal phenomenon. It is characteristic of Soviet steel-smelting complexes.

At the present time, Soviet metallurgical plants are interested in the largest possible increase in the share of pig iron in steel-smelting charges, since one thereby obtains for any given capacity both a larger volume of steel and a lower production cost.

Therefore, there is no reason to assume that scrap will displace pig iron in the steel-smelting charge. There is sufficient reason to foresee a growth in demand for pig iron and, hence, for iron ore.

The real iron-ore base of the USSR is capable of producing 259 million tons of pig iron per annum—almost 2.5 times more than is actually produced at the present time.[106] Hence Soviet ferrous metallurgy's supply of its own iron-ore resources is more than enough to meet the demands of current production, since it is available in virtually unlimited amounts for this growth. And given this supply of raw iron ore, there is a low utilization of the blast-furnace capacities because, as the deputy chairman of Gosplan, V. Vanchikov, observed: "The metallurgical plants have virtually no normal reserves of iron ore in storage"[107]—in other words, because of the shortage of raw iron ore. The quality of iron ore sent for metallurgical production is also declining. The insufficient supply of metallurgical plants with iron ore and the reduction in its quality characteristics are explained, above all, by the poor organization of labor and the low technological level employed in exploiting the iron-ore deposits, and also by the discrepancy between the machinery base of mining enterprises and the dimensions and growing complexities involved in the extraction and enrichment of ores.

Conditions for the functioning of iron-ore industries will, it seems, not improve in the immediate future for the following reasons:

> The demand for iron ore will continue to rise.
>
> The iron content in mine ore in the main iron-ore basins (except the Kursk Magnetic Anomaly, where the exploitation of rich ore deposits is expected) will continue to decline,[108] and hence the burden on enrichment, exceeding its real possibilities, will continue to grow.
>
> Accelerated renewal of machinery and equipment in iron-ore enterprises, and the introduction of new technologies—to judge from the condition of the machine-building sectors that produce mining and enrichment machines—will occur.

The condition of the investment sphere of the economy, which aims toward a redistribution of investment resources both in industry as a whole and within ferrous metallurgy in particular, gives no grounds to expect an increased investment in the iron-ore industry. A reduction in investment activity in recent years has led to the sharp decline in the introduction of production capacities in the production of iron ores: for 1981–85, compared to the preceding five-year period (1976–80), the decline in introduction of new capacities represented a reduction from 134 million tons to 69 million tons.[109]

The decline in productivity in existing open-pit and underground mines, and the reduction in the introduction of new production capacities, create dismal prospects for improving the production of iron ore. Episodic surges may occur, but in general one should expect continuing stagnation in the production of iron-ore raw materials and a continuing deterioration in its supplies for metallurgical plants.

CHAPTER 6

Investment

In the twelfth five-year plan, adopted by the Twenty-seventh CPSU Congress, the chief political decision underlying this plan—the relative shares of national income to be distributed to current consumption and to investment—must have been reached under truly dramatic circumstances. The preceding five-year plan (1981–85) had explicitly targeted an increase in the share of the consumption fund, at the expense of investment.[1] But when anticipated revitalization and increased effectiveness in the investment sphere did not materialize, it proved necessary to increase investments and make cutbacks in consumption. The share accorded to consumption declined from 76 percent in 1980 to 73 percent in 1985. The share of investment going to industries in "Group B" (those producing consumer goods), which was supposed to rise in 1981–85, sank to a postwar low of 4 percent, while the share of investment going to "Group A" industries (those manufacturing producer goods) was at 32 percent. The share of investment in housing construction, health care, trade, and other social and consumer sectors of the Soviet economy fell from 35.4 percent of total investment in 1966–70 to 30 percent in 1981–85.[2]

It was against this backdrop that the Soviet leadership set out its priorities for the twelfth five-year plan. In the realm of macroeconomic choices there appeared to be essentially two alternative courses to be pursued.

The regime could reduce the growth of investment and restructure industry by focusing investment on one sector at the expense of others (on machine building, at the expense of extractive industry, including the oil and gas sectors). Under these conditions, economic growth would—in the short term—decelerate even more substantially. But the concept would be to "retreat now in order to move ahead later."

Or the leadership could increase investment in heavy industry across the board at the expense of consumption and increase restructive industry amid a simultaneous growth of overall production.

In 1982 Vadim Kirichenko, director of a Gosplan research institute, observed that "the time has finally come to make a choice between alternative possibilities in investment policy: either to preserve the tendency to reduce the tempo of increases in capital investment, or . . . shift to a regime of increased investment activity. The turning point in this respect should be the twelfth five-year plan."[3]

In February 1984 Kirichenko insisted on the need to increase the growth of investments in the twelfth five-year plan. In contrast, academician Aganbegyan declared in June that the growth of investment in the twelfth five-year plan would be half that registered in the eleventh.[4] Clearly a debate had commenced. On one side were adherents of the traditional hard line, who insisted on increasing investment at the expense of consumption. On the other side were those who postulated the need for a "radical reform," one that could activate the reserves of the economy. This could raise productivity without increasing investment and thereby permit the maintenance or even raising of the level of consumption, which would in turn make more realistic the effort to expand the use of material incentives to spur effective economic performance.

In a June 1985 speech, Gorbachev seemed to evade this critical issue, although his discussion of various "maneuvers" or changes in the structure of investments could be construed as favoring the reformist approach.[5] But in the fall of 1985—during the final stages of preparation of the twelfth five-year plan—forces favorable to the conservatives appeared to gain the ascendancy. And the new Soviet government team of Premier Nikolay Ryzhkov and Gosplan Chairman Nikolay Talyzin clearly rejected the course of reform and embarked on the second alternative. As Ryzhkov put it at the congress:

> Given its commitment to a course of accelerating [economic growth], the Central Committee of the CPSU has deemed it expedient to increase the tempo of growth of productive capital investment in the twelfth five-year plan. Naturally, this entails certain changes in the proportions of distribution of national income—an increase in the share of accumulation [that is—investment]. This tack is necessary in order to attain both current and strategic goals. In the next [stage] there is the intention to stabilize or even slightly reduce the share of accumulation.[6]

The stress on "accumulation" implied a reduction in the share of consumption, an unpalatable fact Ryzhkov preferred not to state directly.

Two Schools of Thought in Investment Strategy

In theory and practice, Soviet planning gives primary attention to its investment policy for capital formation. The problems of labor and natural resources, by contrast, have always been matters of secondary importance for Soviet economic textbooks and the methodological instructions from Gosplan for the preparation of the five-year plan.

And now, despite the worsening deficit in the labor force and mounting difficulties in the supply of raw materials and labor, the traditional stress on investment in fixed capital has changed but little. The deficit in labor and natural resources is treated as something inevitable, something that has objective causes, and something against which it is simply impossible to fight. The labor shortage is attributed to demographic decline, which, in turn, is purportedly just a consequence of World War II. The deficiencies in natural resources are ascribed to the exhaustion of old deposits in the western regions of the country (oil in Azerbaydjan and the Volga region, coal in the Donets basin, iron ore in the Urals) and the consequent relocation of the fuel and raw material basis of the country to eastern regions, where the new production entails difficulties in the preliminary conquest of new territories under severe climatic conditions.

The people involved in the theory and practice of Soviet economic planning seek to extricate themselves from this situation by optimizing the effectiveness of their investment policies. But this issue has come to provoke serious disagreements among leading experts in the USSR. The key problem is whether, under conditions of reduced investment, one can avoid a further slowdown in economic growth. Let us examine, if only briefly, the two main schools of opinion.

One side[7] holds a view that in essence justifies the slower tempo in investment growth. The argument here runs as follows: the USSR has created enormous fixed capital and productive capacities, and although the investment curve is being reduced, it still has significant reserves in the form of more efficient use of existing productive capacity. Tapping these reserves, moreover, does not require so significant an outlay in new investment. In effect, this school wants to direct investment toward the modernization of existing enterprises and away from increasing the basic capital resources through the construction of renovated enterprises. This policy prescribes an accelerated writeoff of old equipment and the acquisition of new, more modern replacements. A diminished investment curve is fully justified from the point of view of investment theory. Moreover, it should stimulate Soviet economic managers to pursue a more economic and effective utilization of the investment funds that the state does allot.

The opposing school[8] argues that the maximum utilization of existing productive potential reached its outer limits in the mid-1970s. Evidence for that is found in the decline in the use of productive capacity in the late 1970s and early 1980s; one simply cannot squeeze any more juice out of this lemon. Hence unless the negative investment trend is overcome, there is no possibility of preventing a further decline in growth rates for production and national income—and all the consequences that this entails. It therefore seems justified to conclude that we are about to witness, for the first time since the 1920s, a confrontation within the Soviet elites over a cardinal economic issue: investment policy.

Inflation in Investment

What are the real dynamics of investment in the current period? According to official statistics, the average rate of growth in 1981–85 was 3.5 percent.[9] But does this figure take inflation into account? Inflation is, after all, a fact of life in the Soviet economy. It is to be found in both the production and consumption spheres of the economy. One of the leading economists of the Institute for Industrial Economics, Konstantin Val'tukh, on the basis of his calculations came to the conclusion that, compared to 1971–75, in the period 1976–80 "there occurred an absolute reduction in productive capital investments *in real terms*" (emphasis added).[10] Evidently, from this one can infer that, once inflation is taken into account, investments declined.

To answer the question of whether the planned economic development can be achieved under existing investment possibilities, one must consider the actual and anticipated changes in capital intensity resulting from current and planned investment activities. The growing trend toward capital intensity is a characteristic feature of development in Soviet industry over the course of at least the last twenty-five years. In the 1970s the capital intensity of newly introduced capacities rose sharply. The per annum growth rates of capital intensity for the category of basic industrial sectors (ferrous metallurgy, machine building, chemical, coal, construction materials) rose from 5 percent in 1971–75 to 7.4 percent in 1976–80 and, judging by some direct and indirect indicators, has continued to rise in the 1980s.[11] Since the growth tempo for capital intensity exceeds the growth tempo for capital investment, it naturally follows that the quantity of new enterprises and capacities is curtailed.

The research conducted by one of the leading Soviet experts in the investment sphere, Vladimir Fal'tsman (Central Economic-Mathematics Institute, Moscow), has established that the capital intensity of new productive capacity is increased irrespective of any improvement in the quality of production obtained from these new capacities.[12] In other words, if one converts the production obtained to a single qualitative equivalent, then one observes a growth in capital intensity.

The growth in capital intensity of new productive capacities, to a certain degree, is linked to such objective phenomena in the economic development of the USSR as the mechanization of manual labor and the automatization of technological processes (entailing the substitution of capital for labor), the relocation of extractive industry to new regions of the east and northeast (and the consequent need to assimilate new territories and under adverse climatic conditions), and increased expenditure on environmental conservation. To a large degree the growth of capital intensity is explained by the accelerating unit cost of productivity in new machinery. Thus between 1971–75 and 1976–80, expenditures for equipment acquisition (per unit of productive capacity—for example, per ton of steel, kilowatt of electrical energy, cubic meters of reinforced concrete) rose by 72 percent, whereas construction costs rose by only 23 percent.[13]

According to Fal'tsman, one of the basic reasons for the higher costs of equipment is the higher costs per unit of productivity. Moreover, if one sets 100 as the total increase in costs, then the Soviet share of this increase is 34 percent, while 66 percent is attributable to the increased volume and cost of equipment purchased abroad.[14] One of the causes of this, in turn, is the rising cost of imported technology.

Leaving aside the question of the impact of foreign technology, let us consider the rising cost of Soviet machinery. According to calculations made by Fal'tsman, who made an analysis of a representative sample, the cost of domestic machinery (per unit of productivity) rose by 15 percent between 1971–75 and 1976–80—compared to just a 7 percent increase from 1966–70 to 1971–75.[15]

The rising equipment cost per unit of productivity is a complicated phenomenon, resulting from both inflation and objective factors (expenditures to increase labor productivity, to improve quality of production, to economize on raw materials and fuel). Technological progress in Soviet machine building is directed not so much toward labor productivity as toward reduced consumption of fuel, raw materials, and primary industrial products. A Central Statistical Administration study of a series of machine-building sectors found that two-thirds of the real gain in technological progress is directed toward the conservation of resources, only one-third toward higher labor productivity.[16]

The theory and practice of accounting for expenditures on Soviet industrial production does not make it possible to calculate the degree to which the price increase of manufactured machinery is justified by an increase in their productive capacity or qualitative improvement. The absence of established methods to determine prices of production, which would correspond to changes in their real economic utility (in terms of their consumption characteristics), enables machine-building enterprises to make unjustified increases in the price of their machinery.

As is well known, prices of machinery produced in the USSR are regulated by the State Pricing Committee and published in official price lists. As production of machine building improves, the prices are supposed to be adjusted (that is, raised). In practice, however, this adjustment requires numerous technical and bureaucratic approvals, and hence significantly lags behind the production of the modified equipment (one or two years, and sometimes more). In the period prior to the formal issuance of new prices on the official price list, "temporary prices" are in effect, and these are in large measure set arbitrarily. In many cases these prices include a substantial element of pure inflation.

A still greater opportunity for unjustified price increases exists when prices are set for the production of nonstandardized and custom machinery as an individual unit or in small series, for these are not included in the official price lists. The share of such machinery in total Soviet machine building is 42–50 percent.[17] In effect, the price of such machinery is set by an agreement between the producer and the customer. In addition, the basis of such price agreements is the cost of equipment more or less similar in consumption purpose and found on the price list; this price is then adjusted to take into account the real economic return obtained through utilization of the new, modified machine. A selective study by the State Pricing Committee found that the economic return, as calculated by the machine-building enterprise, is overstated by 30–50 percent (sometimes several times) for the production of such equipment.[18] This unjustified, arbitrary increase of the price of equipment not on the price lists is a key cause of inflation in machinery.

Just because it is impossible to determine the expenditures connected with the increase in real economic utility, it does not follow that this always leads to an increase in prices. In a series of cases the contrary occurs. But the factual data obtained through selective studies by the State Pricing Committee show that unjustified price increases do predominate. A study of seven thousand enterprises in 1979 showed that almost half of them raised the prices on what they produced. The State Pricing Committee established that, in the sectors of machine building it had checked, as a whole prices had been raised 56–75 percent. On the basis of the spot check alone, the State Pricing Committee reduced prices of machine-building production by 1.5 billion rubles.[19]

The State Pricing Committee tries to slow down the rising cost of new and, especially, nonstandard equipment by creating what are known as "limit prices." Limit prices, however, cannot restrain the rapidly rising costs of equipment. In the 1981 decree of the CPSU Central Committee and USSR Council of Ministers, "On Measures to Further Improve Project-Estimating Work," the State Pricing Committee, along with the machine-building ministries, was obligated to work out limit prices for equipment on a regular basis—a ceiling above which the price of a certain piece of equipment or machinery is not allowed to rise. These prices, however, have not yet been calculated. This is because, first, a sufficiently reliable methodological basis for these calculations has not yet been drawn up; and second, because it is dangerous to deprive machine manufacturers of additional material incentives. Instead of introducing limitations on price rises, machine-building enterprises received the right—currently on an experimental basis—to impose a 30 percent rise on the price of the machines they produce if they are deemed to be "highly effective."[20]

This was done to stimulate the production of more effective technology, but given the lack of clarity in the definitions and the poorly developed techniques for establishing the effectiveness of new technology, these sorts of incentives for manufacturers of machinery merely provide them with additional opportunities to inflate their prices.

Thus there is good reason to believe that the data provided in Soviet statistical publications on the growth of capital investment (in adjusted prices) by no means take the real rate of investment fully into account. But if these data are corrected, then apparently Konstantin Val'tukh's assertion about the cessation of investment growth in the USSR is fully confirmed.

Reallocation of Investment from Expansion to Replacement

According to the twelfth five-year plan, fixed capital replacement rates will double by 1990 (from 3 percent in 1985 to 6 percent in 1990).[21] Gorbachev announced that the focus of investment policy will shift from "expansion of industrial fixed capital to its modernization."[22] Old equipment should be replaced with the most modern machinery designed to meet the highest technological standards in the world. Implementation of this program requires enormous investment in upgrading of existing capacities and acquisition of new technologies.

Thus important decisions, which at the planning stage constitute the basis for industrial modernization, have been made. But what are the real conditions for their implementations? Does the investment situation in the Soviet industry make it possible to allocate investment to upgrading of existing capacities? Will this much larger amount of investment be used effectively? Is there a strong enough base that could absorb it? Can we expect the machine-building sector to accomplish the tasks facing it?

Giving priority to investment in upgrading of existing capacities (not construction of new ones, as was done during the eleven preceding five-year plan periods) is the fundamental precondition for the implementation of the modernization program. In his report to the Twenty-seventh Party Congress, Prime Minister Nikolay Ryzhkov stated that "a characteristic feature of the new five-year plan is the emphasis on technological rearmament and reconstruction of existing production. The share of capital investment allocated to this purpose will increase from 37 percent in 1985 to 50 percent in 1990. In those branches and regions where capital has become especially obsolete, this number will be even higher."[23]

The course toward priority for investment in upgrading of existing capacities and, accordingly, reduction of the share of new construction was adopted by the Soviet leadership in the early 1970s. But despite the decisions of the Twenty-fourth, fifth, and sixth Party Congresses, and despite the persisting calls to channel the flow of investment into reconstruction and modernization, the share of new construction remained 60 percent in 1985.[24] Whereas in the previous five-year plan period (1981–85), based on published statistics, the share of reconstruction and modernization grew by six percentage points (from 31.6 percent to 37.5 percent), the current five-year plan provides for a 13 percent increase.[25] Achieving this number will require enormous changes in the entire investment sphere of the economy. But first, how accurate is the picture reflected in official Soviet statistics?

One of the most sophisticated specialists in the area of investment statistics, Delez Palterovich of the Institute of Economics of the Soviet Academy of Sciences, hinted in November 1986 that enterprises falsify information concerning investment in modernization. They report construction of new capacities as modernization and reconstruction.[26] Therefore, it is likely that the official Soviet indicators of the share of investment in modernization are higher than the reality.

It should be noted that the Soviet leaders appear to be sensitive to this issue. Perhaps they understand the futility of their efforts. A meeting took place in December 1986 at the Central Committee where the top leadership—M. Gorbachev, N. Ryzhkov, Ye. Ligachev, and L. Zaykov—together with the heads of industrial ministries discussed the economic results of 1986 and measures that need to be taken in order to guarantee the fulfillment of the 1987 plan. One of the issues repeatedly emphasized by the participants of the meeting was that "the bulk of capital investment should be channeled not to the construction of new capacities but to reconstruction and modernization of existing enterprises."[27]

But this direction of the investment policy has met with opposition of Soviet scholars. The December 1986 issue of the leading economic journal, *Voprosy ekonomiki,* contained an article written by a recognized authority in the field of investment planning, Lyudmila Smyshlyayeva. She referred to the proposal to increase significantly the share of investment allocated to reconstruction and modernization as inappropriate.[28] Another prominent expert, L. Braginskiy, wrote in October 1986 in the party's principal ideological journal, *Kommunist,* that "a sharp counterpoising of two basic trends in capital investment—reconstruction and new construction—is economically unfounded."[29]

In the pre-Gorbachev years Soviet experts refrained from criticizing the investment policy of the leadership. But today, in the period of openness, or "glasnost'," some economists feel brave enough to speak out on the subject.

At first glance the effectiveness of such a course of reconstruction seems fully cogent: the time period for obtaining results is shortened and thereby the circulation of capital is accelerated; less is expended for the increase in capacity per unit; the writing off of old technology and its replacement by new machinery is speeded up. All these benefits, however, have a short-term character. From the point of view of long-term results, such a policy has a number of serious negative consequences. As always, when a campaign like this is conducted in the USSR, the limits of economic expediency are ignored. The possibilities for economically effective renovation of many enterprises are limited. From the standpoint of the development of the country's economy as a whole, focusing investment primarily on renovation of existing enterprises—the overwhelming share of which are located in the western regions of the USSR (with exhausted natural resources, overloaded infrastructure, and ecological limitations)—will impede the regional advances that are so vital to Soviet industry. Indeed, this policy will intensify the territorial polarization of economic sectors—a manufacturing industry in the western part of the country, and an extractive industry in the east. And here one must also take into account the enormous distances and serious transportation situation. In a series of sectors of industry, it is either impossible or economically ineffective, through this policy of reconstruction and modernization, to develop new branches and production and to incorporate fundamentally new technology.

Thus the disagreement of leading economic scholars with the leadership's policy of sharp reallocation of investment has been established. Do these and other experts object to the preferential funding of modernization and reduction in the enormous volume of investment in new construction? In principle, they agree that this step is justified and even necessary. Objections are raised to the speed and scale of the implementation of such an ambitious economic plan without adequate preparations. Reading between the lines, we can see that the experts see little possibility of achieving by 1990 the planned targets for capital stock renovation on the basis of a qualitatively new technology. Few believe in the success of the reconstruction and modernization campaign under the conditions in which it is being conducted.

Gorbachev's team inherited from Brezhnev's an idealized, one-sided approach to modernization of industrial enterprises. They see its advantages but do not understand the practical aspects of its implementation given the concrete conditions of the Soviet economy.

In an ideal situation the major portion of capital investment is allocated to acquisition of new equipment and a minor part of it to reconstruction of buildings and other structures. Therefore, as a result of modernization and reconstruction, one unit of added capacity should consume much less capital than as a result of new construction. But in reality most enterprises built after the war and, especially, before the war require a radical reconstruction that is now often more expensive than new construction. It should be noted that many enterprises are located in urban areas and do not have reserve land for territorial expansion.

Proponents of rapid and comprehensive reconstruction and modernization remain undeterred by the lack of success. They attribute it to shortcomings in the work of ministries and enterprises, or individual failures of various officials, and continue to advocate this policy.

There are, however, more objective reasons for the lack of success of this program. The economy's investment sphere was totally unprepared for such a large-scale program. The corresponding scientific, design, planning, and machine-building bases were not reoriented or prepared. The construction industry was not reorganized, nor was it equipped to engage in renovations. Finally, no one established the kind of material stimulation that would compensate for running the risk of not fulfilling the production plan, with all the material consequences resulting therefrom.[30]

The latter constitutes a significant problem. Gosplan does not reduce output targets when it prepares plans for reconstruction and modernization. Indeed, it raises them. There are limits to the ability of an enterprise to function under the conditions of reconstruction when its machinery and various items of equipment are being replaced. At least a partial slowdown of production is unavoidable. In practice, however, enterprises are expected to carry out reconstruction without stopping production, the planned targets for which are not lowered. If their work absolutely must be stopped, permission to do so is sought from the highest authorities. It is practically impossible to carry out a quick and thorough reconstruction and modernization and combine it with continuity of production. The choice is clear: either the plan has to remain unfulfilled or reconstruction has to be stretched out. (Soviet planning officials even have a special term for it: "crawling reconstruction.")[31] Gosplan pressures the ministries, which in turn pressure enterprises to achieve both— plan targets and quick reconstruction. But instead of rebuilding the old structures and replacing old equipment, new shops are being built adjacent to the old ones, which in essence is construction of new capacities. This work is then reported to the central authorities as reconstruction and modernization. Enterprises simply do not have any choice.

Those who are at the top of the economic planning apparatus are not capable of dealing with the tradeoff between accelerated replacement of capital stock and output growth. At any given moment they cannot accept a decline in industrial production because day-to-day interests have always been given top priority by the Soviet leadership. The inability to accept a temporary setback for the sake of a long-term advance has been an inherent feature of the Soviet system. This is also one of the fundamental reasons why the program of industrial modernization has made little progress. But even in an ideal situation it would have been impossible to introduce within the first years of the current five-year plan period changes so deep that they would affect the entire process of investment in industry. It would entail redirecting a process with a seventy-year history and an enormous amount of inertia.

Thus sharp reduction in the introduction of new productive capacities, a shift of emphasis to the modernization of existing capacities, a jump in depreciation rates for outdated fixed capital—all have been written into the twelfth five-year plan. They connote a radical change in the economic proportions and balances that have developed over the course of half a century. Over this period, resources have been directed primarily at expanding fixed capital at the expense of replacing it. This distortion of economically justifiable proportions in the creation of fixed capital, manifested in an artificial increase in net investment, has made it possible to sustain high tempos of growth. But the price has been the accumulation of worn out machinery and old industrial plants. To overcome the inertia of this entire process would require a temporary but abrupt reduction in production and in national income. Past Soviet leaders have never been willing to accept such a decrease in national income. One can question whether Gorbachev is ready to pay this price to redeem the economic sins of his predecessors.

The Slump in Machinery Output and Depreciation Policy

An important obstacle to this path of effective renovation is the inability of Soviet machine building to supply the requisite machinery and equipment—and, especially, the high-tech and advanced technology. One of the chief problems of the Soviet economy today is the decline in the production of machinery and equipment. It is, in fact, a decline without parallel in Soviet economic history. The beginning of the 1980s was marked by a falloff in the production of turbines, locomotives, gas and oil drilling equipment, diesels, electrical motors, metal-cutting machines, and transport and construction equipment, and in a host of other important areas of machine building as well.[32]

The decline was not only quantitative but also qualitative; the number of new models of machines and equipment was reduced, and the share of new products in machine building declined.

Soviet machine building has become less and less capable of satisfying the essential demands of the economy. For example, it met only 70–72 percent of the demand for lift-transport machinery; in the case of warehouse machinery, it satisfied just 30–35 percent of industry requirements. As the president of the Soviet Academy of Sciences, A. Aleksandrov, acknowledged, domestic producers can supply only one-third of the demand for apparatus and high-tech equipment.[33]

The increasingly acute shortage of machines and equipment, as well as the industry's failure to satisfy contemporary standards, is a direct cause of the extraordinarily low rate of depreciation for worn out, outdated capital goods. The amortization reform of 1975, which reduced the normal periods of service for fixed capital, did not lead to the desired results. The writeoff of fixed capital not only failed to accelerate, but actually slowed down to no more than 1 percent per annum. The average service life for industrial equipment rose in the 1970s by 13 percent.[34]

Thus the Soviet strategy for scientific and technical progress calls for an accelerated amortization rate, the introduction of shorter service lives, and a switchover from the existing linear methods of amortizing depreciation to the accelerated method used in industrially advanced states, permitting a faster depreciation rate in the first years of service. The Soviets also specifically cite the American case, where the government encourages accelerated amortization. But as far as the Soviet Union is concerned, there is no way to think about "accelerated depreciation" if the machine-building industry is incapable of producing replacements even on the scale set by depreciation schedules issued ten years ago. And the pragmatists in Gosplan are perfectly well aware of that.

In one of his first programmatic statements, Gorbachev commented: "A primary task of the twelfth five-year plan must be a substantial increase in the coefficient of replacement of equipment."[35] A *substantial* increase, however, would only be possible if the entire amortization policy were overhauled. Would it be wise to expect such a turnaround? The system of amortization currently in force is one of the oldest procedures in Soviet economics (both theoretical and practical). Its essentials were formed by the 1920s, in

the period of industrialization, when the first plan posed the problem of the creation and accumulation of fixed capital, and not its
renewal. In those circumstances a straight-line method of writing off
capital was entirely appropriate. The maintenance of such a system
in present conditions, however, cannot be justified. In order to bring
the amortization mechanism in line with the task of speeding up the
renewal of fixed capital, which Gorbachev has urged (echoing similar calls by Brezhnev and Andropov), it will be essential to change to
a method of accelerated retirement. In addition, it should be noted
that the normative base of the amortization system (amortization
norms or normed periods of service) also fails to meet current demands. Such normatives, calculated on the basis of equipment
being operated in certain typical conditions, also have to allow for
technical progress and for the physical wear and tear of different
units of the capital stock, grouped together on the basis of their
technological characteristics. First, however, such normatives in
practice fail to allow for the individual peculiarities of such enterprises: those many factors that determine the optimal length of service of a particular type of fixed capital in a given set of technological, organizational, climatic, and economic conditions. Second,
these normatives are reviewed and corrected far too infrequently.
Thus the norms that were introduced in the 1930s continued to apply with various adjustments right up to 1963. The norms adopted
in 1963 lasted until 1975. The 1975 norms are in force up until 1988.

The introduction of new norms for amortization is preceded by a
lengthy preparatory period, involving a detailed census of the existing stock, including the determination of its technical and economic
attributes; it is followed by a revaluation of the entire mass of fixed
capital on the basis of the norms' operation at the precise moment
that the revaluation takes place. To have amortization norms in
operation for such lengthy periods in no way corresponds to the rate
of technical progress and turns the comments of Soviet leaders as to
the necessity of accelerating and expanding the rate at which old
capital is retired into mere declarations, devoid of practical significance.

The radical path for the introduction of a more dynamic amortization policy would consist of a shift to techniques of accelerated
amortization, and what sort of objections have been raised by opponents of this method?

The first objection is straightforwardly ideological, without any

practical foundations. It is advanced by the dogmatic Marxist dino-
saurs of Soviet political economy. They associate the use of techniques of accelerated amortization with the interests of capitalist
monopolies, who seek to conceal profits from taxation via amortization, and they categorically reject the possibility of using such
methods in a socialist society. For example, A. Dodonov, who may
be regarded as a representative of this school, tried to show that the
adoption of such methods "is entirely a product of the particular
circumstances of monopolistic economics, serves as a means of
freeing the monopolies from taxation, and is a way of stealing from
the working masses." Thus "this sort of operation is incompatible
with the economic conditions prevailing under socialism."[36] These
Soviet Marxist economists are, one might say, "more Catholic than
the pope." They ignore the clear warnings in the writings of Marx
against falling into the errors of a "vulgar" economist—that is, one
who "is incapable of distinguishing those forms, developing at the
very heart of the capitalist mode of production, which can be looked
at separately and independently of their antagonistic capitalist character."[37]

The opponents of the adoption of methods of accelerated amortization also raise objections of a practical character. They include,
for example, the point that an increase in total amortization in the
first few years after adopting such a method would markedly raise
production costs, thus lowering profits. It follows that there would
not be any additional effect from the appearance of large amortization sums, since these effects will be "eaten up" because of losses
arising from that part of profits left out of the overhaul. Certainly, if
the new method of calculating amortization is imposed on the old
system of normative distribution of profits, the change would have
no serious effect. A genuine change in the amortization mechanism
will take place only when the desired effects are realized, when
there will be introduced corresponding changes in the procedures
for allocating profits. There is no shortage of suggestions and ideas
on how to modernize, coordinate, and improve the efficacy of both
these spheres.

But the most important and serious hindrance to the introduction
of accelerated amortization in the Soviet economy is the inability of
Soviet machine-building and construction industries to satisfy the
demand for capital plant and equipment. That it would reduce
service lives of equipment without having a satisfactory engineering

base is confirmed by the experience of the 1975 amortization reform. The new amortization norms that the sectoral research institutes worked out (on the basis of the nature of the technology and of technical progress) contained suggestions for significant reductions in the equipment service. It was not possible to comply with these suggestions, for one could not simply write off large amounts of equipment without any possibility of replacing them. Gosplan decided to compromise: they left on one side the suggestions from the industrial sectors, but shortened to some extent the length of service. In industry as a whole the normative length of service of fixed capital was shortened from 29.0 to 25.4 years. But this was only a paper reduction: from 1971 to 1980 the average life span of machinery and equipment increased rather than fell, from 12.5 to 14.0 years, while buildings' and installations' average age rose from 36.6 to 43.1 years.[38]

There is no need to show the importance of amortization policy in economics in general, nor for the specific case of a planned economy. The leading problem for Soviet industry at the present time is to hasten the renewal of fixed capital. But Soviet amortization—the engine of capital renewal—is still set at a leisurely pace. A move to accelerated amortization would call for a significant stepping up of this work.

Attitudes toward Imported Technology

There is no reason to expect that in this decade Soviet industry will be able to accelerate the renewal of its machinery base through the efforts of its own machine-building industry. Therefore, the only available path for stopping the slide in its economy is to increase significantly its import of machinery and equipment from Western countries. And it is precisely this tendency that we have witnessed in recent years.

The forced increase in machine imports has had a negative impact on the development of the domestic machine-building industry. In particular, distrust toward equipment produced in the Soviet Union has now become deeply ingrained in the mentality of Soviet plant managers and executives. As a result, there is a distinct tendency to prefer imports, even in those cases where a Soviet equivalent is acceptable and available.

All this has aroused mounting concern in the scientific and economic establishment. At the 1982 annual meeting of the Academy of Sciences, its president, A. Aleksandrov, rebuked Soviet scholars and economic managers because "in a whole range of scientific and technical areas [they] have up to now been too easily inclined to purchase technological methods and equipment abroad. The result has been that in such areas we have not made sufficiently serious attempts to devise our own methods and equipment, or have been too slow in doing so. In our time that could all come back to haunt us."[39]

Most revealing of all, the orientation toward technological and machine imports is undermining the Soviet Union's own scientific-technical potential. Here it has been argued that, if foreign imports are avoided, this will promote domestic efforts to speed up technological progress and, ultimately, lead to an improvement in Soviet science and technology. The director of the Institute of Economics for World Socialist Systems, Oleg Bogomolov, has declared:

> In the West it has become fashionable now to exaggerate the role of imported technology in our scientific-technical development. A sober view of the situation shows, however, that socialist countries were by no means always the winner in this matter. In an effort to receive new technology as fast as possible by importing it from the West, we have sometimes inflicted unjustified harm on the development of our own research and production resources in various branches of industry. Nor should bourgeois ideologists forget that fundamentally new innovations appeared in our technology precisely at those times when the bans on technology imports were especially severe. The difficulties associated with obtaining foreign technology forced us to mobilize our own forces more fully.[40]

Still, the gap between the demands of such officially condoned patriotism and economic reality is steadily widening.

As prominent Soviet economists acknowledge, a restructuring of investment to stimulate machine building will require "a profound economic maneuver."[41] But any such maneuver will, at least in the short run, cause economic growth to slow down even further. Though such reverses will be recouped in the near future, such a maneuver seems hardly conceivable for the Soviet leadership.

Only one alternative is really left: to increase imports of Western technology. There are, of course, certain limitations to this, related in part to the need to import grain and other agricultural products. The experience of recent years, however, shows that equipment imports have been steadily rising, while agricultural imports have actually declined (notwithstanding the fact that domestic harvests have fallen short of their planned objectives). All this suggests the conclusion that the Soviet leadership will even limit grain purchases in order to increase technology and machinery imports. The longer the regime defers restructuring its investment policy to optimize the productivity of its economic structure, and the longer it waits to shift investment resources from primary to advanced industries, the more difficult it will be to halt the country's increasing dependence on Western technology and equipment. Until then, clearly the Soviet Union will not be able to avoid significantly expanding its import of technology from the advanced industrial countries. Such imports, as the criticism cited above suggests, has provoked growing opposition from certain segments of the economic and scientific establishment. But the statistics tell a different story: the economic system requires ever greater imports of Western technology and equipment.

The Diversion of Funds from Repairs to New Capacity

If in studying the investment patterns of Soviet industry we look only at capital investment planned by Gosplan and appearing in the statistics and do not look at the independent investment sphere, we significantly risk underestimating the real growth of Soviet industrial potential. This kind of investment, uncontrolled by any central planning organ, is playing an ever more important role in the growth of industrial capacity, to some extent compensating for the slump in state investment.

In Soviet industry the gap is narrowing between the volume of depreciation deductions for capital repair on the one hand and investment in plant equipment on the other. Over the period 1965–75 depreciation deductions over all industry rose, in relation to annual capital investment, by five percentage points (from 23 percent to 28 percent), while in 1975–83 they went up by nine percentage points (from 28 percent to 37 percent). In ferrous metallurgy depreciation, deductions for repair made up 4 percent of investments in 1978, but 60 percent in 1983.[42]

Major overhaul (*kapital'nyi remont* in Soviet parlance) is the sort of repair in which a piece of equipment is completely dismantled and rebuilt until there is full restoration of its working capacity and original technical specification. In many cases the cost of such overhaul exceeds that of new equipment. For this reason, many Soviet theorists are of the opinion that it would be better to dispense with such unprofitable approaches to the maintenance of productive capacity.[43]

Upgrading and expansion of fixed capital, at the expense and instead of major overhaul, is becoming more widespread, for several reasons. First, in spite of announced intentions at the beginning of the seventies to orient the greater part of investment toward upgrading and "reconstruction" of existing enterprises, the share of upgrading and reconstruction did not exceed 22 percent of all industrial investment in the early eighties, compared to 47 percent for new construction.[44]

Second, when modernization upgrading and reconstruction are carried out on the basis of centrally controlled investment funds, the resulting output gets included in output targets, whereas if it is done by enterprises with their own resources and funds destined for major overhaul, the results of these investments can be concealed, so enterprises can build up reserve capacity, which in some cases reaches considerable proportions. *Pravda* described such a situation as follows:

> Now imagine a factory director who has, say, a particular shop in very poor condition—an entire wall has to be completely rebuilt. A major overhaul? Yes. But what factory director will resist the temptation to renovate his equipment at the same time? But this is reconstruction in the guise of a major overhaul. In the final analysis, there is an increase in productive capacity not accounted for by the [central planning agency] and, as a result, not included in the plan. If the director had done the same equipment renovation under the heading "reconstruction" [that is, out of the centrally allocated investment fund—B.R.], the center would immediately increase the production quota.[45]

Third, the growing autarkical characteristics of contemporary Soviet enterprise have created a material base for self-engineered increases in productive potential, including upgrading at the expense of major overhaul. The tendency to accumulate material reserves from the beginning was dictated by the necessity to protect oneself

from the consequences of uncertain supply and the constant interruptions in the delivery of this or that productive resource. In response to the growing inefficiency of central planning and supply,
the weakening of central control, and the growth of barter, enterprise autarky is gaining ground. V. Fal'tsman of the Central Economic-Mathematics Institute of the Academy of Sciences says of
this phenomenon:

> At the present time associations and enterprises are trying to meet plan
> obligations in conditions of insufficient stability of external economic
> links. In order to increase reliability, these organizations try as much as
> possible to reduce their external exposure. Among other things, en-
> terprises want their own automobiles, repair equipment, tools and
> machinery for reconstruction, construction facilities, woodworking
> equipment, computer technology, and in the case of machine building,
> even steel-making equipment.[46]

In their drive for economic independence, industrial enterprises
try to furnish not only their own industrial goods and services but
also their own agricultural produce. Thus the industrial enterprises
of a large industrial district, Kemerovo in western Siberia—which
contains two of the most important steel plants in the Asian part of
the USSR, the Kuznetskii and the West Siberian—produce on their
own farms 20 percent of the meat of the entire district. The West
Siberian Metallurgical Factory produces for the factory cafeteria
thousands of tons of pork, vegetables, fish, and even honey on its
own land.[47] All this is produced without any capital investment
contribution from central funds, but just out of internally generated
reserves.

In conditions of extremely tight branch management, this phenomenon is abetted by the ministries, which strive to create closed
systems in the industries they run. The central government agencies
(Gosplan, Gossnab) and the Investment Bank are helpless to prevent
this spontaneous decentralization of the allocation and accumulation of material reserves. They limit themselves to noting the increasing scale of the phenomenon, as exemplified in the occasional
sample surveys.

Until recently this increased enterprise autarky was criticized as
extremely harmful to the economy—to be countered in every possible way. In practice this censure took the form of multiple regulations, preventing the enterprise from creating and developing aux-

iliary services with no direct technical connection with the main function of the enterprise.

These measures, however, only partially restrained the spontaneous process, tending to make enterprises more self-sufficient. Current opinion is changing in regard to this phenomenon. In March 1985 *Izvestiia* published an article evoking in nostalgic terms the economic autarky of the Soviet economy during the war years. The building of machinery and equipment in the enterprise, down to the self-engineered production of robots, is not only justified in this article but endorsed as the most advanced and progressive form of production organization, leading to minimal dependence on outside suppliers.[48]

Soviet industrial managers are finding sympathy and tolerance of their attempts to create a diversified industrial subsistence economy inside their factories. A characteristic comment was: "If in striving to fulfill his duty, his plan, an enterprise director or minister feels he has in effect to create his own 'subsistence economy,' he can hardly be blamed for that. He can't force his suppliers to fulfill delivery contracts exactly."[49]

We can perhaps judge something of the extent of the use of depreciation allowances for upgrading by looking at the example of steel plants. In the second half of the seventies centrally allocated investment in open-hearth processes made up only 1 percent of all investment in steel making.[50] At the same time upgrading of a number of open-hearth furnaces converted them into tandem furnaces, significantly increasing capacity. Centrally allocated investment went mainly for higher-priority converters and electric technology, while improvement and capacity increase for blast furnaces were mainly paid for out of depreciation allowances for major overhauls.

That the steel industry has the ability to produce its own machinery is indicated by the fact that 98 percent of the spare parts used in steel plants are produced either in repair enterprises associated with steel plants or in repair shops of the steel plants themselves.[51]

Thus steel factories have ways of getting along without investment allocations from central funds and in many cases without, or with only minor, supplementary material resources. It is thus possible to speak of an auxiliary investment process operating on the side and having real effects on increases in productive capacity. Let us look at concrete examples of steel factories' increasing capacity via depreciation funds and internal reserves.

In the Il'ich steel factory, spending on modernization upgrading absorbed 48 percent of the amortization/depreciation funds destined for major overhauls.[52] At the Nizhne-Tagil'sk steel plant in the Urals in 1981, 28 percent of the funds destined for overhauls were spent on reconstruction and modernization upgrading. Reconstruction of only one open-hearth furnace enabled the factory to increase steel production from 359,000 to 404,000 tons, or by 12 percent.[53] At the Novolipetsk steel plant the capacity of the oxygen converter shop almost doubled as a result of modernization disguised as overhaul, from 2.1 to 4.0 million tons.[54]

The above-mentioned examples describe such significant increases of capacity that it would be unlikely they would not find some reflection in official statistics and be included in production plans. Information about such important cases makes it into the press from time to time (which is how we know about it). It is altogether possible that increases in productive capacity are revealed by the enterprises only very imperfectly. Central authorities are often kept in the dark about smaller-scale improvements that nevertheless produce good results.

Unimpeded dipping into overhaul funds is abetted by the fact that neither the cost nor the profit calculations of the enterprise depends on repairs or overhauls, since these expenditures are included in cost on the basis of official norms for depreciation deductions, not according to their actual amounts.

An attempt to regulate the use of depreciation deductions so as to limit their diversion from maintenance to expansion was made in the regulation on depreciation deductions adopted in connection with the reform of depreciation practices of 1975. This regulation contained a number of significant limits on the rights of an enterprise to dispose of funds of major overhauls, and stressed instead the need for modernization and upgrading of equipment and other elements of fixed capital.[55] But these limits remained on paper. The greater difficulty in obtaining central investment funds, the growing accumulation of internal reserves, the central authorities' weakening grip on expenditures—all these factors contribute to the growth of self-engineered investment using resources supposed to go to major maintenance overhauls.

This substitution of expansion paid for out of overhaul funds in place of centrally organized investment runs counter to the economic nature of this component of cost (sebestoimost'), which is maintenance rather than capacity increase. This theoretical fine point does not influence pragmatic managers. If they now carry out modernization upgrading and reconstruction of fixed capital only partly via depreciation deductions for major overhauls, in the future they intend to switch over entirely to this new system. "It is time for a complete change in attitude to the problem of major overhauls of fixed capital," one well-known manager announced.[56]

One can trace the degree to which Soviet economic theory legitimizes the combination of upgrading and major overhaul—or of carrying out modernization at the expense of overhaul. In the economic encyclopedia published in 1962, modernization upgrading is contrasted with major overhauling of fixed capital, whereas in the 1972 encyclopedia they are combined in the same article.[57] In the 1975 regulation on depreciation deductions, modernization upgrading carried out over the course of major overhauls is allowed to the extent that it does not augment the fixed capital stock, that is, its capacity.

Soviet economists have difficulty explaining the gradual conversion of the capital maintenance system into one of self-engineered capacity expansion. On the one hand, they cannot go against the current in opposing pressures from practical managers who are trying their hardest to expand capacity despite growing shortages of centrally allocated investment while paying no attention to the "laws" of a planned economy or effects of disruption of the "normal" reproductive structure of capital investment. The managers' credo is "Get through today!"

On the other hand, the economists have a hard time fitting the practice of spontaneous, self-generated investment into the canons of Soviet political economy, with its Marxian reproduction schemes and its axiomatic distrust of market forces and concomitant faith in central planning. A leading theoretical specialist on investment, Viktor Krasovskii, is puzzled; he asks whether "the question of switching resources designed for major capital overhauls to more progressive and economical investment channels—modernization upgrading and 'reconstruction' of fixed capital and its capacity—can ever be broached. The answer cannot be simple or one-dimensional."[58] Krasovskii himself declines to suggest a way out.

We have examined an important aspect of Soviet investment practice. We should not exaggerate its scale and importance for augmenting capacity in Soviet industry. It is clear that the main source of capacity increase is centrally allocated investment funds, and that self-generated and engineered investment merely supplements it, mainly offsetting effects of slower growth of transfers from the center. Despite negative consequences (for maintenance), at present the positive benefits seem to outweigh the negative in that independent investment overcomes bottlenecks and creates room for maneuvers, which in extreme situations and at the price of exceptional efforts may be efficiently utilized.

From the point of view of technical progress, however, in the majority of cases self-engineered modernization and upgrading of capacities at the expense of overhauls involves making only limited improvements without affecting the basic level of the equipment's technology. A similar kind of modernization is observed when old machines are not entirely replaced by new ones produced either en masse or individually in specialized machine-building factories, but rather are partially rebuilt on site by the factory's maintenance workers. A typical instance of this sort of modernization upgrading would be conversion rebuilding of old blast furnaces into tandem furnaces. Their capacity in the aggregate was significantly increased, but the basic blast-furnace principle has been fully conserved, and at a time when replacement of the process by the more advanced oxygen and electric processes was announced as one of the major goals of the Soviet steel industry.

Partial rebuilding as opposed to full replacement of old machinery by new is explained, first, by capacity in the capital goods sector which is insufficient for meeting the requirements of what are held to be normal rates of fixed-capital retirement. This is aggravated by the fact that in many cases equipment must be one of a kind, custom made to fit an existing structure, with its topography or production infrastructure.

A second factor is the declining share of new machinery and equipment in the total output of Soviet machine building. According to an evaluation made by the Joint Committee of the State Commission on Science and Technology (GKNT) of the Council of Ministers and Gosplan, based on a 1980 survey of 20,000 categories of capital goods, 29 percent were classified as requiring either modernization upgrading or discontinuation. At the same time, the share of new designs fell between 1970 and 1980 from 4.3 percent to 2.5 percent. Evidence of a rising share of obsolete models of machinery equipment is to be found in the fact that the share of items in total machine building which had been produced continually for more than ten years was 16 percent in 1967, 20 percent in 1971, and 25 percent in 1980.[59]

Third, the enterprise is often not interested or motivated to replace equipment that still works since new equipment filling the same technical function often does not have special engineering or economic advantages and, especially important, is often harder to use and to repair.

The great majority of new machines are destined to equip new enterprises. The rest go for reconstruction and modernization upgrading paid for out of central investment funds. Modernization carried out at the expense of major equipment overhauls uses the resources of specialized machine building to an insufficient degree.

Thus the system of depreciation allowances is not fulfilling its role, which is to regulate the "simple reproduction" of fixed capital, and this has deleterious consequences for the age and quality structure of the capital stock as it expands. Investment practices are running counter to objective demands for intensification of industrial production. Diverting depreciation allowances to capacity expansion when machinery and equipment are both scarce and of insufficiently recent vintage moves the economy away from its avowed goal of faster renewal of the means of production. To speed up introduction of better techniques it would be necessary either to go over to accelerated depreciation schedules or to shorten standard service lives while retaining straight-line depreciation.

Again, however, this would intensify pressure for the forced expansion of capital goods production, including the machine-building sector, which even under the present system of outdated, overlong service lives of equipment is not up to the task. Prominent Soviet economist Solomon Kheinman of the Institute of Economics of the Academy of Science in Moscow mentions in this connection that "our machine building is often unable to accommodate the full increases in capacity in (some) branches, and the necessary rates of renewal of existing capacity."[60]

In the twelfth five-year plan (1986–90), with a view to achieving planned improvements of technology in steel, mining, rail transportation, and other sectors, twelve hundred types of equipment are supposed to be introduced or modified in heavy machine building alone. On the average this would mean that heavy machine building would have to remodel 22 percent of its output every year.[61] Placed against the background of the current day, such a plan appears totally divorced from reality.

The Widening Gap between Investment
Practice and Labor Supply

So far we have treated the investment problem as one of capital proportions alone. Logically, however, the nature and structural dynamics of the investment process affect all other spheres of the economy, including above all the labor force. It would appear at first glance that an economy subjected to strict central control would have every opportunity to match the growth rates and structure of the capital stock to the evolution of labor resources. But this supposition is not borne out in reality. The disproportion between the number of unfilled vacancies and the size of the labor force has become one of the most important and dangerous disproportions in the Soviet economy; it is the worsening of this mismatch which is the best indicator of the lack of realism of Soviet investment plans and practices.

The problem of unfilled vacancies first arose in the 1960s. It was new and unusual, alien to the mentality of Soviet planners and managers who were trained at a time when relative labor abundance, in some periods surplus labor, and capital scarcity were the norm. Even when insufficient labor resources had become the obvious limiting factor on economic growth plans, they continued to be based on a single scarce factor—capital. Proof of this is to be found in Gosplan's methodology for plan formulation, in which a great deal of attention is given to planning needs for and efficiency in the use of capital plant and investment, with incomparably less attention given to planning analogous labor requirements and labor efficiency norms.

Increases in the numbers of jobs to be filled persisted even when the participant rate hit a practical maximum and the annual increment in the labor force declined sharply, to the point of becoming negative in a number of regions. Beginning in the mid-sixties the number of vacancies in jobs began to increase faster in industry than in the labor force as a whole, so that the gap between them is growing. The fraction of jobs on the first shift that remained unfilled was 1 percent in 1967, 4.9 percent in 1970, 7.3 percent in 1975,

9.9 percent in 1980, and it was projected to reach 12.2 percent in 1985.[62]

The growing gap between workers and jobs is basically due to the following factors: first, the reduction in labor supply growth rates is attributable to reductions in the rate of population growth. In the 1970s annual increments to the labor force fell continuously for this reason. Demographic prospects have worsened in the eighties.

For the USSR as a whole, the rate of population increase in the 1980s is approximately a fifth of what it was in the 1970s. In the Ukraine and a few other regions no growth at all is expected in this decade in the population of working age.[63]

The second factor is the inefficiency with which the existing labor force is used. The reasons for this are well known and include poor planning, the difficulty of controlling labor expenditure from the center, and lack of incentive for enterprise managers to release labor. The current plan methodology does not permit the center to determine with any accuracy whether the enterprise really needs as many workers as it says it does, or whether there is featherbedding. The mechanism or rewarding the fulfillment of plans with the smallest possible work force is ineffective. Heads of enterprise in most cases do not want to get rid of surplus laborers; if there are any, they know full well that the wage fund, the prestige and importance of the enterprise, the material appointments and perquisites, the earnings of the managers and the director all depend in large part on the size of the work force. They also know that hidden labor reserves may come in handy should the output plan be raised and in case labor should be needed for agricultural and other tasks unconnected with the main business of the enterprise. The Shchekino Method, introduced in 1967, was supposed to reward reductions in the numbers of workers. It is being applied in only 4 percent of all industrial enterprises.[64]

A second factor is the unfavorable organization and distribution of tasks within factories. In industry 40 percent of workers are engaged in manual labor; in construction, 50 percent. Because of the weak specialization and insufficient mechanization of maintenance, materials handling, transport, and similar tasks, the already large share of auxiliary workers has been steadily rising and has lately matched the share of basic production workers in industry.[65]

A third factor is the poor correspondence between qualifications of the existing labor force and the qualitative demands of the vacancies posted. It would be wrong to underestimate the achievements in general education and specialized preparation of industrial workers. In 1959 401 per 1,000 industrial workers had completed eight to ten years of school, whereas in 1982 800 had. From 1967 to 1981 the number of graduates from professional and technical schools rose 2.2 times to approximately 2.5 million per year. Over the same period the number of workers who raised their professional qualifications on the job rose more than fourfold, to 34.1 million in 1981. Nevertheless, in spite of these impressive figures, professional qualifications lag behind requirements both in quality and quantity.[66]

In the overwhelming majority of enterprises the average skill classification of workers is significantly lower than the average skill classification of the tasks to be filled. The supply of high-grade workers is significantly less than demand and the reverse is the case for lower-grade workers. There is also the matter of low mobility: only 5 percent of industrial workers possess a combination of skills and a wide range of work experience. To a great extent the poor quality of the Soviet labor force with respect to current needs is due to inadequate professional training: too high a fraction of workers—74 percent—received their basic professional training directly on the job, where preparation is considerably worse than in specialized professional schools. There is widespread wastage of higher-qualified workers in low-skill jobs, with engineers and technicians used as ordinary workers.[67]

Fourth, there is the inertial persistence of the old investment pattern, with its failure to react to demographic changes, its continued focus on brand new factories and sections, all of which require additional full-time workers. As some writers have noted, analysis of the structure of investment in the eleventh five-year plan (first half of the 1980s) shows that creation of new jobs with very little release of labor from old jobs has continued to be the basic focus of attention. In connection with this, in the eleventh five-year plan an increase in unfilled industrial vacancies of around 15 percent was expected. It is understandable that investment that raises demand for labor should occur in new industrial regions (Siberia, Kazakhstan, the north of European USSR, Central Asia). But a similar strategy is being followed in old industrial regions. Thus in investment destined for the Ukraine in 1981–85, 13 out of 18 billion rubles required additional workers.[68]

The difficulty is clear. On the one hand, in order to match labor requirements to labor availability, new enterprises should not be built in regions of labor scarcity, but rather be concentrated in regions of relative labor abundance. On the other hand, many of these new enterprises must be located in the eastern regions, which are most affected by labor shortages.

In theory the labor shortage should be conducive to raising the share in investment of reconstruction and modernization upgrading of existing capacity, since these forms of investment raise the capital-labor ratio and possibly release labor for other tasks. First, however, as shown above, the share of investment in reconstruction and modernization upgrading is relatively small compared with investment in new sections and enterprises and is rising only slowly despite an exceptional amount of discussion at the center. Second, reconstruction and modernization upgrading do not always have the desired labor-force effect; they too may increase labor requirements. Thus in enterprises of the Russian Soviet Federal Socialist Republic (RSFSR) which underwent reconstruction in the first half of the seventies, overall labor needs rose by an average of 18 percent.[69]

Thus a paradoxical situation is developing. At a time when claims on investment resources are increasing, capital plant and equipment are not being fully utilized (since they embody a technology that is too labor-intensive). According to a deputy director of a Gosplan research institute in the 1970s, when the demographic situation was still favorable, around 10–12 percent of the increment of fixed capital after allowing for price rises remained unutilized.[70] It is likely that in the 1980s, with the sharp decline in labor-force growth and stagnant capital-labor ratios, stocks of unutilized capital are continuing to grow.

Besides the illogic of spending investment funds on equipment that will stand idle for lack of labor, this excessive investment inevitably has a negative effect on the productivity of workers already working. The effectiveness of workers' output norms and of measures to improve quality of work, tighten technical and labor discipline, reduce turnover, and raise skills are all affected. There are pressures to level wage disparities upward, which raises average wage levels. This is all perfectly natural in a tight labor market: the greater the enterprise's demand for labor, the fewer specific demands will be placed on that labor with respect to qualifications, discipline, performance. What kind of labor discipline can there be when over 30 percent of workers fired for misconduct manage to negotiate higher wages at their new place of work?[71] According to calculations made by Yu. Baryshnikov and I. Malmygin, with a 5 percent vacancy rate in Soviet industry, the rate of utilization of equipment per shift falls 17 percent below the norm; the intensity of effort by workers falls by 20 percent; the average length of time worked in a given plant falls 75–80 percent, while equipment downtime doubles and the average wage goes up by 38 percent.[72]

Such a situation is naturally extremely worrisome to the Soviet leadership. In a document adopted at the Twenty-sixth Party Congress of the CPSU in 1981, "Basic Directions for Economic and Social Development of the USSR for 1981–85 and to 1990," mention was made of the necessity to "take measures to achieve a balance between existing and future labor requirements and labor resources."[73] Judging from the situation at mid-decade, however, this resolution had no impact.

The growing disproportion between labor availability and capital utilization is due in the last analysis to three factors. The first derives from inadequacies at the plan level. The lack of sophistication and the carelessness of economic research and of current and long-term planning, both at the economywide and the sectoral/regional levels, extends to the methods and practices of establishing labor-input norms and thus of the potential for increasing labor productivity. Current and long-term planning from the training and use of skilled labor is particularly poor.

Typical is the remark of an authoritative observer of projected Soviet growth rates and proportions, Yuri Yaremenko, of the Central Economic-Mathematics Institute of the Academy of Sciences of the USSR in Moscow:

> Of three ways of increasing the effective quantity of labor resources— (1) increasing the size of the labor force and the amount of time worked, (2) mobilizing labor reserves being hoarded by enterprises, (3) raising the intensity of work—only the first is of any quantitative significance. In calculating the expected effects of the labor factor on the other economic indicators, instead of three equally important sources, account is taken of only one.[74]

The second factor is that the technology being adopted for replacement investment and for expansion does not provide sufficient savings in labor. The primary task of industrial investment in the

1960s and 1970s was to add to the sheer volume of technical processes, machines, equipment, accompanied by an increase in their complexity. In many cases, the use, servicing, and repair of this fixed capital did not correspond with the newly increased capacity and complexity. Particularly evident was the concentration of energy on developing and perfecting assembly line equipment and process technology, at the cost of a growing backwardness of auxiliary equipment and processes. Mechanization and automation elsewhere are much less evident and productivity is much lower. For example, in the production of rolled steel, in which all basic processes are automated, auxiliary processes, employing mainly manual labor, use around half the labor force.

In this manner, by the end of the 1970s a situation was created in which improvements in labor productivity were being held back by the large number of nonmechanized sections, primarily in auxiliary operations. Poor mechanization of the lowest-priority processes is the main reason why orienting investment toward increasing the unit output of line equipment is having an ever more feeble labor-saving effect.

Mechanization of labor-intensive auxiliary tasks is occurring slowly, not only because primary processes get the lion's share of investment, but also because the various types of equipment in use in many branches of industry work in production cycles that are not fully coordinated with each other, either in output or spatial terms. Between operations there are gaps, filled as a rule by manual labor.

The optimal situation would be complete integration and coordination of the various operations into a single uninterrupted process. Achieving a continuous flow of input and output, however, would require major redesign of equipment and layout. To make any headway in this direction will require a strong injection of computer technology, which the USSR is not in a position to provide for the foreseeable future.

The third factor is, as discussed earlier, the altogether insufficient rates of retirement of old equipment that is unable to handle either quantitative or qualitative increases in the demands made on it.

Investment Activity in Ferrous Metallurgy

We may now look at the most important characteristics of investment activity in the iron and steel industry, while bearing in mind that the overall features of investment activity in Soviet industry as a whole influence this sector as well.

We shall examine the extent to which investment policy corresponds to the principal tasks laid down for the sector: a shift from a quantitative to a qualitative path of industrial growth, and the elimination of disproportions among the capacities of different links in the technological chain. (Bear in mind also that these goals must be pursued while keeping capital spending to a minimum.)

The Distribution of Investment in Ferrous Metallurgy

Since the second half of the 1960s ferrous metallurgy has consistently occupied fifth place among the principal sectors of Soviet industry when it comes to the allocation of investment within industry. It has lagged behind the machine-building, electrical energy, oil and chemical oil technology industries. The share of ferrous metallurgy in industrial investment, however, has declined steadily over the last two decades. It stood at 8.3 percent in 1966–70, 7.6 percent in 1971–75, 6.9 percent in 1976–80, and fell to 6.0 percent in 1981–85. The time when this sector of industry enjoyed priority status in Soviet investment policy lies even farther in the past.[75] In the years of the early five-year plans this sector received 13–15 percent of all industrial investment, taking second place after machine building.[76] One can argue, however, that the position ferrous metallurgy currently occupies in the structure of industrial investment in the USSR is even too high for a modern industrial economy, especially if one considers the fact that extraction and concentration of iron ore accounts for around 30 percent of the sector's investment outlays.

The favorable attitude of the Soviet leadership toward ferrous metallurgy when it comes to allocating investment has to some extent lessened the impact on the sector of the decline in investment that has been characteristic for the economy as a whole in recent years. Ferrous metallurgy was a vanguard sector in the early 1980s, when measured in terms of the rate of growth of investment, falling behind only the oil and gas industries, which received absolute priority. If one compares investment in the years 1980 and 1985, then in electrical energy it rose by 29 percent; in coal, by 21 percent; in the oil and gas industries, by 60 percent; in machine building, by 21 percent; in light industry, by 10 percent; in food, by 9 percent; and in ferrous metallurgy, by 3 percent.[77]

It is true that the flow of investment funds into ferrous metallurgy has been cut back over the course of the 1981–85 five-year plan in comparison with the preceding one. But against the background of a marked slowing in the rate of investment in all sectors of the economy, investment in ferrous metals would seem to enjoy a relatively favored position.

Thus, generally speaking, for an industry that lived under a favorable—even privileged—investment regime for half a century, a shift to moderate annual growth rates would not seem to be too disturbing a development. It implies only a need to reorganize the internal investment structure, to reorient investment policy from quantitative to qualitative priorities.

The principal idea behind the planned development of ferrous metallurgy consists of a shift in production from the quantitative to the qualitative path, in improving the quality and widening the assortment of rolled metal, and in ending the chase after quantitative production targets. One can at least point out that this aim has been voiced by Soviet leaders and is constantly promoted in economic publications and planning documents. Successful pursuit of this course depends on the investment policy in ferrous metallurgy. Has investment policy actually been directed to achieving these tasks? The main conditions for the realization of the above-described program in the sphere of investment are to ensure some correspondence between the way investment is restructured in the various departments of ferrous metallurgy, and an acceleration in the renewal of fixed capital in the enterprises. It follows that we should investigate these key factors.

It can be seen from Table 6.1 that there has been significant change in the distribution of investment within the ferrous metallurgy sector over the course of the period in question. One can identify two distinct and clearly different subperiods. The first, from 1956 to 1975, is characterized by growth in output. In this period there is a rise in the share of investment going to metallurgical production and a reduction in the proportion going to the production of iron ore. Within metallurgical production there is a significant (2.5 times) rise in the share of investment expended on technological processes designed to improve the quality and increase the range of products—what is known as the "fourth division" (chetvertyi peredel).

The second subperiod, from 1976 to 1980, witnesses a decline in production. In this the share of metallurgical production drops

TABLE 6.1
The allocation of investment in ferrous metallurgy by sector (%/billions of rubles)[78]

| | Ferrous metal production (FMP) | | | | | | | | Ferro-alloys production | Iron-ore production | Firebrick production | Scrap preparation | All other | Total in ferrous metallurgy |
	Total in FMP	Iron making	Steel making	Rolled steel production	Quality upgrading and production of finished rolled product	Production and processing of metallurgical coke	Tube making	Cold-drawn wire, nails, bolts, screwnuts, etc.						
1956–60	51.6 / —	16 / —	10.2 / —	16 / —	4 / —	5.4 / —	6.9 / —	2.6 / —	1.4 / —	32.2 / —	2.5 / —		2.8 / —	100.0 / —
1961–65	54.7 / —	15.9 / —	15.6 / —	10.7 / —	7.4 / —	5.1 / —	6.9 / —	2.9 / —	2.6 / —	29.9 / —	3.4 / —		2.6 / —	103.0 / —
1966–70	52.7 / 5.21	11.3 / 1.12	12.0 / 1.19	16.0 / 1.59	9.2 / 0.913	4.0 / 0.397	8.1 / 0.804	4.1 / 0.407	2.4 / 0.238	26.9 / 2.67	2.7 / 0.268	1.1 / 0.109	1.6 / 0.159	99.4 / 9.927
1971–75	55.6 / 7.18	5.6 / 0.722	15.4 / 1.99	20.3 / 2.62	10.6 / 1.37	3.7 / 0.477	8.8 / 1.14	4.0 / 0.516	2.4 / 0.310	24.1 / 3.11	2.3 / 0.297	1.2 / 0.155	1.6 / 0.206	100.0 / 12.901
1976–80 (plan)	55 / 10.4	4.2 / 0.798	14.1 / 2.68	18.3 / 3.48	14.2 / 2.70	4.2 / 0.798	—	—	—	—	—	—	—	100.0 / 19.0
Actual	49 / 7.45	5 / 0.760	17 / 5.58	14 / 2.13	10 / 1.52	3 / 0.456	7 / 1.1	4 / 0.600	4 / 0.60	29 / 4.41	2 / 0.30	1 / 0.150	4 / 0.60	100.0 / 15.202

Note: Percentages do not sum to 100 because of rounding.

sharply, while the share devoted to the production of iron ore rises sharply at almost the same rate. The share of the fourth division declines.

Thus the distribution of investments within ferrous metallurgy in the period 1976–80 is following a pattern different from that which held for the previous twenty years and is, moreover, a pattern that flatly contradicts the declared course of development set for this sector of the economy—improving the qualitative indicators of its output.

How is one to account for this contradiction? A refusal to carry out the tasks set before ferrous metallurgy? That is clearly not the case. A comparison of the two lowest lines of the table shows that the plan did foresee a continued strengthening of investment in the fourth division and a sharp increase in the proportion of resources devoted to its development. But reality overturned the plan's projections. In the mid-1970s there was a growing crisis in the production of iron ore (see above), and in these circumstances the leaders of the ferrous metals industry were obliged to deviate significantly from their established course and divert investment to the aid of the iron-ore industry. It was essential to halt the decline in both the quantity and quality of iron ore.

A second reason for the shift away from investment priority for the fourth division is that metallurgical machine building was unable to cope with the task of delivering equipment in the amounts required by the given level of investment for this part of the technological process. Of course, many factors may serve to explain the inability of metallurgical machine building to provide the necessary quantities of equipment required by the ferrous metallurgy industry—equipment that is among the most complex of all manufactured metallurgical machinery. But the root of the problem, in our view, lies in the lack of material incentives for the engineering factories to produce such equipment. This hidden tendency may be explained in the following manner. The production of metallurgical equipment is planned by the manufacturing plant by weight, in tons. It is widely recognized that planning in tons provides an incentive to increase the output of products that are less labor-intensive, but that are heavier, contain more metal, and do not permit accurate assessment of the productive capacity of the factories. (The latter arises because the method for calculating productive capacity is built upon the principle of defining labor outlays per ton of product.) Equipment for the fourth division is the most labor-intensive, and heavy machine-building plants therefore have little interest in producing it. They prefer to fulfill the plan for the least labor-intensive types of blast furnace equipment, but do not ensure the supply of more labor-intensive equipment for rolling mills and finishing operations.

As a result of the developments in the structure of investment reviewed above and the decline in the rate of growth of investment in ferrous metallurgy as a whole, in 1976–80 (when compared to 1971–75) investment in the production of rolled metal fell by almost 20 percent, while investment in the fourth division rose by a mere 11 percent as against a planned rise of 200 percent. Naturally, such a decline in investment will lead inevitably to the frustration of the program for qualitative improvements in the production of rolled metal and widening the assortment of available products.

Thus it is not appropriate to talk of a particular investment strategy in ferrous metallurgy. In practice, investment in this sector of the economy in the second half of the 1970s has not followed the plans for the development and improvement of production.

Information on the distribution of investment within ferrous metallurgy in the 1980s is not yet available to us. The continuing decline in the rate of growth of investment in industry as a whole, and the continuing difficult situation as regards the production and processing of iron ore, provide the grounds for suggesting that notable changes are unlikely to have occurred. And even if there had been a change in the utilization of rolled metal and in the fourth division, the slackening of investment in these final stages of the technical cycle in the 1976–80 period placed such difficulties in the path of attempts to improve the quality profile and assortment of rolled metal that it would not be possible to have overcome them even in the early 1980s.

Capital Intensity and the Upgrading of Existing Capacities

The distribution of investment within ferrous metallurgy is decided upon, primarily, by the leadership of this industry, that is, by the Ministry of Ferrous Metallurgy. When apportioning investments to the ministry (these funds being in theory intended to facilitate the fulfillment of the output plan), Gosplan assumes that they will be used to maximum effect. By this is meant the minimum outlay required for the maintenance and increase of a unit of capacity. The desire to reduce the capital coefficient is a thread running through all the methodologies and normative materials of Gosplan. Any increase in capacity must be as capital-saving as possible.

Ferrous metallurgy is one of the most capital-intensive sectors of Soviet industry, and one in which the capital coefficient has been rising for over a quarter of a century. The rise in capital outlays on the production of steel has had a substantial influence on the rise in capital intensity of industrial products in the Soviet economy as a whole. If one includes in one's calculations the investments in associated industrial sectors which provide the metallurgical plant with its materials, fuel, external transport services, and so forth, then the cost of capacity to produce 4–5 million tons of rolled metal in a modern metallurgical factory stood at some 1.5–2.0 billion rubles in the second half of the 1970s.[79]

The factors influencing the rise in the capital coefficient (discussed above) are also fully at work in ferrous metallurgy. The price set for metallurgical equipment manufactured in the USSR per unit of capacity rose on average by 15 percent in the period 1975–80. Capital investments designed to improve the quality and assortment of rolled metal rose (per unit of capacity) by 60 percent between the periods 1971–75 and 1976–80. We should note that the rise in the costs of equipment shows up equally across all the indices. For example, the cost of 1 ton of equipment for the converter shop in the Cherepovets plant, laid down between 1976 and 1980, was 18 percent higher than the cost of similar equipment introduced in the Novolipetsk plant (1972–75).[80]

It is clear that the level of capital outlays on new capacity does not depend solely on movements in the prices of equipment. More significant influence is exercised by such features of the installation process as the nature of the expansion in capacity (the building of a new enterprise or shop versus the modernization and reconstruction of the existing plant), the scale of production, and the specific features of the natural environment and regional economy. These indicators of the development of ferrous metallurgy are all connected and interrelated.

The main theme of investment policy in the 1970s and 1980s has been the concentration of resources on the modernization of existing capacity rather than the creation of new facilities. The Soviet leadership has long sought to realize this idea of switching investment over to the reconstruction of existing enterprises. Published statistics have created the illusion that this idea has been translated into reality. Among the various sectors that make up the Soviet ferrous metals industry, the one receiving the largest share of investments has been that described as "technical reequipping, reconstruction, and expansion of existing production." In the course of the 1970s it grew from 60 percent to 80 percent.[81] Toward the end of the 1970s, however, one began to see increasing evidence in the press to the effect that in actual fact the proportion of investments going to the modernization of existing capacity was considerably less than these figures would imply. The predominant trend is in fact toward new construction, spatially linked to existing enterprises and undertaken under the rubric of reconstruction and expansion. Earlier in this book we discussed the reasons industrial managers prefer to erect new capacity rather than modernize the old. Sometimes, in fact, conflicting information appears, revealing the true state of affairs. Thus, for example, one of the directors of the state institute for the design of metallurgical plants, P. Shiryaev, stated that "about 7 percent is directed toward reconstruction and 93 percent to new construction"[82]—and the reference is to the same period (the 1970s) when the Central Statistical Administration figures we quoted above showed reconstruction funds rising from 60 percent to 80 percent of total investments. On the basis of an examination of technical-economic designs, plant designer Shiryaev considers the growing practice of expanding plants on sites adjacent to existing capacity to in fact amount to "new construction"—while branch directors are writing it into their planning and statistical materials as "reconstruction and expansion."

Substitution of concepts leads to a substitution of meaning. This form of reconstruction is transformed from a means of economizing on investment resources to an expensive form of increasing capacities.

A study of the effectiveness of capital investments in metallurgical plants during 1966–80, carried out by the Central Economic Scientific Research Institute of the RSFSR Gosplan, showed that capital investments per ton of increase in output at new plants were about 55 percent of those for the reconstruction and expansion of existing enterprises.[83] The authors of this study reached the conclusion that the branch had gone beyond the limits of economic effectiveness of the reconstruction of existing plants. Nevertheless, this method of increasing production capacity was included in all plan variants for the 1980s.

The primary factor accounting for the greater capital intensity of reconstruction of old metallurgical capacity when compared with the cost of new projects is the need to replace large amounts of fixed capital in the course of the reconstruction, including industrial buildings and facilities. In theory, the advantage of reconstruction over new building lies precisely in the significantly lower share of investments devoted to construction work, leaving the lion's share for the acquisition of equipment. In practice, however, more money is spent on construction in investment projects involving the reconstruction or replacement of metallurgical plants than goes on equipment purchases. Moreover, it is even higher than the corresponding proportion of expenditure in the erection of new capacity. In 1977 58.8 percent of investment expenditures in reconstruction projects in metallurgical plants went on construction work, 58.3 percent of that in new construction projects and 65 percent in replacement projects.[84]

In his meeting with workers at the Dnepropetrovsk metallurgical factory in June 1985, Mikhail Gorbachev remarked:

> Plans have not been met in ferrous metallurgy in recent five-year plans. Nowadays this sector more and more frequently disrupts the rhythm of our economy. While this was objectionable before, how much more unacceptable it must be when serious challenges are facing our machine-building industry. The causes of the current situation stem from the slow rate at which the sector's fixed capital has been renewed. Yet at the same time a huge quantity of resources has been devoted to repairing them.[85]

Over the course of the last decade the retirement of fixed capital due to wear and tear has been considerably less than allowed for by the norms. The amortization fund for replacement has only been utilized at 15–35 percent of the prescribed rate. The rate of replacement of old fixed capital in ferrous metallurgy is roughly two times lower than in Soviet industry as a whole. In metallurgical factories roughly 10 percent of capital investments are spent on replacement of old fixed capital, while according to expert opinion the proportion should be on the order of 25–30 percent.[86]

To meet the normed rate for the writing off of fixed capital in ferrous metallurgy (as of the early 1980s) required the withdrawal, on average, of 5 percent of the equipment (by value) per year. The actual rate of retirement, however, was a little over 1 percent, while in the core areas of metallurgical production it was even lower (amounting to 0.4–0.6 percent in rolling shops).[87]

In order to increase fivefold the rate of retirement of equipment it is necessary to create the corresponding capacity in metallurgical machine building to make up for the withdrawn capacity. The nature and rate of growth of metallurgical machine building have not been such as to prepare it for this task. Considerable increases in investment would be needed if this sector of engineering were to be raised to the required level. The situation dictates that investment in metallurgical machine building should grow at a faster rate than investment in ferrous metallurgy itself. In reality, however, the level of investment in metallurgical machine building is not particularly high in relation to the level of investment in ferrous metallurgy, and it is tending to decline.[88] The available production capacity in machine building is not such as to provide for the development of new, advanced technologies in ferrous metallurgy. Given the current availability of hard currency, imports of equipment from either Eastern Europe or the advanced Western economies will not be sufficient to improve the situation significantly.

We should bear in mind that 90 percent of the equipment acquired by ferrous metallurgy is assigned for the construction of new capacity, and not replacement. Thus there are no grounds for expecting that in the 1980s there will be the required acceleration in the withdrawal and replacement of fixed capital in metallurgical factories which Gorbachev was calling for—neither in the economic nor in the technological sense.

Such a considerable accumulation of old fixed capital naturally leads to sizable and growing expenditure on maintenance. The share of spending on capital repairs in actual outlays on capacity maintenance in ferrous metallurgy is 2.5 to 3.0 times higher than on replacement.[89] Huge outlays on the repair of old equipment do not make economic sense. For example, total annual spending on the repair of fifty-three old rolling mills producing together some 2 million tons of rolled metal per year amounted to some 20 million rubles. They are spending in two and a half years an amount equal to the cost of a modern rolling mill capable of producing 4 million tons per year.[90] The rate of increase of spending on repairs has exceeded the rate of growth of investments of ferrous metallurgy. From 1976 to 1980 repair outlays were 50 percent higher than investment in ferrous metallurgy. We should add that maintenance of equipment and other types of fixed capital occupies 45 percent of all workers in this industrial sector, which is 70 percent more than the number directly working on the technological processes.[91]

Thus increasing the scale of reconstruction work in ferrous metallurgy represents not a more capital-saving way to increase capacity and improve product quality than does the construction of new capacity, but the very opposite. It is actually more wasteful of capital than is new construction. As is true for industry as a whole, in order to enable reconstruction of existing plants to economize on capital while meeting quantitative and qualitative targets, one would need to see extraordinary efforts and a radical reorganization of many aspects of the investment sphere (investment planning, the design of capacity, metallurgical machine building, organization of construction, incentive systems). Nevertheless, in our opinion the determination shown by the new Soviet leadership to carry out the course they have outlined within existing enterprises does not provide a solution to these problems. Gorbachev's newly appointed minister of Ferrous Metallurgy, Serafim Kolpakov (the former director of the flagship plant of the metallurgical industry in Novolipetsk), will doubtless try to implement his boss's plans, despite the lack of preparedness of the related elements of the economy's industrial and investment spheres.

Can the modernization of old capacity be a more effective way of meeting the demands being placed upon ferrous metallurgy than new construction? Given the specific circumstances under which the upgrading of old capacity is taking place, the state of metallurgical machine building, and the fact that 90 percent of its output is produced for the erection of new facilities rather than reconstruction, and if one allows for the unavoidably extensive reconstruction of buildings which must take place despite the constraints imposed by the need to keep the enterprises running, then one can see that this road is more difficult, more lengthy, and more capital-intensive. Such a course would also lead to the maintenance of the existing geographical distribution of ferrous metallurgy, contradicting the idea of opening up metallurgical capacity in new industrial regions with incommensurably better natural conditions for the development of metallurgical production and with growing shortages of rolled metal.

TABLE 6.2
Proportion of enterprises with annual output over 3 million tons
(in percent of total number of enterprises)[92]

	1960	1965	1970	1975	1980
Cast iron	42.6	59.1	75.9	89.2	90.4
Steel	45.5	68.6	68.9	82.0	83.2
Prepared rolled metal	13.8	42.4	59.8	73.5	77.7

TABLE 6.3
The factory concentration of metallurgical production in the USSR
(in millions of tons)[93]

	1960	1965	1970	1975	1980[b]
Cast iron	$\frac{44.8^a}{1.7}$	$\frac{61.6}{2.3}$	$\frac{81.8}{2.9}$	$\frac{98.9}{3.7}$	$\frac{118.2}{4.4}$
Steel	$\frac{45.9}{1.7}$	$\frac{67.5}{2.5}$	$\frac{90.5}{3.2}$	$\frac{113.6}{4.2}$	$\frac{138.2}{5.1}$
Prepared rolled metal	$\frac{32.4}{1.2}$	$\frac{48.3}{1.8}$	$\frac{66.4}{2.4}$	$\frac{95.1}{3.1}$	$\frac{100.4}{3.7}$

[a]Numerator = total production; denominator = average per enterprise.
[b]Estimated.

Concentration of Production

Let us turn now to the concentration of production. The course of maximal transfer of investment to existing plants will lead to an even higher level of territorial concentration of metallurgical production. In the period from the middle of the 1950s to the end of the 1970s the average capacity of metallurgical plants in the USSR increased sixfold. The proportion of enterprises with an annual output in excess of 3 million tons shifted in the period 1960–80 as shown in Table 6.2. At the beginning of the 1980s enterprises produced over 3 million tons of cast iron per year, including nine producing over 5 million tons and two (Magnitogorsk and Krivoi Rog factories) more than 12 million tons.

Table 6.3 illustrates the growing concentration of production of the basic types of output of metallurgical plants over the course of two decades.

There has been a growing tendency for metallurgical factories to grow in size. It seems appropriate at this point briefly to indicate the underlying causes and consequences of this excessive concentration of production, which is characteristic of Soviet industry as a whole and is found in ferrous metallurgy. From the very first stages of its development Soviet industrial planning has proceeded on the assumption of the incontrovertible advantages of industrial concentration and increasing scale of production. From the first five-year plan through to the present day the Soviet press discusses the achievements of the economy with proud boasts of having created enterprises and production units (furnaces, turbines, cement works) which are the "largest in the USSR," "the biggest in Europe," or "the largest in the world."

Research on the economic effectiveness of industrial concentration over the decades has pointed in one direction. Statisticians and economists, with few exceptions, have consistently shown the advantages of large over small operations. This work, however, has proceeded on the basis of such haphazard methods that in fact it is not valid to draw either negative or positive conclusions from the body of research.

In our view, "gigantomania" in Soviet industry can be attributed to the following factors. The first, in the sphere of economic theory, stems from Marx's theory of concentration, which the Soviets interpret to be arguing for the virtually limitless expansion of production. The advantages of concentration are highlighted, and the limits to its effectiveness are not examined. The law of superiority of large-scale production is viewed as absolute. They ignore the point (made also by Lenin) that this law works only if all other circumstances can be taken as equal—which is by no means always the case in practice.

Second, there is the question of the way industrial enterprises are designed. Planned increases in production are easier to obtain, from the designers' point of view, in the large-scale plants. It is easier at the project stage to come up with ideal-looking indicators, which will earn rewards for the designers. It often happens that designs substantially understate the outlays and length of time required for construction (which then turn out to be completely unrealizable), and this is easier to do the bigger the scale of the operation being designed.

Third, one must examine the centralized management of industry. Gosplan and the ministries prefer to create large enterprises, because in a system of highly centralized planning it is easier for the center to direct a small number of large enterprises.

Underlying the growth in the capacity of enterprises is the growth in capacity of individual units of equipment, embodying technical progress. The optimum size of an enterprise from an economic point of view, however, is by no means determined solely by technical capabilities, but also depends on differences between various regions and locations in terms of the availability of fuel and raw materials, the level of demand, size and composition of the work force, and more. It is also extremely important to calculate the likely length of construction (the larger the scale, the longer it will take to build), maintaining a balance between different parts of the enterprise. Given the huge size of the territory of the USSR, great significance must be attached to transport conditions and freight costs. These factors are not adequately taken into account in the calculations made to estimate the economic justification for enterprise reconstruction and expansion involving an increase in scale.

The overconcentration of metallurgical enterprises has serious consequences for both ferrous metallurgy and the whole Soviet economy. One of the most important factors in attempting to raise the productivity of Soviet industry is the question of improving the territorial distribution of steel production—that is, its deconcentration given current economic conditions and the transport situation in the USSR. If one examines the location pattern of the steel industry, one can perceive a distinct contradiction between the requirements for the optimal territorial structure of production on the basis of the economy and military-strategic interests of the USSR, on the one hand; and on the other hand, bureaucratic interests dictated by the ministry.

The production of prepared rolled metal rose by some 2.5 times in the USSR as a whole between 1960 and 1980, including a rise of 2.4 times in the Siberian zone (including the far east). Most (85–87 percent) of the cast iron, steel, and rolled metal is produced in the European part of the USSR. The proportion of rolled metal produced in this region has fallen slightly, from 88.6 percent in 1960 to 85.6 percent in 1980. To be more precise: the share of output in the central European region and Siberia rose by 3.8 percent, while the shares of the south and Ural-Volga regions declined by 1.4 percent and 5.5 percent, respectively.[94]

One cannot but consider the rise in the share of the Asiatic regions of the USSR (Siberia, far east, Kazakhstan, and Central Asia) of only three percentage points over two whole decades as insufficient when it comes to improving the territorial balance of the Soviet economy. Maintaining the dominant role of the European part of the USSR in the production of steel at a certain level is valid, given the traditionally high demand for steel in the region and the availability of more than sufficient material resources. Such insignificant improvements in the territorial structure of production, however, hinder the goal of advancing the development of the economic potential of the eastern regions of the USSR, where the demand for steel is growing, and where the potential of nature—fuel and material resources—are also favorable for the creation of large-scale metallurgical capacity. The growing imbalance between production and demand, especially as regards the range of types of rolled metal, amounts to dozens of millions of tons. The excessive concentration of production of steel leads to an increase in the average distance that iron ore, scrap, and fuel are carried. Thus from 1960 to 1975 average freight distance of raw materials rose by 40 percent.

The increase in unit size of basic metallurgical equipment and plant capacity as a whole weakens its flexibility and maneuverability, the ability to quickly master new types of products, to produce the sort of relatively small items that may be required or to widen the range of products. This inability leads, as was noted above, to excessive use of steel in metalworking, machine-building, and construction enterprises—and to a high level of concentration of the harmful effects that blight the surrounding environment.

The course that the Ministry of Ferrous Metallurgy is following— the further concentration of production, expanding the capacity of existing enterprises—and which received a new emphasis in Gorbachev's economic program, has attracted its share of critics from the ranks of Soviet experts independent of the ministry. For example, Boris Zherebin, former director of the Kuznetsk metallurgical factory and currently professor at the Moscow Steel and Alloys Institute, characterized the ministry's investment policy this way:

> The policy of the Ministry of Ferrous Metallurgy is incorrect. For the past twenty years they have only talked about the construction of new plants, while in practice continuing to expand the old ones. But we are talking about the limits to the concentration of capacity, about atmospheric pollution, and about people's health. Why despoil these areas? Such factories become poorly managed. No matter what sort of director is appointed to such superenterprises, they invariably lose their effectiveness, resulting ultimately in direct losses for the Soviet economy. In my view, the shift to metallurgy to the east has now come to a halt.[95]

No less definitive a statement on this issue came from academician
Abel Aganbegyan:

> The ministry lost its strategy for developing the industry. From the
> point of view of today's planners, the idea for the Uralo-Kuznetsk
> combine would not work. They'd consider it inefficient. Efficient for
> them would be an orientation toward the southern Ural region; there
> was a construction base there, manpower, a railroad, a lot of ore. But
> no, then it was into the swamp to build a city, to build a railroad.
> Colossal funds were needed. There were people opposed to such a
> decision. But then the idea of greater profitability was put forward.
> Under this flag there occurred many changes and actions that to other
> contemporary economists seem inexplicable. Now it is hard to imagine
> building a city like Komsomolsk-na-Amure in the taiga just to accom-
> modate one plant. Planners now approach things somehow from a
> utilitarian viewpoint: we'll get a blast furnace here, a mill there, save a
> million here. But meanwhile many regions in Siberia and the far east
> have been put in a difficult position.[96]

After examining the available materials on the main features of
investment activity in ferrous metallurgy (from the second half of
the 1970s), we have come to the conclusion that its most characteristic element is the total break between actual practice and the Soviet
leadership's scenario of development for this sector of the economy.

According to the scenario, the cornerstone of development in
ferrous metallurgy (and its main function today) is to repudiate the
drive for quantitative indicators of production growth and to redirect efforts toward a qualitative improvement in production and
an expansion in the variety of its production. In practice, however,
Soviet investment activity is primarily directed toward achieving
greater quantitative growth (in accordance with the earlier fetish for
"tons" irrespective of utility or quality); investment in technologies
that would provide higher qualitative indices of production is being
reduced.

Moreover, according to the scenario, the technological reconstruction (which is necessary for achieving this primary goal) is to
be accomplished with smaller expenditures of resources by max-
imizing investment in the updating of existing capacities and by
minimizing investment in the creation of new capacities. In practice, however, it is precisely the reconstruction of old capacities that
is proving more capital-intensive and complicated, and here the
explanation rests in the lack of preparedness in the pertinent economic sectors of the machine-building and construction industries.

Furthermore, according to the scenario, investment in ferrous metallurgy should be distributed internally in such a way that it will stimulate the accelerated liquidation of worn out, antiquated fixed capital. In practice, however, the lion's share of investments are directed toward the introduction of new fixed capital amid the conservation and accumulation of old fixed capital. That in turn means enormous and constantly increasing expenditures for their repair and maintenance.

It should be noted that ferrous metallurgy is by no means unique. An investment process that operates according to past inertia (and in no way corresponds to the real needs for modernization and structural improvements) is in fact intrinsic to industry in the USSR and to most of its sectors.

The foregoing comments pertain to investment from centralized state sources. But the independent investment activity of enterprises is making the investment flow more substantial and is creating auxiliary capacities through the partial modernization of old equipment that is being renovated and repaired. A significant segment of these increases in productive capacities remain concealed from the central administration and constitute unreported reserves of enterprises. At the same time, however, the resources required to sustain such capacities are declining, and the exhaustion of fixed capital is steadily rising.

Considered more broadly, all this creates a strange picture of a simple and expanded reproduction of fixed capital. It is directly contradictory to the theoretical constructs of Soviet political economy, which is of course based on Marx's schemes of economic reproduction. It is therefore no easy task, especially for Soviet theoretical economists, to make sense of what is emerging, or to design a model that replicated the real reproduction of capital under these distorted conditions in the contemporary Soviet economy.

Solving the cardinal problems in ferrous metallurgy does not depend, however, merely on internal investment strategies. On the contrary, implementation of a program to achieve technological modernization in this sector is a highly complex, multifaceted problem. In the first instance, it is essential to achieve the corresponding development in metallurgical machine building, even if that must be done at the expense of reducing the investment share given directly to ferrous metallurgy itself.

That would, of course, entail the highly disagreeable result of a transitory decline in steel production. But a serious reconstruction of the existing investment proportions is in fact only possible if the Soviet leadership consciously accepts the need to plan a temporary reduction in the production of certain sectors of the economy (in this case, of ferrous metallurgy). The whole question is whether it has the capacity to make such a decision, which is so politically and economically difficult.

Conclusion

In order to assess the supply of steel and hence fulfillment of the plan to accelerate machine building in the second half of the 1980s, we shall focus on the quantitative and qualitative indices for production of rolled steel (see Chapter 2 for more details). This is a matter of cardinal importance, and Gorbachev has explicitly termed it the key element in any improvement of the Soviet economy.

Under the level of production set in the plan, the supply of steel for machine building depends on a number of factors. The most important of these are: (1) changes in the proportions of the production of rolled steel and output in machine building; (2) changes in metal-consumption levels in the production of machinery; and (3) changes in the structure of consumption of materials for machine building—replacement of steel with other materials, such as plastics, synthetics, aluminum, and composite materials. What are the real prospects for a controlled, directed alteration of these factors in a way that would allow the steel deficit to be eliminated?

To answer that question, let us first compare the trends in machine-building output and rolled-steel production for the period after elimination of the Khrushchevian Sovnarkhozy—that is, during the period of Soviet industrial development under its existing organizational structure, 1966–83. The results show that the tempo of production growth of these industrial sectors was essentially the same: the average annual growth rate was 3–4 percent.[1] Hence this main factor, taken by itself, offers no advantage for the development of machine construction.

With respect to the second factor (the intensity of metal consumption), Chapter 1 of this book pointed out that metal-consumption intensity has tended to decline, but that the real achievements here were insignificant. According to Fal'tsman's data, in the period 1966–83 the net rate for metal-consumption intensity declined by 15 percent over an eighteen-year period—that is, less than 1 percent per annum.[2] Prime Minister Ryzhkov told the Twenty-seventh Party Congress that in the twelfth five-year plan period a 40–45 percent increase in the machine-building output must be accompanied by a mere 9 percent increase in the production of steel.[3] Ryzhkov stressed in his speech that growth in the machine-building sector should be achieved with the help of a more economical use of steel. Let us note that the shortage of steel has always been one of the main reasons for not fulfilling production plans cited by the Soviet machine builders. The current five-year plan has placed an unprecedented emphasis on the efficient use of steel. Specific targets for steel have been incorporated into the plan of every machine-building ministry. In 1985 the statistical yearbook *Narodnoye Khozyaystvo SSSR* published for the first time a special table dealing with "steel wastage in machine building and metalworking."[4] Judging by the data reported in that table, the share of steel wastage in total steel consumption is 22 percent and has remained constant for twenty-five years (since 1960).

Thus in the twelfth five-year plan period the machine-building sector must plan to satisfy its demand for steel not so much by getting more metal but by using it more efficiently. For example, according to the current five-year plan, one of the main machine-building branches—heavy machine building—must satisfy 75 percent of its new demand for steel by economizing. The use of steel in that branch of industry can be illustrated by the following statistics: in the production of locomotives 290 kilograms of every ton of steel is wastage; in the production of diesel engines 560 kilograms of every ton is wastage.[5]

Judging by published statistics, there has been an improvement in the use of steel in the machine-building sector. But even these statistics indicate that the improvement is nowhere near the plan targets.[6]

Is Soviet machine construction capable of making such a reduction in the metal-consumption intensity of its production? Soviet experts testify to the fact that this industrial sector is in fact not prepared for so revolutionary a change. To attain the planned transition to more efficient utilization of metal it would be necessary to modernize the technology of metal finishing, to introduce fundamental changes in the methods and norms for machine building, to improve the organizational structure, and to create an economic mechanism to regulate the process of metal consumption and conservation. There are no grounds to expect that, under the existing technological level of Soviet machine-tool building, and under the conditions of the existing economic system, it will be possible to achieve goals of so broad a scale in the next five-year plan. Taking into account the foregoing, we find that the plan to accelerate development in machine construction by means of a reduced shortfall in steel is utterly divorced from reality and has little prospect of realization.

As for the third factor (the substitution of other materials), it is important to emphasize that a cautious approach to the use of materials has been one of the distinctive features of the Soviet economy. Indeed, when measured against each unit of national income, materials (measured in weight) are 50 percent greater than in other industrially advanced nations. The fact that steel accounts for an excessively high share (95 percent) of the materials used by the machine-building sector, and the fact that the utilization of other materials (for example, plastics, aluminum, nonferrous metals, and composites) is developing at a snail's pace, means of course that the Soviets have great difficulty producing those categories of machines and equipment of greatest importance for their economy—as in electrical, computer, and energy sectors.

But a more intensive substitution of other construction materials for steel has been impeded by the lack of a clear policy in this sphere by the top leadership in Soviet industry. To be sure, top party and state directives ritualistically reaffirm the need to make more extensive use of substitute materials for steel in both the machine-building and construction industries. Nevertheless, such declarations are offset by widespread skepticism among influential figures of the technocratic elite toward the technical advantages of these materials and to the expediency of using them to replace steel. Thus one of the most authoritative Soviet experts, Lev Zusman, expressed it this way: "Alongside the underestimation of the competitiveness of steel, one finds clear overestimation of certain construction materials used as substitutes." On the basis of his own calculations, Zusman came to the conclusion that "in the foreseeable future it is hardly possible to anticipate any substantial replacement of steel with aluminum, titanium, and plastics."[7] Apparently, his assessment of the situation is realistic.

"The country is hungry for metal," declared Stalin's Central Committee at the outset of industrialization in 1929.[8] The same statement can be made by the Gorbachev leadership almost half a century later. It is no secret that the five-year plans of industrialization failed, and that shortages of metal had a lot to do with it. Judging by reports in the Soviet press, in 1987 the situation was no better.[9] Many industrial and construction enterprises cannot fulfill their production plans due to the shortage of metal. Even such giants of Soviet machine building as the Minsk Tractor Plant "are literally suffocating without steel," wrote *Sotsialisticheskaya industriya* in April 1987.[10] All signs indicate that the "hunger for metal" is disrupting the ambitious twelfth five-year plan as well.

Gorbachev has replaced the leadership of the steel industry, including the minister. These measures, however, appear to have had little effect on the way in which the steel industry functions. The growth of quantitative indicators has continued, (steel output grew by almost 4 percent in 1986), but no serious qualitative changes have been introduced. The accumulated burden of problems of the steel industry cannot be eased either by changes in its leadership or by transfer of enterprises to self-financing or by any other palliative measures intended to improve its management. As in the Soviet industry as a whole, the fundamental problems of this branch are rooted in the Soviet economic system. The longer the radical reform, or in other words transition to a market economy, is postponed, the more remote the eradication of the "hunger for metal" appears.

Notes

Introduction

1. P. Sopin, "Plany i tumany," *Izvestiya*, January 18, 1988.
2. Yu. Kurbatov, "Metall: Kachestvo—rezerv ekonomii," *Sotsialisticheskaya industriya*, January 30, 1988.
3. *Narkhoz*, 1970, p. 190; *Narkhoz*, 1980, p. 158; *Narkhoz*, 1985, pp. 140, 142.
4. Ibid.; *Narkhoz*, 1985, p. 141; *Ekonomicheskaya gazeta*, No. 51, 1985, p. 6.

Chapter 1. Dynamics and Peculiarities of Steel Consumption in the USSR

1. V. Efimov, "Effectivnost' metallopotrebleniya," *Planovoe khozyaistvo*, No. 8, 1983, p. 33. This translation and all translations hereafter are the author's.
2. A. Polyak, *Uluchshenie ispol'zovaniya metalla v narodnom khozyaistve SSSR*, Moscow, Nauka, 1971, p. 33; A. Kamalov et al., *Analiz structury proizvodstva i potrebleniya chernykh metallov v SSSR* Moscow, Metallurgiya, 1980, p. 19.
3. *KPSS v rezolyutsikyakh i resheniyakh S"ezdov, konferentsiy i plenumov TsK*, No. 10, 1969–71, p. 402; No. 12, 1975–77, p. 229; No. 14, 1980–81, p. 267.
4. Boris Rumer, *Investment and Reindustrialization in the Soviet Economy*, Boulder, Colorado, Westview Press, 1984, p. 2; *Narkhoz*, 1985, p. 363.

5. Narkhoz, 1980, p. 333; Pravda, November 20, 1981.

6. Rumer, Investment and Reindustrialization, p. 18.

7. Val'tukh, "Investitsii—dvigatel' ekonomiki," EKO, No. 3, 1982, p. 5.

8. Narkhoz, 1980, p. 347.

9. KPSS v rezolyutsiyakh, No. 10, p. 383; No. 12, p. 200; Narkhoz, 1980, p. 164; Narkhoz, 1985, p. 129.

10. Narkhoz, 1980, p. 338; Narkhoz, 1985, p. 368.

11. KPSS v rezolyutsiyakh, No. 10, p. 385; No. 12, pp. 206–7.

12. Organizatsiya i planirovanie otraslei narodnogo khozyaistva, No. 36, Kiev, 1974, p. 137.

13. Ibid.

14. Kamalov et al., Analiz, p. 19; Polyak, Uluchshenie, p. 20.

15. Narkhoz, 1981, pp. 205, 379; Narkhoz, 1985, pp. 153, 373.

16. A. Tokarev, "Vozmozhnosti ratsional'nogo ispol'zovaniya resursov v stroitel'stve," Planovoye khozyaistvo, No. 8, 1983, pp. 13–14.

17. L. Zusman, "Metalloemkost' obschehestvennogo proizvodstva," Voprosi ekonomiki, No. 3, 1981, p. 83.

18. Ibid.

19. N. Mel'nikov, "Ekonomiya metalla, vyigrysh vo vremeni," EKO, No. 9, 1980, p. 4.

20. N. Smelyakov, "S chego nachinaetsya rodina," Moscow, Politizdat, 1975, p. 224.

21. I. Pashko, "Rezervy snizheniya materialoemkosti," EKO, No. 3, 1976, p. 31; Organizatsiya i planirovanie otraslei narodnogo khozyaystva, 41, Kiev, 1975, p. 43.

22. L. Zusman, "Metalloemkost': Tekhnika i ekonomika," EKO, No. 4, 1980, p. 142.

23. Ibid.

24. Kamalov et al., Analiz, p. 19; Narkhoz, 1975, p. 247.

25. N. Safronov et al., "Rezervy proizvoditel'nosti truda v promyshlennosti SSSR," Sotsialisticheskii trud, No. 7, 1983, p. 12.

26. Polyak, Uluchshenie, p. 78.

27. N. Ryzhkov, "Kachestvo mashin i material'nye resursy," Planovoe khozyaistvo, No. 9, 1981, p. 19.

28. Ibid.

29. N. Ryzhkov, "Metally i mashiny," Planovoe khozyaistvo, No. 12, 1980, p. 16.

30. A. Myrtsimov, "Chernoi metallurgii intensivnyi put' razvitiya," EKO, No. 4, 1980, p. 129.

31. Ibid.

32. I. Kazanets, "Osnovnye zadachi chernoi metallurgii na sovremennom etape," Stal', No. 9, 1977, p. 770.

33. Ryzhkov, "Metally i mashiny," p. 18.

34. Ibid.; Narkhoz, 1980, p. 158; Narkhoz, 1985, p. 141.

35. Stal', No. 1, 1978, p. 79.

36. G. Kurbatova, "Mashinostroenie i investitsionnye protsessy," *EKO*, No. 3, 1982, p. 77.

37. I. Pashko, "Resursy ekonomii metalla i povyshenie ego kachestva," *Planovoe khozyaistvo*, No. 7, 1981, p. 81.

38. Ibid.

39. *Sotsialisticheskaya industriya*, August 21, 1982, p. 2.

40. Ibid.

41. M. Kaganskii, "Defitsit otvetstvennosty," *Material'no-tekhnicheskoe snabzhenie*, No. 11, 1981, p. 28.

42. *Sotsialisticheskaya industriya*, September 3, 1982, p. 2.

43. Ibid., September 2, 1982, p. 2.

44. Ibid., September 3, 1982, p. 2.

45. Ibid., September 2, 1982, p. 2.

46. E. Kubrin, "Rol' material'nykh zapasov v povyshenii effectivnosti obshchestvennogo proizvodstva," *Ekonomicheskie nauki*, No. 7, 1981, p. 55.

47. I. Starostin, "Zanaryadka metalloprokata i privedennie tonny," *Material'no-tekhnicheskoe snabzhenie*, No. 3, 1983, p. 20.

48. Krepit' Distsipliny Postavok, ed., *Material'no-tekhnicheskoe snabzhenie*, No. 3, 1983, p. 4.

Chapter 2. Qualitative Achievements of Soviet Steel Production

1. *Sotsialisticheskaya industriya*, October 25, 1984.

2. *Metallurg*, No. 1, 1983, p. 1.

3. N. Sklokin, *Ekonomicheskie problemy povysheniya kachestva i razvitiya sortamenta chernykh metalloy*, Moscow, Metallurgiya, 1978, p. 94; A. Sokolov and G. Filosofov, "Povyshaya kachestvo metalla," *Material'no-tekhnicheskoe snabzhenie*, No. 10, 1981, p. 18.

4. L. Spivakovskii, "Vygodnyi i nevygodnyi prokat," *Sotsialisticheskaya industriya*, March 19, 1982.

5. Ibid.; I. Kazanets, "Osnovnye zadachi chernoi metallurgii na sovremennom etape," *Stal'*, No. 9, 1977, p. 770.

6. Spivakovskii, "Vygodnyi i nevygodnyi prokat."

7. N. Tulin, *Perspektivy razvitiya kachestvennoi metallugii SSSR*, Moscow, Metallurgiya, 1983, p. 25; *Narkhoz*, 1981, p. 183.

8. *Narkhoz*, 1981, p. 149; A. Kamalov et al., *Analiz struktury proizvodstva i potrebleniya chernykh metallov v SSSR*, Moscow, Metallurgiya, 1980, p. 55.

9. Kamalov et al., *Analiz struktury*, p. 55; Tulin, "Perspektivy," pp. 25, 149.

10. *Sotsialisticheskaya industriya*, October 25, 1984; *Narkhoz*, 1983, p. 153; Kamalov et al., *Analiz struktury*, p. 46.

11. A. Kablukovskii, "Razvitie vnepechnykh sposobov rafinirovaniya stali," *Metallurg*, No. 4, 1980, p. 25.

12. M. Malakhov, "Vnedrenie dostizhenii nauki i techniki na predpriyatiyakh chernoi metallurgii," *Stal'*, No. 7, 1982, p. 93; Tulin, *Perspektivy*, p. 158; N. Sklokin and L. Makarov, "Osnoynye napravleniya technicheskogo perevooruzheniya chernoi metallurgii," *Metallurg*, No. 1, 1983, p. 2.

13. "Promyshlennost' SSSR," Moscow, *Statistika*, 1964, p. 169; *Narkhoz*, 1970, p. 193; *Narkhoz*, 1985, p. 141. Data on the production of sheet metal with a thickness of more than 5 millimeters were last given in 1978; at the time it was 14.1 million tons—that is, production had increased 260 percent since 1960 (*Narkhoz*, 1978, p. 147).

14. S. Gubert, "Osnovnye napravleniya razvitiya chernoi metallurgii na 1981–1985," *Stal'*, No. 8, 1979, p. 570.

15. R. Arutyunov, "Marshrutami tekhnicheskogo progressa," *Vestnik mashinostroeniya*, No. 6, 1983, p. 3.

16. I. Morozov, "Metalloemkost' mashin i normy," *Voprosy ekonomiki*, No. 12, 1980, p. 53.

17. I. Uzlov, "Effektivnyi put' povysheniya kompleksa svoisty massovykh vidov metalloproduktsii," *Metallurg*, No. 11, 1981, p. 5.

18. V. Bakhtinov and Yu. Bakhtinov, *Proizvodstvo ekonomichnykh profilei prokata*, Moscow, Metallurgiya, 1984, p. 4.

19. Calculated on the basis of number in *Narkhoz*, 1970, p. 192; 1975, p. 246; 1980, p. 158; 1983, p. 153; and *Stal'*, No. 2, 1976, p. 98; No. 9, 1977, p. 770.

20. N. Tikhonov, "Chernaya metallurgiya i technicheskii progress promyshlennosti," *Stal'*, No. 10, 1977, p. 873; A. Kugushin, "Zadachi ostraslevoi nauki v svete reshenii 26 s"ezda KPSS," *Stal'*, No. 9, 1981, p. 2.

21. *Narkhoz*, 1981, p. 183.

22. *Metallurg*, No. 8, 1983, p. 32; N. Mityaev, "Osnovnye proizvodstvennye fondy chernoi metallurgii," Metallurgiya, 1977, p. 143.

23. *Stal'*, No. 8, 1979, p. 606.

24. Estimated from data in Kamalov et al., *Analiz Struktury*.

25. D. Tursunov et al., "Ekonomicheskaya effectivnost' kontrolya kachestva tolstolistovogo prokata," *Organizatsiya i planirovanie otraslei narodnogo khozyaistva*, Kievskii Universitet, No. 52, 1978, p. 109.

26. *Metallurgicheskaya i gornorudnaya promyshlennost'*, No. 4, 1981, p. 4.

27. Kamalov et al., *Analiz Struktury*, p. 18.

28. *Sotsialisticheskaya industriya*, August 22, 1984, p. 1.

29. A. Shoifot, "Vlozheniya i otdacha," *EKO*, No. 3, 1981, p. 97.

30. A. Tselikov, "Effektivnost' novykh protsessov i agregatov," *EKO*, No. 3, 1976, p. 26.

31. *Stal'*, No. 10, 1982, p. 90.

32. *Pravda*, November 9, 1985, p. 3.

33. *KPSS v rezolyutsiyakh i resheniyakh*, Moscow, Izdatel'stvo Politicheskoi Literatury, No. 12, 1978, p. 196; No. 14, 1982, p. 243; *Narkhoz*, 1983, p. 153.

34. Gubert, "Osnovnye napravleniya," p. 570.

35. *Narkhoz*, 1983, p. 153.

36. *Sotsialisticheskaya industriya*, October 25, 1984.

37. *Pravda*, November 9, 1985, p. 2.

Chapter 3. Soviet Steel Plants

1. G. Bobylev et al., *Povyshenie rentabel'nosti proizvodstva v chernoi metallurgii*, Moscow, Metallurgiya, 1976, p. 144; V. Cheplanov and G. Sorokina, *Osnovnye narodno-khozyastvennye i otraslevye faktory povysheniya rentabel'nosti proizvodstva v chernoi metallurgii*, Moscow, Metallurgiya, 1985, p. 37; *Stal'*, No. 4, 1983, p. 5. See notes 16, 25, and 26, below.

2. *Stal'*, No. 1, 1976, p. 66.

3. N. Gurov, "K novym vysotam," *Metallurgicheskaya i gornorudnaya promyshlennost'*, No. 2, 1975, p. 12.

4. Yu. Zateishchikov, "Sovershenstvuya kontrol' za postavkami," *Material'no-tekhnicheskoe snabzhenie*, No. 5, 1982, p. 46. Bobylev, *Povyshenie rentabel'nosti proizvodstva*, p. 144.

5. "Steel Industry in Brief," Japan, Institute for Iron and Steel Studies, 1977.

6. *Stal'*, No. 5, 1982, p. 42.

7. Estimated by experts.

8. *Stal'*, No. 1, 1976, p. 4.

9. G. Matukhno, "Est' 200 millionov tonn krivorozhskoi stali," *Metallurg*, No. 12, 1982, p. 12.

10. *Metallurgicheskaya i gornorudnaya promyshlennost'*, No. 2, 1975, p. 12.

11. Ibid., No. 4, 1978, p. 10.

12. *Stal'*, No. 2, 1977, p. 99.

13. G. Vasilenko and V. Frolov, "Pochemu kominatu trudno?" *EKO*, No. 11, 1982, p. 79; *Stal'*, No. 2, 1983, p. 46.

14. *Ocherki ekonomiki Sibiri*, Novosibirsk, Nauka, 1980, p. 184. A. Kamalov et al., *Analiz Struktury proizvodstva i potrebleniya chernykh metallov v SSSR*, Moscow, Metallurgiya, 1980, p. 18.

15. *Stal'*, No. 1, 1976, p. 46.

16. *EKO*, No. 12, 1979, p. 39; *Razvitie metallurgii v Ukrainskoi SSR*, Kiev, Naukova Dumka, 1980, p. 7; *Metallurgicheskaya i gornorudnaya promishlennost'*, No. 4, 1978, p. 2; *Stal'*, No. 12, 1980, p. 1047; *Sotsialisticheskaya industriya*, April 26, 1983, p. 1; *Metallurg*, No. 12, 1982, pp. 9, 12,

16; Narodnoye khozyaystvo Kazakhstana, 1983, p. 45; Stal', No. 9, 1981, p. 3.

17. Razvitie metallurgii v Ukrainskoi SSSR, p. 300.

18. Stal', No. 8, 1982, p. 70; Metallurg, No. 8, 1983, p. 44.

19. Metallurg, No. 12, 1982, p. 7.

20. Stal', No. 2, 1979, p. 85; Metallurgicheskaya i gornorudnaya promyshlennost', No. 4, 1981, p. 4; Metallurg, No. 8, 1983, p. 1.

21. Ya. Kulikov, "Zadachi chernoi metallurgii Ukrainy v 1980s," Metallurg, No. 4, 1980, p. 10; Stal', No. 2, 1977, p. 99.

22. N. Tereshko, "Magnitka: chto za gorizontom?" EKO, No. 3, 1984, p. 141.

23. Stal', No. 1, 1982, pp. 1, 23; Stal', No. 2, 1982, p. 5; Stal', No. 8, 1977, p. 681; Stal', No. 4, 1982, p. 1; Metallurg, No. 7, 1981, p. 41; M. Berkovich, "Kombinat na ploshchadi pobed," EKO, No. 2, 1978, p. 96.

24. Sotsialisticheskaya industriya, March 24, 1982, p. 2.

25. EKO, No. 12, 1979, p. 29; Razvitie metallurgii v Ukrainskoi SSR, pp. 7, 454; Stal', No. 1, 1982, p. 76; Metallurg, No. 12, 1982, p. 8; Stal', No. 11, 1977, p. 953; Stal', No. 2, 1983, p. 48; Metallurg, No. 8, 1983, p. 38; Metallurg, No. 8, 1982, p. 20; Stal', No. 8, 1982, pp. 70, 71; Metallurgicheskay i gornorudnaya promyshlennost', No. 4, 1980, p. 63.

26. Metallurg, No. 12, 1982, p. 26; Stal', No. 4, 1982, p. 6; Zakavkazskii ekonomicheskii raiion, Moscow, Nauka, 1973, p. 53; Stal', No. 12, 1982, p. 11.

27. Stal', No. 10, 1982, p. 90; N. A. Tikhonov, Soviet Economy, Moscow, Novosti, 1983, p. 93.

28. I. Ustiyan, "Moldaavaskaya SSR v edinom narodno-khozyaistvennom komplekse strany," Kommunist Moldavii, No. 6, 1983, p. 14; G. Serov, "Kapital'nym vlozheniyam-vysokuyu effektivnost," Kommunist Belorussii, No. 1, 1983, p. 42; A. Tselikov, "Predposylki sozdaniya metallurgicheskoro proizvodstva novogo tida," Vestnik Akademii Nauk SSSR, No. 7, 1983, p. 25; Pravda, July 6, 1984, p. 1; V. Zimin, "Perspektivy stroitel'stva nebol'shinkh peredel'nykh zavodov," Planovoe khozyaistvo, No. 12, 1978, p. 129.

29. Stal', No. 8, 1981, p. 36; Metallurg, No. 4, 1983, p. 4; Stal', No. 7, 1978, p. 578.

30. Stal', No. 3, 1982, p. 48.

31. Stal', No. 5, 1983, p. 95; Sotsialisticheskaya industriya, April 20, 1982, p. 2.

32. Stal', No. 10, 1975, p. 939.

33. Ibid.

Chapter 4. Capacity Utilization

1. Pravda, December 28, 1982.

2. Val'tukh, "Investitsii-dvigatel' ekonomiki," EKO, No. 3, 1982, p. 15.

3. V. Kirichenko, "O nekotorykh voprosakh," *Planovoe khozyaistvo*, No. 9, 1982, p. 62.

4. *Stal'*, No. 4, 1979, p. 242; N. Ivantsova, "Nauchno-teknicheskii progress v chernoi metallurgii," *Voprosy ekonomiki*, No. 2, 1985, p. 54.

5. B. Martynov, "Uluchshenie ispol'zovaniya proizvodstvennykh moshchnosteiy," *Voprosy ekonomiki*, No. 4, 1977, p. 79.

6. *Metodicheskie ukazaniya k razrabotke gosudarstvennukh planov ekonomicheskogo i sotsial'nogo razvitiya SSR*, Moscow, Ekonomika, 1980, p. 186.

7. *Intensifikatsiya i rezervy ekonomiki*, AN SSSR, Institut Ekonomiki, Moscow, Nauka, 1970, p. 219.

8. N. Sklokin et al., *Osnovnye fondy i proizvodsturnnye moshchnosti chernoi metallurgii*, Moscow, Metallurgiya, 1968, p. 169; M. Mityaev, *Osnovnye proizvodstvennye fondy chernoi metallurgii*, Moscow, Metallurgiya, 1977, p. 173.

9. Sklokin, *Osnovnye fondy*, pp. 168–202.

10. Ibid.

11. M. Barun, *Osnovnoi kapital promyshlennosti SSSR*, Moscow, Cosizdat, 1930, p. 151.

12. Mityaev, *Osnovnye proizvodstvennye fondy*, p. 173.

13. Quoted by John Norton in *Measures of Productive Capacity*. Hearing before the Subcommittee on Economic Statistics to the Joint Economic Committee, Congress of the United States. 87th Congress, 2d Session, Washington, D.C., 1962, p. 100.

14. Ibid., pp. 4–5.

15. *Ispol'zovanie proizvodstvennykh moshchnostei v promyshlennosti*, Kiev, Maukova Dumka, 1979, p. 11.

16. Ibid.

17. Sklokin et al., *Osnovnye fondy*, p. 159.

18. *Stal'*, No. 1, 1982, p. 76.

19. *Metallurg*, No. 8, 1981, p. 6; *Narodnoye khozyaistvo Ukrainskoi SSR*, p. 111.

20. *Sotsialisticheskaya industriya*, December 14, 1982.

21. Ia. Kvasha, *Rezervnye moshchnosti*, Moscow, Nauka, 1971, p. 38.

22. Ibid., p. 15.

23. *Pravda*, October 24, 1983, p. 2.

24. Mityaev, *Osnovnye proizvodstvennye fondy*, p. 131; Sklokin et al., *Osnovnye fondy*, p. 96; *Razvitie metallurgii v Ukrainskoi SSR*, Kiev, Naukova Dumka, 1980, p. 446.

25. *Sotsialisticheskaya industriya*, May 4, 1982.

26. *Narkhoz*, 1978, pp. 146, 149. *Narkhoz*, 1982, pp. 144–145.

27. N. Lelyukhina, *Ekonomicheskaya effektivnost' razmeshcheniya chernoi metallurgii*, Moscow, Nauka, 1973, p. 256; *Stal'*, No. 4, 1980, p. 266.

28. *Metallurgicheskaya i gornorudnaya promyshlennost'*, No. 5, 1976, p. 3; Lelyukhina, *Ekonomicheskaya effektvnost'*, p. 34.

29. *Razvitie metallurgii v Ukrainskoi*, p. 459; Mityaev, *Osnovnye pro-izvodstvennye fondy*, p. 131.

30. Sklokin et al., *Osnovnye fondy*, p. 95.

31. *Narkhoz*, 1982, p. 145.

32. *Stal'*, No. 1, 1982, p. 26; No. 2, 1982, p. 30; No. 3, 1982, p. 12; No. 10, 1982, p. 15; No. 11, 1982, p. 17; No. 1, 1983, p. 11; No. 5, 1983, p. 32.

33. Ibid., No. 10, 1982, pp. 14–15.

34. Ibid., No. 1, 1983, p. 11.

35. *Metallurg*, No. 7, 1981, p. 21.

36. *Razvitie metallurgii v Ukrainskoi*, p. 442.

37. *Stal'*, No. 8, 1981, p. 11.

38. Ibid., No. 1, 1981, p. 26.

39. Ibid., No. 1, 1982, p. 31.

40. Ibid., No. 10, 1982, p. 15.

41. *Metallurgicheskaya i gornorudnaya*, No. 1, 1977, p. 1.

42. *Stal'*, No. 4, 1980, p. 266.

43. Ibid.

44. Ibid., No. 5, 1983, p. 81; No. 12, 1982, p. 4; No. 5, 1979, p. 347; *Razvitie metallurgii v Ukrainskoi*, p. 512; *Report of Energy Efficiency in Soviet Ferrous Metallurgy*, Battelle Columbus Laboratories, Contr. no. 80N–383100–000, table III–8, p. 47.

45. *Stal'*, No. 7, 1981, p. 3.

46. Ibid., No. 4, 1982, p. 36.

47. *Metallurg*, No. 6, 1982, p. 20.

48. Ibid., No. 1, 1983, p. 1.

49. V. Andreev, *Osnovnye problemy tekhnicheskogo progressa i ekono-miki chernoi metallurgii SSSR*, Moscow, Metallurgiya, 1976, p. 174.

50. *Stal'*, No. 1, 1976, p. 20.

51. Ibid., No. 6, 1980, p. 450.

52. Ibid., No. 1, 1976, p. 29.

53. Ibid., No. 8, 1981, p. 70.

54. Ibid., No. 1, 1983, p. 94.

55. Andreev, *Osnovnye problemy*, p. 186; *Stal'*, No. 2, 1979, p. 111.

56. *Stal'*, No. 8, 1981, p. 70.

57. *Razvitie metallurgii v Ukrainskoi*, p. 511.

58. *Stal'*, No. 2, 1977, p. 98; No. 3, 1982, p. 2.

59. G. Sergeev et al., *Effektinnost' vyplavki elektrostali*, Moscow, Metal-lurgiya, 1977, p. 9.

60. *Stal'*, No. 3, 1982, p. 2.

61. Ibid., No. 10, 1979, p. 756.

62. Ibid., No. 8, 1981, p. 42.

63. *Metallurg*, No. 3, 1982, p. 1.

64. *Sotsialisticheskaya industriya*, November 27, 1983, p. 1.

65. *Metallurg*, No. 3, 1982, p. 30.

66. *Stal'*, No. 1, 1984, p. 2.

67. *Metallurg*, No. 12, 1982, p. 26; *Sotsialisticheskaya industriya*, November 27, 1983.

68. *Metallurgicheskaya i gornorudnaya*, No. 2, 1983, p. 42.

69. *Razvitie metallurgii v Ukrainskoi*, p. 334; G. Bobylev et al., *Povyshenie rentabel'nosti proizvodstva v chernoi metallurgii*, Moscow, Metallurgiya, 1976, p. 150.

70. *Ekonomicheskaya gazeta*, No. 34, 1983, p. 2.

71. K. Zhilyaev et al., *Ekonomiya material'nykh resursov v chernoi metallurgii*, Moscow, Metallurgiya, 1979, p. 56.

72. *Stal'*, No. 11, 1982, p. 23.

73. *Metallurg*, No. 7, 1981, p. 29.

74. *Razvitie metallurgii v Ukrainskoi*, p. 478.

75. *Stal'*, No. 8, 1981, p. 73.

76. G. Bobylev et al., *Povyshenie*, p. 66.

77. *Stal'*, No. 7, 1983, p. 2.

78. *Trud*, January 10, 1984.

79. N. Tulin et al., *Persektivy razvitiya kachestvennoi metallurgii SSSR*, Moscow, Metallurgiya, 1983, p. 47.

80. *Metallurgicheskaya i gornorudnaya promyshlennost'*, No. 4, 1976, p. 71.

81. International Institute of Steel (IIS), *Commentary Techno-Economic Report*, February 1982, XI–2, p. 4.

82. *Stal'*, No. 10, 1979, p. 751.

83. Ibid., No. 9, 1978, p. 801.

84. Ibid., No. 2, 1979, p. 112.

85. Ibid., No. 9, 1983, p. 3.

86. Ibid., No. 2, 1979, p. 112.

87. Ibid., No. 11, 1981, p. 9.

88. *Razvitie metallurgii v Ukrainskoi*, p. 475; *Stal'*, No. 11, 1981, p. 10.

89. *Razvitie metallurgii v Ukrainskoi*, p. 474.

90. *Stal'*, No. 11, 1981, p. 10.

91. Ibid., No. 12, 1982, p. 43.

92. *Kommunist*, No. 3, 1984, p. 114.

93. N. Sklokin, *Ekonomicheskie problemy privysheniya kachestva i razvitiya sortamenta chernykh metallov*, Moscow, Metallurgiya, 1975, p. 114; *Stal'*, No. 7, 1982, p. 4.

94. *Ekonomicheskaya gazeta*, August 24, 1983, p. 1.

95. *Metallurgicheskaya i gornorudnaya promyshlennost'*, No. 2, 1983, p. 42.

96. Andreev, *Osnovnye problemy*, p. 18.

97. *Stal'*, No. 1, 1982, p. 47.

98. *Metallurgicheskaya i gornorudnaya promyshlennost'*, No. 2, 1983, p. 61.

99. *Stal'*, No. 1, 1982, p. 47.

100. Ibid., No. 7, 1981, p. 3.

101. Ibid., No. 11, 1977, p. 1012; No. 5, 1979, p. 355; No. 5, 1979, p. 42.

102. Ibid., No. 12, 1982, p. 4.

103. *Organizatsiya truda v chernoi metallurgii: Sbornik trudov*, No. 6, 1977, Moscow, Metallurgiya, p. 10.

104. *Ekonomika chernoi metallurgii: Sbornik trudov*, No. 6, 1976, Moscow, Metallurgiya, p. 276.

105. Ibid., p. 277.

106. *Izvestiya Vuzov, chernaya metallurgiya*, No. 5, 1983, p. 139.

107. Ibid.

108. Ibid.

109. *Sotsialisticheskaya industriya*, October 6, 1983.

110. *Organizatsiya i planirovanie otraslei narodnogo khozyaistva*, No. 59, 1980, Kievskiy Universitet, p. 76.

111. *Metallurgicheskay i gornorudnaya promyshlennost'*, No. 3, 1983, p. 61.

112. *EKO*, No. 1, 1983, p. 43.

113. *Stal'*, No. 7, 1981, p. 75.

114. Ibid., No. 1, 1976, p. 28.

115. *Narkhoz*, 1980, pp. 158, 328.

116. *Kapital'noe stroitel'stvo v SSSR*, Moscow, Statistika, 1961, p. 135; *Narkhoz*, 1970, p. 475; 1978, p. 334; 1979, p. 358; 1980, p. 328.

117. Ibid.

118. *Narkhoz*, 1980, pp. 158, 328; *Stal'*, 1982, p. 4; No. 5, 1983, p. 87; *Metallurg*, No. 1, 1983, p. 1; *Ekonomicheskaya gazeta*, No. 34, August 1983; *Ekonomiya material'nykh resursov v chernoi metallurgii*, Moscow, Metallurgiya, 1979, pp. 36, 37, 44; N. I. Minenko et al., *Proizvoditel'nost' truda v chernoi metallurgii SSSR*, Moscow, Metallurgiya, 1978, p. 12; Mityaev, *Osnovnye proizvodstvennye fondy*, p. 178.

119. B. Lavrovskiy, *Analiz sbalansirovannosti proizvodstvennykh moshchnostey v promyshlennosti SSSR*, Moscow, Nauka, 1983, p. 78.

120. Ibid.

121. Ibid.

122. Boris Rumer, "Soviet Investment Policy: Unresolved Problems," *Problems of Communism*, September–October 1982, p. 59.

123. Ibid.

124. Lavrovskiy, *Analiz*, p. 96.

Chapter 5. Iron-Ore Resources and Their Utilization

1. Yu. Chernegov, "Skudeyut li nedra?," *EKO*, No. 2, 1985, p. 131.

2. Calculated on the basis of the data in G. Mirlin, "Mineral'nye resursy i ekonomika," *Planovoye khozyaistvo*, No. 8, 1983, pp. 38, 41.

3. A. Arbatov and A. Mukhin, "K formirovaniyu dolgosrochnoi strategii," *Ekonomika i matematicheskiye metody*, No. 1, 1987, p. 65.

4. *EKO*, No. 3, 1976, p. 32.

5. *Promyshlennost' SSSR*, Moscow, Statistika, 1964, p. 37; *Narodnoye khozyaistvo SSSR v 1985 godu*, p. 96.

6. *Voprosy ekonomiki*, No. 12, 1982, p. 65.

7. A. Arbatov, "Problemy obespecheniya ekonomiki SSSR mineral'nym syr'yom," *Voprosy ekonomiki*, No. 1, 1987, p. 40.

8. V. Sidorova, "O normativnoi baze dlya dolgosrochnogo planirovaniya razvitiya zhelezorudnoi promyshlennosti," *Gornyi zhurnal*, No. 5, 1979, p. 15.

9. Ibid.

10. *Proizvodstvo, nakoplenie, potreblenie*, Moscow, Ekonomika, 1965, pp. 20, 56, 57.

11. Ibid., p. 165.

12. Ibid.

13. Ibid., pp. 166–167.

14. *Narodnoe khozyaistvo SSSR v 1985 godu*, pp. 100, 112, 117, 125.

15. See N. Ryzhkov, *Doklad, XXVII s"ezd KPSS: Stenograficheskii otchet*, Moscow, 1986.

16. *Sotsialisticheskaya industriya*, April 26, 1987, p. 1.

17. N. Smelyakov, "Razvitie otechestvennogo exporta," *Kommunist*, No. 14, 1984, p. 43.

18. *Sibir' v edinom naronokhozyaistvennom komplekse*, Novosibirsk, Nauka, 1980, p. 134. A. Makarov and A. Vigdorchik, *Toplivno-energeticheskii kompleks*, Moscow, Nauka, 1979, p. 17.

19. P. Lomako, "Po-khozyaiski, kompleksno ispol'zovat' syr'yo," *Ekonomicheskaya gazeta*, No. 39, 1984.

20. Arbatov and Mukhin, "K formirovaniyu dolgosrochnoi strategii," p. 71.

21. Ibid.

22. *Pravda*, June 12, 1985, p. 1.

23. Arbatov, "Problemy obespecheniya ekonomiki," p. 40.

24. M. Kiabbi, "Effektivnost' upravleniya prirodopol'zovaniem i kompleksnoe osvoenie nedr," *Voprosy ekonomiki*, No. 6, 1982, p. 41.

25. A. Tselikov, *Puti ekonomii metalla*, Moscow, Mashinostroenie, 1974, p. 5.

26. V. Vinogradov, "Zhelezorudnye resursy SSSR," *Razvedka i okhrana nedr*, No. 7, 1981, p. 22.

27. S. Kadetov, "Narodno-khozyaistvennye problemy razvitiya chernoi metallurgii," *Voprosy ekonomiki*, No. 3, 1982, p. 54.

28. P. Shiriaev, E. Iarkho, and Iu. Borshch, *Metallurgicheskaya i ekonomicheskaya otsenka zhelzorudnoi bazy SSSR*, Moscow, Metallurgiya, 1978, p. 10.

29. Ibid., p. 10; V. Popov, "Mineral'no-syr'evye resursy strany, ikh ispol'zovanie," *Planovoe khozyaistvo*, No. 4, 1981, p. 36.

30. Ibid.

31. Shiriaev et al., *Metallurgicheskaya i ekonomicheskaya otsenka*, pp. 11–12; N. Lelyukhina, *Ekonomicheskaya effektivnost' razmeshcheniya chernoi metallurgii*, Moscow, Nauka, 1973, p. 138.

32. V. Vinogradov, "Intensifikatsiya proizvodstvennogo potentsiala gornorudnoi promyshlennosti," *Gornyi zhurnal*, No. 10, 1983, p. 9.

33. Lelyukhina, *Ekonomicheskaya effektivnost'*, pp. 133–34.

34. V. Kornienko, "Syr'evye resursy i nekotorye voprosy kompleksnogo ispol'zovaniya nedr Krivbassa," *Gornyi zhurnal*, No. 10, 1983, p. 9.

35. L. Lubenets, "Itogi i zadachi podzemnykh rabot v krivorozhskom basseine," *Gornyi zhurnal*, No. 5, 1981, p. 15.

36. Lelyukhina, *Ekonomicheskaya effektivnost'*, p. 139.

37. Ibid., pp. 145–46.

38. *Sotsialisticheskaya industriia*, June 19, 1983.

39. Siberia connotes here the entire territory east of the Urals up to the Pacific Ocean—that is, those areas that Soviet economic geography defines as western Siberia, eastern Siberia, and the far east.

40. *Ocherki ekonomiki Sibiri*, Novosibirsk, Nauka, 1980, p. 185.

41. Lelyukhina, *Ekonomicheskaya effektivnost'*, pp. 150–55.

42. A. Kononov, "Perspektivy sozdaniya syr'evoi bazy chernoi metallurgii v zone Baikalo-Amurskoi magistrali," *Gornyi zhurnal*, No. 1, 1984, p. 13.

43. *Sibir' v edinom narodno-khozyaistvennom komplekse*, Novosibirsk, Nauka, 1980, pp. 167–80.

44. Kononov, "Perspektivy sozdaniya," pp. 13–14.

45. *Ocherki ekonomiki Sibiri*, pp. 182–83.

46. Sources: A. Astakhov, *Fondootdacha v gornorudnoi promyshlennosti*, Moscow, Nedra, 1978, p. 196; *Gornyi zhurnal*, No. 12, 1982, pp. 3–4; No. 7, 1983, p. 8; No. 3, 1982, p. 3.

47. *Stal'*, No. 12, 1982, pp. 1–4; *Narkhoz*, 1970, p. 190; 1983, p. 154; *Ekonomicheskaya gazeta*, No. 5, 1985, p. 6.

48. *Gornyi zhurnal*, No. 4, 1980, p. 6.

49. Ibid.

50. Ibid., No. 9, 1984, p. 8.

51. V. Andreev, *Osnovnye problemy tekhnicheskogo progressa i ekonomiki chernoi metallurgii SSSR*, Moscow, Metallurgiya, 1976, p. 271.

52. *Kommunist Ukrainy*, No. 2, 1982, p. 62.

53. *Gornyi zhurnal*, No. 1, 1983, p. 3.

54. Ibid., No. 5, 1981, p. 23.

55. Ibid., No. 7, 1983, p. 8.

56. Ibid., No. 2, 1983, p. 30.

57. N. Feitel'man, "Ekonomicheskaya otsenka prirodnykh resursov," *Voprosy ekonomiki*, No. 10, 1980, p. 72.

58. *Gornyi zhurnal*, No. 4, 1981, p. 11.

59. Ibid., No. 2, 1983, p. 33.

60. *Ekonomicheskaya gazeta*, No. 52, 1979.

61. *Gornyi zhurnal*, No. 2, 1983, p. 31.

62. Ibid., No. 2, 1983, p. 33.

63. *Metallurgicheskaya i gorno-rudnaya promyshlennost'*, No. 1, 1983, p. 49.

64. *Gornyi zhurnal*, No. 1, 1983, p. 18.

65. Ibid.; *Metallurgicheskaya i gorno-rudnaya promyshlennost'*, No. 4, 1982, p. 39.

66. *Gornyi zhurnal*, No. 1, 1983, p. 18.

67. Ibid., No. 3, 1984, p. 4.

68. Ibid.

69. Ibid., No. 3, 1982, p. 9.

70. Ibid., No. 8, 1984, p. 4.

71. Ibid., No. 3, 1982, p. 9.

72. Ibid., No. 4, 1981, p. 36.

73. Ibid., No. 8, 1980, p. 5.

74. Ibid., No. 3, 1982, p. 11.

75. Ibid., No. 3, 1982, p. 9.

76. Ibid., No. 5, 1982, p. 10.

77. Ibid., No. 3, 1982, p. 18.

78. V. Vanchikov, "Chernaya metallurgiya SSSR v 1983 g," *Metallurg*, No. 2, 1983, p. 2.

79. *Gornyi zhurnal*, No. 5, 1981, p. 15.

80. Ibid., No. 4, 1981, p. 12.

81. Ibid., No. 3, 1982, pp. 10–11.

82. Andreev, *Osnovnye problemy*, p. 269.

83. Sources: N. Bannyi et al., *Ekonomika chernoi metallurgii SSSR*, Moscow, Metallurgiya, 1978, p. 82; *Gornyi zhurnal*, No. 12, 1982, p. 3.

84. Kadetov, *Narodno-khoziaistvennye problemy*, p. 56.

85. V. Cherkasov, "Put'k rude," *Pravda*, April 19, 1983.

86. V. Cherkasov, "Vokrug rudy," *Pravda*, February 17, 1984.

87. A. Yanshin, "Zachem vezti rudu na Ural?" *Pravda*, February 4, 1981.

88. Ibid.

89. Kadetov, *Narodno-khoaziaistvennye problemy*, p. 57.

90. Andreev, *Osnovnye problemy*, pp. 282–89.

91. Ibid.

92. V. Vanchikov, "Chernaya metallurgiya," p. 2.

93. Sources: I. P. Bannyi et al., *Ekonomika chernoi metallurgii SSSR*, Moscow, 1978, p. 84; *Gornyi zhurnal*, No. 4, 1981, p. 27; *Stal'*, No. 12, 1982, p. 3.

94. Vanchikov, "Chernaya metallurgiya," p. 2.

95. Ibid.

96. L. Zusman, *Metalloemkost' obshchestvennogo proizvodstva*, Moscow, Metallurgiya, 1982, p. 31.

97. N. Tulin et al., *Perspektivy razvitiia kachestvennoi metallurgii SSSR*, Moscow, Metallurgiya, 1983, p. 48.

98. Ibid., p. 47.

99. Ibid., pp. 50–51.

100. Petropavlovskaya and Fal'tsman, "Vtorichnye resursy," p. 46.

101. Ibid., p. 47.

102. S. Anisimov, "Planirovanie proizvodstva i snizhenie materialopotreblennia," *Material'no-technicheskoe snabzhenie*, No. 12, 1983, p. 21.

103. N. Ivantsova, "Nauchno-tekhnicheskii progress v chernoi metallurgii," *Voprosy ekonomiki*, No. 2, 1985, p. 49.

104. Petropavlovskaya and Fal'tsman, "Vtorichnye resursy," p. 48.

105. Ibid.

106. Kadetov, *Narodno-khoziaistvennye problemy*, p. 59.

107. Vanchikov, "Chernaya metallurgiya," p. 2.

108. *Gornyi zhurnal*, No. 5, 1979, p. 16.

109. *Narkhoz*, 1978, p. 334; 1983, p. 349.

Chapter 6. Investment

1. See N. Tikhonov, "Doklad," in *XXVI s"ezd KPSS: Stenograficheskii otchet*, Moscow, Izdatel'stvo politicheskoi literatury, 1981, p. 17.

2. *Narkhoz*, 1985, pp. 410, 367.

3. V. Kirichenko, "O nekotorykh voprosakh dal'neishego sovershenstvovaniya planirovaniya i upravleniya khozyaistvom," *Planovoe khozyaistvo*, No. 9, 1982, p. 62.

4. V. Kirichenko, "Sovershenstvovanie investitsionnogo protsessa," *Izvestiya Akademii Nauk SSSR*, Seriya ekonomicheskaya, Moscow, No. 2, 1984, p. 15; A. Aganbegyan, "Vaznye positivnye sdvigi," *EKO*, No. 6, 1984, p. 10.

5. *Literaturnaya gazeta*, June 12, 1985, p. 1.

6. "Report of the Chairman of the USSR Council of Ministers N. I. Ryzhkov," *Pravda*, March 4, 1986.

7. See, for example, A. Bushinskii and S. Kheinman, "Ob intensifikatskii i investitsiiakh," *EKO*, No. 10, 1983, pp. 144–48.

8. See, for example, K. Val'tukh, "Investitsii—dvigatel' ekonomiki," *EKO*, 1982, p. 3.

9. *Narkhoz*, 1985, p. 363.

10. Val'tukh, "Investitsii-dvigatel' ekonomiki," *EKO*, No. 3, 1982, p. 19.

11. V. Fal'tsman and A. Kornev, "Reesrvy snizheniya kapitaloemkosti moshchnostei promyshlennosti," *Voprosy ekonomiki*, No. 6, 1984, p. 32.

12. Ibid., p. 38.

13. Ibid.

14. Ibid.

15. Ibid., p. 40.

16. V. Fal'tsman, "Moshchnostnoi ekvivalent osnovnykh fondov," *Voprosy ekonomiki*, No. 8, 1980, p. 130.

17. Fal'tsman and Kornev, "Rezervy snizheniya kapitaloemkosti moshchnostei promyshlennosti," p. 38; V. Shtanskii, "Fakticheskaya effectivnosti dapitalovlozhenii," Voprosy ekonomiki, No. 2, 1975, p. 29.

18. L. Rozenova, "Tsena i effektivnost' produktsii mashinostroeniya," Voprosy ekonomiki, No. 2, 1984, p. 30.

19. E. Karlik and D. Demidenko, "O zatratakh na povyshenie kachestva produktsii," Voprosy ekonomiki, No. 9, 1983, p. 69.

20. M. Yartsev, "Tsena proekta," Sotsialisticheskaya industriya, April 18, 1984, p. 2.

21. Quoted in L. Smyshlyayeva, "Sovershenstvovaniye struktury kapital'nykh vlozheniy i osnovnykh fondov," Voprosy ekonomiki, No. 12, 1986, p. 133.

22. Mikhail Gorbachev, "Politicheskiy doklad Tsentral'nogo Komiteta KPSS XXVII s"yezdu Kommunisticheskoy Partii Sovetskogo Soyuza," in XXVII s"yezd Kommunisticheskoy Partii, vol. 2, Moscow, Politizdat, 1986, p. 20.

23. Nikolay Ryzhkov, "Ob osnovnykh napravleniyakh ekonomicheskogo i sotsial'nogo ra-vitiya SSSR na 1986–1990 gody i na period do 2000 goda," in XXVII s"yezd Kommunisticheskoy Partii, vol. 2, Moscow, Politizdat, 1986, p. 20.

24. Narodnoye khozyaistvo SSSR v 1985 g., Moscow, Finansy i Statistika, 1986, p. 52.

25. Ibid.

26. Delez Palterovich, "Proizvodstvennyy apparat i intensifikatsiya," Voprosy ekonomiki, No. 11, 1986, p. 40.

27. Pravda, December 26, 1986, p. 1.

28. Smyshlyayeva, "Sovershenstvovaniye struktury," p. 137.

29. L. Braginskiy, "Nauchno-tekhnicheskiy progress i voprosy rekonstruktsii," Kommunist, No. 15, 1986, p. 38.

30. Boris Rumer, Investment and Reindustrialization in the Soviet Economy, Boulder, Colorado, Westview, 1984, p. 36; Braginskiy, Nauchno-tekhnicheskiy progress, p. 40.

31. A. Tsygichko, "Vyvod iz ekspluatatsii ustarevshikh sredstv Truda," Planovoye khozyaistvo, No. 4, 1985, p. 88.

32. Narkhoz, 1982, pp. 253, 155, 158, 159.

33. A. Aleksandrov, "Vstupitel'noe slovo na godichnom obshshem sobranii Akademii Nauk SSSR," Vestnik Akademii Nauk SSSR, No. 6, 1982, p. 11.

34. D. Chernikov, "Nauchno-tekhnicheskii progress i strukturnye sdvigi v obshchestvennom proizvodstve," Ekonomika i matematicheskie metody, No. 4, 1984, p. 594.

35. M. Gorbachev, "O sozyde ocherednogo XXVII s"ezda," Pravda, April 24, 1985, p. 1.

36. A. Dodonov, "O nekotorykh problemakh teorii amortizatsii," Ekonomicheskie nauki, No. 5, 1973.

37. K. Marx and F. Engels, *Sochineniya*, tom 25, chast' 1, p. 426.

38. Chernikov, "Nauchno-technicheskii progress," p. 594.

39. *Vestnik Akademii Nauk, SSSR*, No. 6, 1982, p. 10.

40. O. Bogomolov, "Real'nyi podkhod i politicheskii avantyurism," *Trud*, July 3, 1982.

41. Chernikov, "Nauchno-tekhnicheskii progress," p. 599.

42. V. Krasovskii, "Novyi khozyaistvennyi mekhanizm i. povyshenie effektivnosti kapital'nykh vlozhenii," *Planovoe khozyaistvo*, No. 3, 1980, p. 44; idem, "Intensifikatsiya ekonomiki i problemy kapital'nogo remonta," *Planovoe khozyaistvo*, No. 7, 1983, p. 14.

43. Yu. Lyubimtsev, *Tsikl vosproizvodstva i amortizatsiya osnovnykh fondov*, Moscow, Ekonomika, 1973, p. 78.

44. *Tendentsii i factory povyshenia effektivnosti obshcheestvennogo proizvodstva*, Moscow, Nauka, 1984, p. 82.

45. G. Ovhcarenko, "Rekonstruktsiya," *Pravda*, April 7, 1984.

46. This list could be greatly expanded. V. Fal'tsman, A. Ozhegov, "Vybytie osnovkykh fondov: Investitsionnye vozmozhnosti i orgranicheniya," *Voprosy ekonomiki*, No. 6, 1983, p. 65.

47. "Pervye shagi podsobnykh khozyaistv," *EKO*, No. 6, 1984, pp. 125, 126.

48. O. Latsis, "Polonimsya i pouchimsya," *Izvestiya*, March 31, 1985.

49. V. Volkonskii, "Ekonomicheskaya otvetstvennost'," *EKO*, No. 1, 1985, p. 98.

50. N. Ivantsova, "Nauchno-tekhnicheskii progress v chernoi metallurgii," *Voprosy ekonomiki*, No. 2, 1985, p. 53.

51. Ibid., p. 54.

52. Krasovskii, "Intensifikatsiya ekonomiki," p. 14.

53. *Metody i praktika opredeleniya effektivnosti kapital'nykh vlozhenii i novoi tekhniki*, No. 3, Moscow, Nauka, 1984, p. 53.

54. B. Sheinkin, "Izderzhki neravnoi otvetstvennosti," *Sotsialisticheskaya industriya*, May 14, 1983.

55. D. Palterovich, "Funktsii amortizatsii v ekonomicheskom mekhanizme," *EKO*, No. 3, 1975, pp. 38, 39.

56. Sheinkin, "Izderzhki."

57. "Politicheskaya ekonomiya," *Ekonomicheskaya entsiklopediya*, Moscow, Entsiklopediya, 1972, p. 53; "Promyshlennost' i stroitel'stvo," *Ekonomicheskaya entsiklopediya*, Moscow, Entsiklopediya, 1962, p. 70.

58. Krasovskii, "Intensifikatsiya ekonomiki," pp. 15, 16.

59. N. Ryzhkov, "Kachestvo mashin i material'nye resursy," *Planovoe khozyaistvo*, No. 9, 1981, p. 13; D. Palterovich, "Obnovlenie oborudnovaniya," *Planovoe khozyaistvo*, No. 9, 1980, p. 105.

60. S. Kheinman, "Organizatsionnostrukturnye faktory ekonomicheskogo rosta," *EKO*, No. 6, 1980, p. 59.

61. L. Busyatskaya, "Povorot k zakazchiku," *Sotsialisticheskaya industriya*, April 13, 1985.

62. Yu. Baryshnikov and I. Malmygin, "Sbalanzirovannost' rabochikh mest i trudovykh resursov," *Sotsialisticheskii trud*, No. 9, 1983, p. 39.

63. N. Panteleev and V. Andrienko, "Rezervy Ekonomii truda i stimulirovanie ikh ispol'sovaniya," *Sotsialisticheskii trud*, No. 2, 1985, p. 107.

64. Ibid., p. 110.

65. Baryshnikov and Malmygin, "Sbalansirovannost'," p. 38.

66. Ibid., p. 37.

67. Ibid., p. 39; Panteleev and Andrienko, "Rezervy," p. 109.

68. Panteleev and Andrienko, "Rezervy," p. 107; Baryshnikov and Malmygin, "Sbalansirovannost'," p. 40.

69. Baryshnikov and Malmygin, "Sbalansirovannost'," p. 40; R. Tikidzhiev, "Voprosy sbalansirovannosti vosproizvodstva osnovnykh fondov i trudovykh resursov," *Planovoe khozyaistvo*, No. 12, 1981, p. 45.

70. D. Chernikov, "Nauchno-tekhnicheskii progress i strukturnye sdvigi v obshchestvennom proizvodstve," *Ekonomiko-matematicheskie metody*, No. 4, 1984, p. 594.

71. Panteleev and Andrienko, "Rezervy," p. 108.

72. Baryshnikov and Malmygin, "Sbalansirovannost'," p. 39.

73. *Materialy XXVI s"ezda KPSS*, Moscow, Politizdat, 1981, p. 141.

74. Yu. Yaremenko, "Metodologicheskie problemy narodnokhozyastvennogo prognozirovaniya," *Ekonomiko-matematicheskie metody*, No. 3, 1984, p. 402.

75. *Narkhoz*, 1980, p. 338; 1983, p. 361; 1985, p. 368.

76. *Kapital'noe stroitel'stvo: Statisticheskii sbornik*, Moscow, Gosstatizdat, 1961, p. 66.

77. *Narkhoz*, 1985, p. 368.

78. Sources: N. Bannyi et al., *Ekonomika chernoi metallurgii SSSR*, Moscow, Metallurgiya 1978, p. 131; *Narkhoz*, 1980, p. 338; L. Bufetova, *Narodnokhozyaistvennaya otsenka tekhnicheskogo progressa v otrasli*, Novosibirsk, Nauka, 1982, p. 72; V. Shtanskii, "Formirovanie i puti snizheniya udel'nykh kapital'nykh vlozhenii v chernoi metallurgii," *Stal'*, *Narkhoz*, 1982, p. 31; N. Mityaev, *Osnovnye proizvodstvennye fondy chernoi metallurgii*, Moscow, Metallurgiya, 1977, p. 35.

79. Bannyi et al., *Ekonomika*, p. 7.

80. Fal'tsman and Kornev, "Rezervy," p. 39; Shtanskii, "Formirovanie," p. 82.

81. *Narkhoz*, 1980, p. 339.

82. *Metody i praktika*, No. 28, Moscow, Nauka, 1976, p. 49.

83. Ibid., No. 26, p. 119.

84. V. Fal'tsman and A. Ozhegov, "Proportsii v razvitii mashinostroeniya i stroitel'stva," *Izvestiya Akademii Nauk SSSR, Seriya ekonomicheskaya*, No. 2, 1981, p. 67.

85. *Kommunist*, No. 10, 1985, p. 9.

86. Z. Tsimdina et al., *Modelirovanie razvitiya i razmeshcheniya proizvodstva v chernoi metallurgii*, Novosibirsk, Nauka, 1977, p. 31.

87. E. Lovchinovskii, "Upravlenie vosproizvodstvom osnovnych fondov chernoi metallurgii," *Planovoe khozyastvo*, No. 6, 1984, pp. 12, 13; Tsimdina et al., *Modelirovanie*, p. 31.
88. G. Kurbatova, "Mashinostroenie i investitsionnye protsessy," *EKO*, No. 3, 1982, p. 72.
89. Bufetova, *Narodno-khozyastvennaya otsenka*, p. 71.
90. Tsimdina et al., *Modelirovanie*, p. 31.
91. Lovchinovskii, *Upravlenie*, p. 12.
92. Bannyi et al., *Ekonomika*, p. 272.
93. Ibid., p. 271.
94. V. Pitatelev and V. Sidorova, "Razmeshchenie chernoi metallurgii," *Planovoe khozyaistvo*, No. 4, 1981, p. 80.
95. "Sud'ba veterana," *EKO*, No. 2, 1978, pp. 117, 118.
96. Ibid., p. 126.

Conclusion

1. As the dynamic for machine-building output, we are not using the data given in Soviet statistical yearbooks (where data are given in terms of value of production and hence are not adequately corrected for inflation), but the data given by Vladimir Fal'tsman of the Central Economic-Mathematics Institute in Moscow. Fal'tsman, who draws upon statistical data that are evidently unpublished, measured the growth in production for machine tools according to their main parameter—productivity. In our opinion, this is the most reliable and only possible natural index for measuring dynamics of machine production at the macroeconomic level. See V. Fal'tsman and N. Petropavlovskaya, "Metody prognozirovaniya metalloemkosti produktsii mashinostroeniya," *Izvestiya Akademii Nauk SSSR, Seriya ekonomicheskaya*, No. 3, 1985, p. 79.

2. Ibid.
3. N. Ryzhkov, *Doklad, XXVII s"ezd KPSS: Stenograficheskii otchet*, Moscow, 1986, p. 28.
4. *Narkhoz*, 1985, p. 59.
5. "Na zavode vstretimsya," *Pravda*, May 26, 1986.
6. *Pravda*, January 18, 1987, p. 2.
7. L. Zusman, *Metalloemkost' obshchestvennogo proizvodstva*, Moscow, Metallurgiya, 1982, p. 208.
8. *KPSS v rezolyutsiyakh i reshaniyakh*, vol. 4, Moscow, Izdatel'stvo politicheskoy literatury, 1970, p. 284.
9. See, for example, *Pravda*, editorial, May 22, 1987; A. Pasechnik, "Lyubov' k premial'nym," *Sotsialisticheskaya industriya*, May 13, 1987.
10. O. Zharko, "Ob"yedinit' usiliya," *Sotsialisticheskaya industriya*, April 16, 1987.

Index

Library of Congress Cataloging-in-Publication Data

Rumer, Boris Z.
  Soviet steel.

  (Studies in Soviet history and society)
  Bibliography: p.
  Includes index.
  1. Steel industry and trade—Soviet Union. I. Title. II. Series: Studies in Soviet
history and society (Ithaca, N.Y.)
  HD9525.S652R86   1989   338.4′7669142′0947   88-47745
  ISBN 0-8014-2077-6